Thirteen Strategies

to **Measure**

College Teaching

Other books by Ron Berk:

Humor as an Instructional Defibrillator
Professors Are from Mars®, Students Are from Snickers®
The Michelangelo Code
Tuesdays with Dr. Phil
The Greed-Driven Life
The North-South-East-West Beach Diet
The Story of Watergate's Strep Throat
It Takes a Shopping Mall
My Life: The Slimeball Years
Harry Potter Gets Lasik®
Me: The Owner's Manual
The One-Minute Meeting
The Muppets Take Biloxi
The Catcher in the Pumpernickel
Watermelons of Wrath
The 7 Habits of Highly Infected People
The 8th Habit: From Infection to Sick Leave

Thirteen Strategies
to **Measure**
College Teaching

A Consumer's Guide to Rating Scale Construction,
Assessment, and Decision Making for Faculty,
Administrators, and Clinicians

RONALD A. BERK

with a Foreword by Mike Theall

Sty/us

STERLING, VIRGINIA

Published by Stylus Publishing, LLC
22883 Quicksilver Drive
Sterling, Virginia 20166-2102

Book design and composition by Susan Mark
Coghill Composition Company
Richmond, Virginia

Library of Congress Cataloging-in-Publication-Data

Berk, Ronald A.
    Thirteen strategies to measure college teaching : a consumer's guide to rating scale construction, assessment, and decision making for faculty, administrators, and clinicians / Ronald A. Berk.—1st ed.
        p.   cm.
    ISBN 1-57922-192-0 (cloth : alk. paper)—ISBN 1-57922-193-9 (pbk. : alk. paper)
    1. College teachers—Rating of.   2. Teacher effectiveness.   I. Title.
LB2333.B47 2006
378.1'224—dc22

                                        2005036250

ISBN: 1-57922-192-0(cloth) / 13-digit ISBN: 978-1-57922-192-8
ISBN: 1-57922-193-9 (paper) / 13-digit ISBN: 978-1-57922-193-5

Printed in the United States of America

All first editions printed on acid-free paper that meets the American National Standards Institute Z39-48 Standard.

First Edition, 2006

10   9   8   7   6   5   4   3   2   1

To Ella Madelyn Heiliger,
my FAVE granddaughter

CONTENTS

TABLES, FIGURES, CHECKLISTS, AND MEMORY JOGGERS

Tables

Figures

Checklists

Memory Joggers

ACKNOWLEDGMENTS

W hat are the chances your name is mentioned here? If you don't know me, ZIPPO! If you do know me, MAYBE. If you actually reviewed some of this stuff, DEFINITELY!

As you're probably aware, writing a book of this height, weight, girth, shape, density, and hue is a piece of cake. Actually, it requires a support network of colleagues, friends, family, animals, vegetables, minerals, and extraterrestrials. It also means a commitment to writing every day and in every place, whether in the office, in the hospital sitting in pre-op for brain transplant surgery, at Midas Muffler® waiting to have my midas replaced, or at home in front of my desktop in my undershorts eating chocolate frosting out of a can with my fingers. It's a tough job.

First, I want to acknowledge those special VIPs and directors of conferences on teaching and assessment who have allowed me year after year to present plenary addresses or workshops on most of the topics covered in this book and on humor. Their encouragement and supportiveness have meant a lot to keep this content alive and kicking.

- *Milt Cox*, Director, Lilly Conference on College Teaching
- *Gregg Wentzell*, Program Editor, Lilly Conference on College Teaching, and Managing Editor, *Journal on Excellence in College Teaching*
- *Ronald Harden*, General Secretary, Association for Medical Education in Europe Conference
- *Pat Lilley*, Administrator, Association for Medical Education in Europe Conference, and Managing Editor, *Medical Teacher*
- *Bill Gorth*, President, National Evaluation Systems
- *Dick Allan*, Vice President, National Evaluation Systems

- *Paula Nassif,* Vice President, National Evaluation Systems

Second, to those colleagues in the United Kingdom and Canada who unselfishly gave me an online crash course on "360° assessment" and/or provided scales on which they have conducted research to use as examples in appendix B, I express my unselfish appreciation with a big American imported panda bear hug. They are *Julian Ancher, Bryan Burford, Anne Hesketh, Jocelyn Lockyer,* and *David Wall.*

Third, there are several peers who endured the punishing experience of actually reading earlier, less funny drafts of the chapters, but nonetheless furnished highly constructive, very thoughtful, and valuable feedback. These professionals deserve no less than a pithy T-shirt or an all-expense-paid trip to Cleveland. The general reviewers of the entire book were *Marie Nolan* and *Laura Border.* My technical reviewers for chapters 7–9 were *Bob McMorris, John Mattar, John Silvestro,* and *Marty Karlin.* My humorist buddy *Roz Trieber* held me accountable for the types of jokes I used and my writing style. Her support was invaluable throughout the three-year duration of the project.

Fourth, at Johns Hopkins, I thank my associate dean *Anne Belcher* for permitting me to air the scales and report forms in appendices A and C, which were developed in our school over the past five years. *Donnell James,* my administrative assistant, word-processing guru, and friend, prepared the entire manuscript, including the thousands of tables, checklists, memory joggers, figures, appendices, and references. I made him cry only once, and he considered violence only twice. I am deeply indebted to him for his work on this book and his unwavering support and loyalty.

This book would not have been possible without my publisher *John von Knorring's* appreciation of my warped mind. Amazingly, he still continues to publish my books on humor, and this one, on a "serious" topic but with loads of humor, when other publishers wouldn't touch them. John truly understands the value of humor in all that we do as academicians and he wouldn't let me write a book without it. I am also extremely grateful to my production editor *Judy Coughlin* and copyeditor *Amy Chamberlain* for their meticulous work and special care of my manuscript through the most critical stages of the publication process.

Despite the roles that all of the aforementioned persons played in the production of this book, there is always the possibility of substantive and editorial errores or omis sions. None of these people is responsible. Ultimately, there is only one person who should be held totally accountable for the mistakes in this book, and that person, of course, is Dick Cheney.

Finally, bringing a book like this to completion is not without personal sacrifice. I express an uppercase, boldface, 16-pt font **THANK YOU** to my wife *Marion* for her patience, indefatigable support, and encouragement. I also thank my two incredible daughters, *Boo Boo* (a.k.a. Marissa) and *Cori* (a.k.a. Corinne), who are endless sources of joy, laughter, and inspiration in my life; my fun-loving, supportive, terrific son-in-law *Chris*, for taking tender loving care of Cori and Ella; and my *mommy* for always being there and providing support in so many ways.

A FOREWORD (IN BERKIAN STYLE)

MIKE THEALL

A funny thing happened on the way to this foreword (insert an appropriate ba-da-boom "rimshot" here). Well, actually, it happened just about a year ago, right before I was scheduled to leave for a conference. A small section of lumen in my right descending coronary artery tore, releasing a minute amount of atherosclerotic plaque and creating a blockage that generated some classic symptoms (why accept everyday symptoms when you can have classic ones?). This was unpleasant, of course (who wants to miss a paid trip to a professional meeting in Montreal?), but it was also frustrating because I had been eating my fruit and vegetables, ingesting appropriately prescribed chemicals, and getting a modicum of exercise. But that's another story, and given Ron Berk's (2002) coincidentally prescient suggestions about the use of humor as a defibrillator, there is a connection. But the real question is, "Why should you care about that heart-wrenching experience when this book is about measuring college teaching?" HINT: It's not because evaluating teaching is also a frequently heart-wrenching experience.

The answer is that Ron Berk's approach is very much like that used to evaluate my dramatic sojourn into cardiac catheterization. There was an immediate response based on my symptoms, and equally rapid use of various tests to more definitively ascertain the problem. Data were regularly collected. There was a kind of "360°, multisource assessment." Some of it was very quantitative. For example, there was detailed chemical analysis of various naturally occurring and commercially produced compounds, with results expressed in appropriately scientific and metric terms. Attention was paid to things like the HDL/LDL ratio (kind of like GPA, GRE, SAT, and other academic indicators).

Other data were surprisingly qualitative. Denzin and Lincoln (2000) would have loved it. People asked me, "How do you feel?" on an almost hourly basis.

I provided a self-reported, narrative response and (believe it or not) my assessment was accepted at face value. Some data were in the form of responses to survey questions such as, "On a scale of 1 to 10, where would you place your pain?" This would be analogous to asking a faculty member something like, "So, did you enjoy preparing for tenure?" I also regularly received feedback on my "performance," but not all of it was immediately understandable. "Your enzyme count was 143," they said. This didn't do a lot for my peace of mind until a knowledgeable expert interpreted the data and informed me that a count of 1,500 was usually expected after similar incidents. It also helped to know that the lower the count, the better. Additionally, when my situation stabilized after a few days, I was able to return to normal activities given my commitment "not to overdo it"; to a careful regimen that included strengthening/improvement activities; and to a follow-up rehabilitation program and checkups on a regular basis.

And perhaps most interesting, when it was all over, I was asked to complete an "evaluation" of the care I had received. Small sample issues aside, this was a chance to register a *post hoc* opinion based on sufficient time for reflection. It was certainly not a "popularity contest." All in all, the intensity of the surveillance, the continuous monitoring of changes, and the establishment of a program for improvement provide an analog for the emphasis of this book.

The point here, is not, as some critical wags would say, that evaluating college teaching is hazardous to your health, but rather to indicate that what is often done in faculty evaluation is much less thorough or precise than it could be. For the sake of maintaining the health of our academic enterprise, we should be paying a lot more attention to multiple indicators of effectiveness, we should be providing people with understandable information, and we should be offering expert assistance in using that information to foster improvements and/or to make important professional life decisions. As the demand for accountability in higher education grows (talk about adding stress to an already stressful situation), it becomes more and more important to be able to gather and use valid and reliable information, and to develop programs and processes that support and sustain faculty vitality rather than constraining it or creating additional roadblocks to success.

So, with this in mind (and with Berk as a model), I offer the following:

Top Ten Reasons Why You Should Read This Book

10. You are a statistician or psychometrician and you are excited by this stuff. (Please seek immediate psychological help.)

9. You are a student of statistics at Johns Hopkins who has no choice. Bucko is forcing you to buy it for his course. (You can always sell it to the next victim.)

8. You are a faculty member with a morbid sense of curiosity. (Scatology hasn't worked for you to date.)

7. You are an administrator with a penchant for "evidence" (whether you understand it or not).

6. You are a friend of Ron Berk's and you want to help him build his retirement nest egg and achieve professional credibility. (Why?)

5. You work for the publisher and you want to insure your own future. (At least this is understandable.)

4. You are a humanities professor and you want to see how the other half lives. (Remember, a little knowledge is dangerous. You might get quantified.)

3. You are essentially a masochist. (Refer to the suggestion in #10)

2. The term "Rasch modeling" suggests there will be risqué photos of Tyra Banks embedded in the text. (One can always hope.)

And the number one reason for buying/reading this book (drum roll please)

1. You care about your teaching and you want to know how to assess and improve it. (Thank you.)

But seriously, folks . . . (I had to say that after using the opening line in this foreword) . . . this is a text for those who want no-nonsense guidelines for measuring teaching effectiveness. OK, OK . . . "no nonsense" is the wrong descriptor for the work of a man who has equated professors and students with candy bars (Berk, 2003), but there is a legitimate reason for telling academics how to measure teaching. It is that even though more than five decades of research have shown us how to do it well, that research has not made its way into our operational consciousness and day-to-day practice. Quite simply, this often puts faculty careers at risk. It also doesn't give evaluators and institutions a leg to stand on if things get nasty.

A foreword should at least mention what's in the book. I do that now in full recognition of the fact that you just saw the Table of Contents, and that this may be redundant. Nonetheless, I would like to point out a few highlights worth considering. First, Berk's list of strategies is (as advertised) one of the most complete discussions of these issues available. Second, the organization of the book matches the steps one would take to determine which strategies are most appropriate in determining what process to use, and then, in constructing instruments that will produce valid and reliable results. Third, Berk begins each chapter with notes to faculty and administrators about the applicability of the content to their respective purposes and interests. Fourth, though there are necessary technical issues to present, Berk avoids psychometric excesses that would make the material less readable. Fifth, as in previous work, Berk is willing to break the rules of academic writing in order to hold the reader's attention. He dares to be funny. Some would call this "iconoplastic" (isn't that when someone breaks a cheap picture of a religious figure at the Dollar Saver store?), but I call it downright brave for, as Berk has often said, "Isn't 'funny statistician' an oxymoron?" Well, acne and IQ aside, the "bottom line" (to use Berk's indicator for the meat of each chapter) is that this book can be used by both novices and experienced practitioners as a guide to better practice. That's why it is worth reading.

So, you've bought the book. Now, read it and try to help your institution, college, or department do a better job of measuring and improving teaching. Your colleagues, your students, and your institution should thank you for it. If not, then they should read the book too. If they refuse, then "throw the book at them." If your aim is true, at least you'll get your money's worth from the satisfaction of knowing you have made "a dent" in poor daily practice.

References: (Are you serious?)

Berk, R. A. (2002). *Humor as an instructional defibrillator*. Sterling, VA: Stylus.

Berk, R. A. (2003). *Professors are from Mars®, students are from Snickers®*. Sterling, VA: Stylus.

Denzin, N. K., & Lincoln, Y. S. (Eds.). (2000). *Handbook of qualitative research*. Thousand Oaks, CA: Sage.

Mike Theall is Director, Center for the Advancement of Teaching
And Learning at Youngstown State (CATALYST),
and associate professor of education,
Youngstown State University, Youngstown, Ohio

Thirteen Strategies
to Measure
College Teaching

INTRODUCTION

Disclaimer

You know those excellent books on faculty evaluation (Arreola, 2000; Braskamp & Ory, 1994; Centra, 1993; Seldin, 1995), in which the author reviews piles of research and presents Dumpsters® of evidence to proffer models and methods for evaluating faculty teaching, scholarship/research, service, and practice? You know which ones? Huh? Huh? Well this book is nothing like those. Neither is it a feel-good, inspirational work that provides you with heaps of useful information to change your academic life or lose weight or grow hair. Writer to reader, let's not kid ourselves. I know you didn't pick up this book because you couldn't find Kierkegaard or your favorite Shakespearean play. Lower your expectations. This volume just deals with how to measure teaching performance: traditional face-to-face classroom teaching, blended face-to-face and Web-based teaching, online teaching, and clinical teaching of physicians, nurses, and other health care professionals. The measurement strategies also apply to other faculty, administrator, and clinician competencies.

 ## ~~CLIFFS~~ BERK'S NOTES

Faculty—Unless you've been in a coma, beamed down from another galaxy, or returned from that long-dreamed-of trip to Uzbektripgatchastan, you know the impact of your teaching on your students. They evaluate it, you evaluate it, and your boss evaluates it. The results are used to help you improve the quality of your teaching. Your boss may draw on that same information as well as other evidence to decide your annual contract renewal, merit pay raise, and/or whether he or she should recommend you for promotion and tenure. All of these decisions about your teaching affect your future. How good is the evidence currently being used for those decisions? Does the word *BLECCCH* roll off your tongue? The problem is that many of the rating scales that are employed to gather this evidence are poorly constructed. If they were bridges, they would probably collapse. This book will describe the procedures for building rating scales and using multiple sources of evidence (13 possible sources) for more accurate, reliable, and fair decisions than those being made at numerous institutions right now. It will arm you with the tools to make this happen.

Administrators—If you are a dean, associate dean, program director, or department head or chair, or run a small country, you probably evaluate the teaching performance of your faculty. You may be using student ratings and other evidence to render decisions about their annual retention or dismissal and merit pay as well as whether they should be recommended for promotion and tenure. These are all high-stakes decisions that you take very, very, very seriously. What is the quality of the evidence that provides the foundation for those decisions? Is it adequate? Can it be improved? Are your decisions fair or biased? Could you defend them in a court on *Law & Order* (which is based on that popular TV sitcom *Happy Days*)? It all depends on the evidence and how you interpret it. This book will supply you with the guidelines to develop and use multiple sources of evidence to make better decisions than the ones you may be currently making. The progress and success of your faculty hinge on what you do.

Intended Readership

These Berk's Notes will appear at the beginning of every chapter throughout the book to provide you with a terse digest of the specific content you need to know in that chapter. They will tailor the procedures for *you*, my favorite reader who actually shelled out a wad of your hard-earned green stuff for this book. If you're as overcommitted as I am, you don't have time to fiddle around with material that is irrelevant to your interests or responsibilities. My motto for this book is "Get to the point, Bucko. Don't waste my time."

Whether you're a faculty member, an administrator, a transacademician (both faculty and administrator), or a clinician, I couldn't possibly know your individual needs on the topic of measuring teaching effectiveness, didactic and/or clinical.

Having been a professor for 30 years and an assistant dean for teaching, I can only guess the roles you assume in the process using my psychic-horoscopic techniques. I realize this is a shotgun approach, but hopefully some of my buckshot will spray your way with information you can use. (*Clinician Alert*: Although the central focus of this book is on teaching effectiveness, all of the scaling rules and strategies [for overview, see Memory Jogger 2.1, p. 49] apply to any professional job where the goal is to measure "effectiveness" in terms of job behaviors and outcomes. I have included specific applications in the health care professions for fear that my white-coated, scalpel-wielding, clinical-type colleagues would whip me with their stethoscopes or shoot me with tranquilizer darts during a presentation if I didn't pay homage to their disciplines.)

Rationale

And lo, as darkness fell over my first disclaimer box and Berk's Notes, there were distant sounds: EEEWs, AAAHs, YIIIKES! It is the official start of this book. And hark, the next paragraph will unleash unto this land and all of the academicians who actually bought this book a new beginning, thereof. How's that for a snappy opening?

Teaching is one major component among the 75 components in a faculty member's job description. An instructor's performance in the classroom may be evaluated by current students, peers, outside experts, self, administrators, alumni, or even aliens. If you're in the health care professions, the evaluators of your clinical teaching and performance may be students, colleagues, nurses, attending physicians, consultants, patients, pharmacists, licensing or certification boards, or ambulance chasers. The individual or collective opinions of other people furnish the information for faculty to improve their own teaching or clinical performance and for administrators and promotions committees to make employment decisions about their future. There is no 100-item multiple-choice employment test with a new writing section, administered online on a rainy Saturday morning in a test center, that will measure teaching or clinical competence.

FACTOID #1

The assessment of teaching rests almost entirely on the judgments of people above, below, and on the same level of faculty.

Ruminate over that factoid for a moment. Oh, take five, and get a cáffé móchá látté mácchíátó cáppúccínó décáf véntí brévé while you're at it. There is no known objective method for measuring teaching performance. The trick is to find a *sound, defensible strategy for combining multiple sources of "informed" judgment* for reaching those decisions. The target outcome of this book is to arm you with high-quality tools for these sources of evidence to produce alternative configurations for the decisions you have to make.

So, how do you assess teaching effectiveness with enough evidence to make decisions accurately, reliably, and fairly? That seems to be the question leading into this paragraph. No one seems to know the answer, but everyone takes a stab at it. There are a variety of opinions on what to use and how to interpret the results. However, there is a humongous gap between what the experts recommend and what is actually occurring in practice. A survey of liberal arts colleges in the United States (which is located in Western Europe) indicated that more than 76% use rating scales of one kind or another to evaluate teaching performance (Seldin, 1999a). The *rating scale* is the appropriate instrument because that's its sole purpose in life, its *raison d'être*, which is French for "lame excuse for interrupting the flow of this paragraph." These colleges are measuring the opinions of different respondents about the quality of teaching.

This book describes the procedures for developing any rating scale to measure teaching performance and the assessment process by which faculty and administrators use the scores for decision making. It is a *basic training manual for all faculty and administrators*, albeit a consumer's guide to the assessment of teaching effectiveness. If you have no need to inspect, select, adapt, critique, or write items for a rating scale, or make decisions about teaching or clinical performance, then STOP READING NOW. Close the book. I stillll seeee yooou. This book's not for you. Sell it on e-Bay or use it to kill bugs or small rodents.

At present, how do institutions of higher education develop these scales to assess teaching effectiveness? Several rely on available on-campus experts in measurement and statistics to deal with the technical issues or hire off-campus consultants to get the job done. In some cases, there may even be centers for evaluation, teaching excellence, or faculty development with personnel who will develop the instruments and administer the evaluation system. However, there are so many scales, so little time (Wait! That's not the right ending . . . Where's the rest of this sentence? Oh, here it is.) that we use to measure the performance of individuals and programs that those experts may not always be the most appropriate resource. A few of these scales usually supply documentation for the excruciatingly painful accreditation process, which involves all faculty and administrators.

Unfortunately, these resources are either not available or not accessible at all institutions. More important, *faculty and administrators need to be active participants in the assessment process.* They both make decisions based on the results and are directly affected by the consequences of those decisions. At some point, they will have to provide item content, write items, review items, approve items and the final scale, administer the scale, interpret the results, receive feedback, give feedback, and, in some cases, suffer the slings and arrows of outrageous scores. Their involvement as the primary stakeholders in assessing teaching effectiveness must be secured. Faculty jobs are at stake.

FACTOID #2

Many rating scales and item banks currently being used to make decisions about faculty members contain flawed, inappropriate, insensitive, unreliable, inaccurate, and/or putrid items that can yield unfair and biased ratings of their teaching performance.

Although 76% of liberal arts colleges use rating scales for employment decisions, only 14% conducted research to gather validity evidence on the scale scores (Seldin, 1999a). Quality control in scale construction seems to be falling through the cracks. In some cases, it's as if someone with the IQ of a starfish threw a bunch of items together. However well meaning, such products are unacceptable. It seems that only faculty evaluation researchers take notice or care about this problem. Rarely do faculty and administrators express concern over scale quality.

The precise wording of the statements and anchors on a rating scale is crucial to maximizing the validity and usefulness of the scores. *Seemingly small changes in wording can cause huge differences in responses.* Yet, typically, writing the items is considered to be the easiest part of scale development, so that too often it may receive the least attention, when, in fact, it should receive the most. An arrogant faculty member has commented, "After all, how difficult could it be to write items for a rating scale? There are scales everywhere to use as examples. Faculty committees do it all the time." Other faculty and administrators are probably thinking those same three sentences in cartoon-type bubbles over their heads—maybe not with the quotation marks, though. (*Grammatical Note*: English professors call this sentence structure a *corpuscular transitive embolus*.) Further, the items on available scales may not even reflect the up-to-date research and best practices in college teaching.

Purposes of the Book

There are six purposes for the writing of this book: (1) to present a state-of-the-art synthesis of the literature on the measurement of teaching effectiveness, (2) to evaluate the merits of 13 methods to measure teaching performance, plus a bonus method on clinical teaching and competence, (3) to provide step-by-step procedures for faculty to develop, test, and analyze scales for those methods, (4) to recommend guidelines for faculty and administrators to interpret scale scores for decision making, (5) to penetrate the cob-webbed, crust-encumbered craniums of those academicians who still believe student ratings are sufficient to evaluate teaching, and (6) to generate enough royalties for the gasoline to drive to a Hummer® (which is a military acronym for "Mobile Army Surgical Hospital") dealership and test-drive the H3, to experience the amazing ride that has been described as "surprisingly similar to that of a full-size luxury sedan dragged across a boulder field on its roof."

My use of humor will probably blow a hole in the propriety of extant volumes on faculty evaluation and scaling through which you could drive a 16-wheeler. In fact, many of you who have read my previous books and the articles on my Web site (www.ronberk.com) can judge how much I have matured as a humor writer. Actually, I haven't matured one ounce. Maturity is a crippling disability for a humorist. This disability is like obesity for jockeys, narcolepsy for pilots, or ethics for politicians. It's extremely difficult to stay serious for long periods of time, like for a paragraph or two. By the way, the coverage of technical topics in the book, such as item analysis, validity, and reliability, is drop-dead hilarious if you like irreverent humor. You'll laugh so loudly that the hot coffee you're drinking will spray out of your nostrils all over your laptop. Further, those topics are treated conceptually for the statistically challenged, to furnish faculty and administrators with a basic understanding for decision making.

Content Organization

This book is divided into nine chapters. The first chapter provides an overview and critique of 13 possible sources of evidence recommended in the literature to measure teaching performance. Those sources should prompt a reaction and decision from even the most emotionally constricted academics, those whose faces usually convey a Botox®-type paralysis, but without the injections. Once a tentative selection of sources has been determined, the task of custom building the scales to measure the desired teaching behaviors begins. The scale development process is outlined at the outset of chapter 2 in Memory Jogger 2.1. Chapters 2 through 6 give the detailed prescription for reaching scaling heaven. They cover how to operationally define teaching or clinical effectiveness, write scale statements, pick the appropriate anchors, structure the items to maximize reliability and minimize bias, assemble the draft scale, and decide on paper-based or online administration.

I'm sorry to interrupt this section, but it's time for a commercial break right now. (*Commercial Break*: "Would you like to save 50% or more off your long-distance telephone bill?" The next time a dinnertime telemarketer asks you this question, answer: "NO, I want a gigantic bill. I love mega-overage. In fact, I often place totally unnecessary calls to distant continents just to jack it up." That response works every time. This has been a public service announcement by your FAVE author.) It's time to resume with chapters 7 through 9. Chapter 7 explicates the procedures for mini- and monster-size field tests to gather data on the items to see if they work. This is the most techie chapter, but specific directions for faculty and administrators on the first page will get you through what you need to know. Chapter 8 applies the results of the field tests to the criteria for validity and reliability evidence. The chapter 9 finale and fireworks display jog you through all of the possible formats for reporting and interpreting the scale scores. It concludes with a stepwise presentation of how the model for using multiple sources of evidence recommended at the end of chapter 1 can be applied to a variety of individual faculty and program decisions. The norm-referenced and criterion-referenced score-interpretation approaches for summative decisions, in particular, are unlike any described in available books on the evaluation of teaching effectiveness. Sample "home-grown" scales from my institution and several scales from institutions in the United Kingdom are given in appendices A and B. Plus, a few score report formats are displayed in appendix C for your perusal.

Unique Contribution

There are 10 unique characteristics of the rating scale construction sections in this volume: (1) the compilation of 28 rules for writing statements and choosing anchors, (2) the description of five different types of anchors and a hectillion examples, (3) the pretests in several chapters so you can skip over material you already know, (4) the checklists for critiquing items, (5) the loads of "humorous" concrete examples to illustrate the rules, (6) the memory joggers, (7) the research-based answers to the most thorny questions and issues in scale construction, (8) the guidelines for online scale administration, (9) the sample "faculty-developed" scales from several institutions, and (10) the detailed recommendations for rendering formative, summative, and program decisions. Further, every step in the process follows the national *Standards for Educational and Psychological Testing* (AERA, APA, & NCME Joint Committee on Standards, 1999). Appropriate research-based "gold standards" for scale construction and employment decision making are cited throughout the book to justify the procedures that are recommended.

1

TOP 13 SOURCES OF EVIDENCE OF TEACHING EFFECTIVENESS

 SECURITY ALERT

Homeland Security government leaders, as you have requested, I hereby report "suspicious activity" to 800-492-TIPS. I inform you of this chapter. It qualifies for an index alert level of "EEEEEEE," which is so high only dogs can detect it. If this doesn't qualify as suspicious activity, then I don't know what would. Can you believe the title above? Me neither. Just knock me over, slap me silly, and kick me until I bleed from my ears. Yup, that's what I typed: *13*, a baker's dozen. A virtual smorgasbord of data sources is waiting for you to make your move. How many can you name other than student ratings? How many are currently being used in your department? Could you pick 'em out of a lineup? That's what I thought. By the time you finish this chapter, your toughest decision will be (Are you ready? Isn't this exciting?): "Should I slog through chapter 2?" WRONGORINO! It's: "Which sources should I use?"

 BERK'S NOTES

Faculty—If you like to be evaluated by people, are planning a shopping spree for a method to measure teaching effectiveness in your department/school, or are considering techniques other than student ratings, you're in the right chapter. This is where the action begins. So you are clear on the decisions you want to make about *your* teaching performance and those that are made by your chair or dean, read the sections "Teaching Effectiveness" and "A Unified Conceptualization" to put all of this in context. Then tackle the 13 "sources," paying particular attention to the ones intended for teaching improvement. Table 1.1 lists all sources, the players involved, and types of decisions. Focus on those with an "F" for *formative* in the last column. Each source is described briefly and then evaluated in terms of available research and current practices. The "Bottom Line" recommendations and last two sections should help guide your specific choice(s). Be selective. Don't pick everything in the store—I mean chapter. You might also want to peek at the surprise BONUS strategy to challenge your thinking about how to measure on-the-job performance, especially if you're in the health professions.

Administrators—If you are involved in developing or selecting a rating system to evaluate your faculty, this chapter has your name on it (somewhere). Start with the kind of decisions *you* need to make, such as summative (whatever that is), and an assessment model for those decisions. Those topics are covered in the first sections, on teaching effectiveness and unified conceptualization. Then you're ready to snoop around the 13 sources of evidence to identify which ones are most appropriate for your faculty, department/school, and budget. Review table 1.1 before snooping. Note those sources with an "S" for *snooping*—I mean *summative*—in the last column. In case you are also interested in using these sources for program decisions related to accreditation review, check out the "P" sources as well. Make sure to read the "Bottom Line" recommendations and the last two sections in the chapter before you make your selection. The bonus strategy after the 13 sources is also worth your time. It will give you a new perspective on how to assess faculty performance as well as your own. See you at the end of the chapter.

A Few Ground Rules

Have you finally calmed down from the shock of the chapter title? Terrific. Before I get to the 13 "you know whats," I need to set a few ground rules. First, the importance of assessing teaching effectiveness needs to be clear in terms of the decisions that affect us. Second, the entire measurement process to develop the scales and other tools must be guided by an independent set of professional standards and accumulated research evidence, not my whimsical imagination. Finally, student ratings and all of the other sources of evidence need to fit into an assessment model that facilitates the decisions to be made.

Teaching Effectiveness: Defining the Construct

According to Seldin (1998), more than 15,000 studies have been published on the topic of teaching effectiveness. Why is assessing *teaching effectiveness* so important? Because the evidence produced is used for important decisions about an instructor's future in academe. HEEEELLO! It can be used to whack us. Teaching is the major criterion (98%) in assessing overall faculty performance in liberal arts colleges compared to student advising (64%), committee work (59%), research (41%), publications (31%), and public service (24%) (Seldin, 1999a). Although these figures may not hold up in research universities, teaching is still a primary job requirement and criterion on which most faculty members are assessed.

There are two types of *individual* decisions:

1. *Formative decisions.* These are decisions faculty make to improve and shape the quality of their teaching. It is based on evidence of teaching effectiveness they gather to plan and revise their teaching semester after semester. The collection of evidence and the subsequent adjustments in teaching can occur anytime during the course, so the students can benefit from those changes, or after the course in preparation for the next course.

2. *Summative decisions.* These decisions are rendered by "da boss," the administrative-type person who controls an instructor's destiny and future in higher education. This individual is usually the dean, associate dean, program director, department head or chair, or emperor/empress. This administrator uses evidence of an instructor's teaching effectiveness to "sum up" his or her overall performance or status to decide about contract renewal or dismissal, annual merit pay, promotion, and tenure. Although promotion and tenure decisions are often made by a faculty committee, a letter of recommendation by the dean is typically required to reach the committee for review. These summative decisions are high-stakes, final employment decisions reached at different points in time to determine an instructor's progression through the ranks and success as an academician or pain in the butt. These decisions have an impact on the quality of an instructor's professional and personal lives.

The various sources of evidence for teaching effectiveness may be employed for either formative or summative decisions or both. Several of the sources can also be used for *program decisions.* Those decisions relate to the curriculum, admissions and graduation requirements, and program effectiveness. They are NOT

Personal life is limited to three hours per week at research universities, unless that time is used for fundraising.

---

individual decisions; instead, they focus on processes and products. The evidence usually is derived from various types of faculty and student input and employers' performance appraisal of students. It is also collected to provide documentation to satisfy the criteria for accreditation review.

National Standards

There are national professional standards for how teaching effectiveness or performance should be measured: the *Standards for Educational and Psychological Testing* (AERA, APA, & NCME Joint Committee on Standards, 1999). They can guide the development of the measurement tools, the technical analysis of the results, and the reporting and interpretation of the evidence for decision making.

The *Standards* address *what* is measured and then *how* to measure it:

WHAT—The content of any tool, such as a student, peer, or administrator rating scale, requires a thorough and explicit definition of the cognitive knowledge, skills, and abilities (KSAs), and other characteristics and behaviors, such as initiative, self-confidence, motivation, and professionalism, that describe the job of "effective teaching" (Standards 14.8–14.10).

HOW—The data from a rating scale or other tool that are based on the systematic collection of opinions or decisions by raters, observers, or judges hinge on their expertise, qualifications, and experience (Standard 1.7).

Spencer and Spencer (1993) have defined a *competency* as "an underlying characteristic of an individual that is causally related to criterion-referenced effective and/or superior performance in a job or situation" (p. 9). They identified 21 common competencies grouped into six clusters: achievement and action; helping and human service; impact and influence; and managerial, cognitive, and personal effectiveness. All of these areas need to be considered in defining the *what*. These authors note: "You can teach a turkey to climb a tree, but it is easier to hire a squirrel" (p. 294). In other words, squirrelly faculty will possess the teaching competencies that can be assessed; the turkeys will need to be trained in those competencies. Tell your search committee to hunt down and hire squirrels rather than turkeys. You'll save yourself a lot of faculty development time and cost. Save the turkeys (and cranberries) for Thanksgiving, not your department. Translating job competence into measurable behaviors of teaching performance will be examined in chapter 2.

Student and peer direct observations of *what* they see in the classroom furnish the foundation for their ratings. However, other sources, such as student outcome data and publications on innovative teaching strategies, are indirect, from which teaching effectiveness is inferred. These different data sources vary considerably in how they measure the *what*. We need to be able to carefully discriminate among all available sources.

Beyond Student Ratings

Historically, student ratings have dominated as the primary measure of teaching effectiveness for the past 30 years (Seldin, 1999a). In fact, they have placed the assessment of teaching in a metaphorical cul-de-sac for decades. Only recently has there been a trend toward augmenting those ratings with other data sources of teaching performance. Such sources can serve to broaden and deepen the evidence base used to evaluate courses and to assess the quality of teaching (Arreola, 2000; Braskamp & Ory, 1994; Knapper & Cranton, 2001; Seldin & Associates, 1999).

Several comprehensive models of "faculty evaluation" have been proposed (Arreola, 2000; Braskamp & Ory, 1994; Centra, 1993; Keig & Waggoner, 1994; Romberg, 1985; Soderberg, 1986). They include multiple sources of evidence with greater weight attached to student and peer input and less weight attached to self-evaluation, alumni, administrators, and others. All of these models are used to arrive at formative and summative decisions.

A Unified Conceptualization

Consistent with the consensus of experts in the field of faculty evaluation, I propose a *unified conceptualization of teaching effectiveness*, whereby evidence is collected from a variety of sources to define the construct and to make decisions about performance. Those sources may or may not be weighted. Placing value judgments on the relative worth of different sources may be somewhat arbitrary.

Much has been written about the merits and shortcomings of the various sources of evidence currently being employed. Put simply: There is no perfect source or combination of sources. Each source can supply unique information, but also is fallible, usually in a way different from the other sources. For example, the unreliability and biases of peer ratings are not the same as those of student ratings; student ratings have other weaknesses. By drawing on three or more different sources of evidence, the *strengths of each source can compensate for weaknesses of the other sources*, thereby converging on a decision about teaching effectiveness that is more accurate and reliable than one based on any single source (Appling,

Naumann, & Berk, 2001). This notion of *triangulation* is derived from a compensatory model of decision making.

Given the complexity of measuring the act of teaching in a real-time classroom environment, it is reasonable to expect that *multiple sources can provide a more accurate, reliable, and comprehensive picture of teaching effectiveness than just one source*. However, the decision maker should integrate the information from only those sources for which validity evidence is available (see Standard 14.13). The quality of the sources chosen should be beyond reproach, according to the *Standards*.

Assessment is derived from two Latin words: *assidere*, meaning "your big keester," and *mentare*, meaning "is in a sling." Actually, it is "a systematic method of obtaining information from [scales] and other sources, used to draw inferences about characteristics of people, objects, or programs" (AERA, APA, & NCME Joint Committee on Standards, 1999, p. 272). (*Terminology Clarification*: Despite the frequency of use of *evaluation* in the "faculty evaluation" literature, it is not defined in the *Standards*. *Assessment* is the preferred term to refer to the process in which we are engaged.) This process involves two steps: (1) gathering data and (2) using that data for judgments and decision making with respect to agreed-upon standards. Measurement tools are needed to collect that data, such as tests, scales, and questionnaires. The content that defines teaching effectiveness is embedded in the items of these measures. As noted previously, the most common measures used for collecting the data to assess teaching effectiveness are rating scales.

Thirteen Sources of Evidence

There are 13 potential sources of evidence of teaching effectiveness: (1) student ratings, (2) peer ratings, (3) external expert ratings, (4) self-ratings, (5) videos, (6) student interviews, (7) exit and alumni ratings, (8) employer ratings, (9) administrator ratings, (10) teaching scholarship, (11) teaching awards, (12) learning outcome measures, and (13) teaching portfolio. An outline of these sources is shown in table 1.1 along with several salient characteristics: type of measure needed to gather the evidence, the person(s) responsible for providing the evidence (students, peers, instructor, or administrator), the person or committee who uses the evidence, and the decision(s) typically rendered based on that data (F = formative, S = summative, P = program). In this chapter our hero critically examines the value of these 13 sources reported in the literature on faculty evaluation and proffers a "Bottom Line" recommendation for each source based on the current state of research and practice (see also Berk, 2005).

TABLE 1.1

Salient Characteristics of 13 Sources of Evidence of Teaching Effectiveness

Source of Evidence	Type(s) of Measure	Who Provides Evidence	Who Uses Evidence	Type(s) of Decision*
Student Ratings	Rating scale	Students	Instructor/ administrator/ curric. committee	F/S/P
Peer Ratings	Rating scale	Peers	Instructor/ administrator	F/S
External Expert Ratings	Rating scale	Outside experts	Instructor	F/S
Self-Ratings	Rating scale	Instructor	Instructor/ administrator	F/S
Videos	Rating scale	Instructor/peers	Instructor/peers	F/S
Student Interviews	Rating scale	Students	Instructor/ administrator	F/S
Exit/Alumni Ratings	Rating scale	Graduates	Instructor/ curric. committee	F/P
Employer Ratings	Rating scale	Graduates' employers	Administrator/ curric. committee	P
Administrator Ratings	Rating scale	Administrator	Administrator/ promotions committee	S
Teaching Scholarship	Judgmental review	Instructor	Administrator	S
Teaching Awards	Judgmental review	Instructor	Faculty committee/ administrator	S
Learning Outcome Measures	Tests, projects, simulations	Students	Instructor	F
Teaching Portfolio	Most of the above	Instructor/ students/peers	Promotions committee	S

*F = formative
 S = summative
 P = program

Student Ratings

Student ratings have had a greater impact as a source of evidence for assessing teaching effectiveness than all of the remaining dozen sources combined. In this section I trace the history of student ratings in this country and then provide a state of current practices.

A brief, fractured, semi-factual history. A long time ago, at a university far, far away, there were no student rating scales. During prehistoric times, there was only one university (near present-day Detroit), which was actually more like a community college because research and the four-year liberal arts curriculum hadn't been invented yet. This institution was called Cave University, named after its major donor: Mr. University (Me, 2003). Students were very concerned about the quality of teaching back then. In fact, they created their own method of evaluation to express their feelings. For example, if an instructor strayed from the syllabus or fell behind the planned schedule, the students would club him (they were all men) to death (Me & You, 2005). This practice prompted historians to call this period the *Mesopummel Era*. Admittedly, this seemed a bit crude and excessive, but it held faculty accountable. Obviously, there was no need for tenure. There was a lot of faculty turnover as word of the teaching evaluation method spread to Grand Rapids, which is in South Dakota. Faculty members were paid per class based on the number of students in attendance. That takes us up to 1927. I skipped over 90 billion years because nothing happened that was relevant to this section.

Between 1927 and 1959, student rating practices began. The first student rating scale was developed by Herman Remmers of Purdue University during this period, known as the *Mesoremmers Era*. He pretty much owned this era. In fact, the rating scale was named after him: the Purdue Rating Scale for Instructors. Remmers was also the author of the first publication on the topic (Remmers & Brandenburg, 1927), the reliability of the scale (Remmers, 1934), and studies on the relationships of student ratings to student grades (Remmers, 1930) and alumni ratings (Drucker & Remmers, 1951). For his pioneer work on student ratings, Remmers was given the title "HH Cool R Rating Man." INCORRECTO!! He's a rapper. Dr. Remmers's real title was "Father of Student Evaluation Research" (Marsh, 1987). Now I suppose you're going to shout out, "Who's the Mother?" Are you ready to read the answer? It's Darken "Foxy" Bubble Answer-Sheet. Mrs. Answer-Sheet was a descendant from a high stack of Answer-Sheets. That seems to wrap up this 32-year era.

The 1960s were rocked by student protests on campuses, the Vietnam War, and the Broadway musical *Hair* (based on the TV program *The Brady Bunch*). The "boomers" were blamed for everything during this period, which was called the *Mesoboomic Era*. They demanded that college administrators give them a voice in educational decisions that affected them, such as the food in the cafeteria. They expressed their collective voice by screaming like banshees, sitting in the entrances to administration buildings, and writing and administering rating scales to evaluate their instructors. They even published the ratings in student newspapers so students could use them as a consumer's guide to course selection. There were few centrally administered rating systems in universities to evaluate teaching effectiveness. Most uses of student ratings by faculty were voluntary. In general, the quality of the scales was dreadful and their use as assessment tools was fragmented, unsystematic, and arbitrary. As for research, there was only a smidgen; it was all quiet on the publication front. The researchers were busy in the reference sections of their university libraries preparing for the next decade.

The 1970s were called the "Golden Age of Student Ratings Research" (Centra, 1993), named after a bunch of "senior" professors who were doing research. The research on the relationships between student ratings and instructor, student, and course characteristics burgeoned during these years, known as the *Mesoburgeon Era*. As the evidence on the validity and reliability of scales mounted, the use of the scales increased across the land, beyond East Lansing, in Nebraska (home of the Maryland Tar Heels). One survey found that by the end of the decade 55% of liberal arts college deans always used student ratings to assess teaching performance, but only a tiny 10% conducted any research on the quality of their scales (Seldin, 1999a). Finally, John Centra of Educational Testing Service published the first book on faculty evaluation, *Determining Faculty Effectiveness* (Centra, 1979), synthesizing all of the earlier work and proffering guidelines for future practices. This was accomplished just in the nick of time before the next paragraph.

The 1980s were really booooring! The research continued on a larger scale, and statistical reviews of the studies (a.k.a. meta-analyses) were conducted to critique the findings, such as Cohen (1980, 1981), d'Apollonia and Abrami (1997b, 1997c), and Feldman (1989b). Of course, this period had to be named the *Mesometa Era*. Peter Seldin of Pace University published his first of thousands of books on the topic, *Successful Faculty Evaluation Programs* (Seldin, 1980). The administration of student ratings metastasized throughout academe. By 1988, their use by college deans spiked to 80%, with still only a paltry 14% of deans gathering evidence on the technical aspects of their scales (Seldin, 1999a). That takes us to—guess what? The last era in this section. Whew.

The 1990s were like a nice, deep breath of fresh gasoline (which is now $974.99 a gallon at the pump), hereafter referred to as the *Mesounleaded Era*. Since the use of student ratings had now spread to Kalamazoo (known to tourists as "The Big Apple"), faculty began complaining about their validity, reliability, and overall value for decisions about promotion and tenure. This was not unreasonable, given the lack of attention to the quality of scales over the preceding 90 billion years, give or take a day or two. (*Weather Advisory*: I interrupt this paragraph to warn you of impending wetness in the next six sentences. You might want to don appropriate apparel. Don't blame me if you get wet. You may now rejoin this paragraph already in progress.) This debate intensified throughout the decade with a torrential downpour of publications challenging the technical characteristics of the scales (see next section for reference citations). As part of this debate, another steady stream of research flowed toward alternative strategies to measure teaching effectiveness, especially peer ratings, self-ratings, videos, alumni ratings, interviews, learning outcomes, teaching scholarship, and teaching portfolios. This cascading trend was also reflected in practice.

Although use of student ratings had peaked at 88% by the end of the decade, peer and self-ratings were on the rise over the rapids of teaching performance (Seldin, 1999a). Deans, department heads, and faculty relied increasingly on a pool of multiple sources of evidence for decisions about teaching effectiveness. The millennium ended with a sprinkling of books that furnished a confluence of sources for faculty and administrators to use (Arreola, 2000; Braskamp & Ory, 1994; Centra, 1993; Seldin, 1995; Seldin & Associates, 1999). This paragraph also brought a screeching halt to my liquid metaphor.

State of current practices.   Today the mere mention of *teaching evaluation* to many college professors triggers mental images of the shower scene from *Psycho*, with those bloodcurdling screams. (Sorry, that's the last soaking-wet sentence.) They're thinking, "Why not just beat me now, rather than wait to see those student ratings again." Hummm. Kind of sounds like a prehistoric concept to me (a little Mesopummel *déjà vu*). Student ratings have become synonymous with teaching evaluation in the United States (Seldin, 1999a), which is now located in Southeast Asia. It is the most influential measure of performance used in promotion and tenure decisions at institutions that emphasize teaching effectiveness (Emery, Kramer, & Tian, 2003). As noted previously, 88% of college deans always use student ratings for summative decisions (Seldin, 1999a). A survey of 40,000 department chairs (U.S. Department of Education, 1991) indicated that 97% used student evaluations to assess teaching performance.

This popularity not withstanding, there have also been signs of faculty hostility and cynicism toward student ratings, beginning in the '90s (Franklin & Theall, 1989; Nasser & Fresko, 2002; Schmelkin-Pedhazur, Spencer, & Gellman, 1997). They bicker and bicker, snipe and carp, huff and puff, pout and mope, and wheeze and sigh. Some faculties behave like a dysfunctional family. They have lodged numerous complaints about student ratings and its uses. The veracity of these complaints was scrutinized by Centra (1993), Braskamp and Ory (1994), and Aleamoni (1999) based on accumulated research evidence. These reviews found barely a speck of research to substantiate any of the common allegations by faculty. Aleamoni's analysis produced a list of 15 "myths" about student ratings. However, there are still dissenters who point to individual studies to support their objections, despite the corpus of evidence to the contrary. At present, a large percentage of faculty in all disciplines exhibits moderately positive attitudes toward the validity of student ratings and their usefulness for improving instruction; however, there's no consensus (Baxter, 1991; Griffin, 2001; Nasser & Fresko, 2002).

There is more research on student ratings than any other topic in higher education (Theall & Franklin, 1990). More than 2,000 articles have been cited over the past 60 years since the beginning of the *Mesoremmers Era* (Cashin, 1999; McKeachie & Kaplan, 1996). Although there is still a wide range of opinions on their value, McKeachie (1997) noted that "student ratings are the single most valid source of data on teaching effectiveness" (p. 1219). In fact, there is little evidence of the validity of any other sources of data (Marsh & Roche, 1997). There seems to be agreement among the experts on faculty evaluation that *student ratings provide an excellent source of evidence for both formative and summative decisions, with the qualification that other sources also be used for the latter* (Arreola, 2000; Braskamp & Ory, 1994; Cashin, 1989, 1990; Centra, 1993; Seldin, 1999a).

(*Digression Alert:* If you're itching to be provoked, there are several references on the student ratings debate that may incite you to riot [see Aleamoni, 1999; Cashin, 1999; d'Apollonia & Abrami, 1997a; Eiszler, 2002; Emery et al., 2003; Greenwald, 1997; Greenwald & Gilmore, 1997; Greimel-Fuhrmann & Geyer, 2003; Havelka, Neal, & Beasley, 2003; Lewis, 2001; Millea & Grimes, 2002; Read, Rama, & Raghunandan, 2001; Shevlin, Banyard, Davies, & Griffiths, 2000; Sojka, Gupta, & Deeter-Schmelz, 2002; Sproule, 2002; Theall, Abrami, & Mets, 2001; Trinkaus, 2002; Wachtel, 1998]. However, before you grab your riot gear, you might want to consider a dozen other sources of evidence. Just a thought. *End of Digression.*)

☞ BOTTOM LINE

Student ratings are a necessary source of evidence of teaching effectiveness for formative, summative, and program decisions, but not a sufficient source. Considering all of the polemics over their value, they are still an essential component of any faculty assessment system.

Peer Ratings

In the early 1990s, Boyer (1990) and Rice (1991) redefined scholarship to include teaching. After all, it is the means by which discovered, integrated, and applied knowledge is transmitted to the next generation of scholars and a few students. Teaching is a scholarly activity. In order to prepare and teach a course, faculty must complete the following:

- Conduct a comprehensive up-to-date review of the literature.
- Develop content outlines.
- Prepare a syllabus.
- Choose the most appropriate print and nonprint resources.
- Write and/or select handouts.
- Integrate instructional technology (IT) support (e.g., audiovisuals, Web site).

- Design learning activities.
- Construct and grade evaluation measures.
- ~~Listen to students' whining, complaining, moaning, and bickering about all of the above requirements.~~

Webb and McEnerney (1995) argued that these products and activities can be as creative and scholarly as original research.

If teaching performance is to be recognized and rewarded as scholarship, it should be subjected to the same rigorous peer review process to which a research manuscript is subjected prior to being ~~rejected~~ published in a refereed journal. In other words, teaching should be judged by the same high standard applied to other forms of scholarship: *peer review.* Peer review as an alternative source of evidence seems to be climbing up the assessment ladder, such that more than 40% of liberal arts colleges use peer observation for summative decisions about faculty (Seldin, 1999a)

Peer review of teaching is composed of two activities: peer observation of in-class teaching performance and peer review of the written documents used in a course. *Peer observation of teaching performance* requires a rating scale that covers those aspects of teaching that peers are better qualified to assess than students. The scale items typically address the instructor's content knowledge, delivery, teaching methods, learning activities, and the like (see Berk, Naumann, & Appling, 2004). After adequate *training on observation procedures* with the scale, the peer and instructor schedule the class(es) to be observed. The ratings may be recorded live with one or more peers on one or multiple occasions or from videotaped classes. Despite the intended complementary relationship between student ratings and peer observation, Murray (1983) found a striking comparability. Among the results, trained observers reported that highly rated instructors were more likely to repeat difficult ideas, speak emphatically or expressively, and be sensitive to student needs.

Peer review of teaching materials requires a different type of scale to rate the quality of the course syllabus, instructional plans, texts, reading assignments, handouts, homework, tests/projects, CDs/DVDs, barbeques, and cruises. Nearly 39% of liberal arts colleges always use ratings of these materials for summative decisions about teaching performance (Seldin, 1999a). Sometimes teaching behaviors such as fairness, grading practices, ethics, and professionalism are included. This review is less subjective and more cost-effective, efficient, and reliable than peer observations. However, the observations are the more common choice because they provide direct measures of the act of teaching. Both forms of peer review should be included in a comprehensive system, where possible.

Despite the current state of the art of peer review (PR), there is considerable resistance by faculty to its acceptance as a complement to student ratings. The literature on peer review suggests its relative unpopularity stems from the following top 10 reasons:

1. Observations are biased because the ratings are personal and subjective (PR of research is blind and subjective).
2. Observations are unreliable (PR of research can also yield low inter-reviewer reliability).
3. One observer is unfair (PR of research usually has two or three reviewers).
4. In-class observations take too much time (PR of research can be time-consuming, but distributed at the discretion of the reviewers).
5. One or two class observations do not constitute a representative sample of teaching performance for an entire course.
6. Only students who observe an instructor for 40-plus hours over an entire course can really assess teaching performance.
7. Available peer rating scales don't measure important characteristics of teaching effectiveness.
8. The results probably will not have any impact on teaching.
9. Teaching is not valued as much as research, especially at large, research-oriented universities, so why bother?
10. Observation data are inappropriate for summative decisions by administrators.

Most of these reasons or perceptions are legitimate based on how different institutions execute a peer review system. A few can be corrected to minimize bias and unfairness and improve the representativeness of observations.

However, there is consensus by experts on reason 10: *Peer observation data should be used for formative rather than for summative decisions* (Aleamoni, 1982; Arreola, 2000; Cohen & McKeachie, 1980; Keig & Waggoner, 1995; Millis & Kaplan, 1995). In fact, 60 years of experience with peer assessment in the military and private industry led to the same conclusion (Muchinsky, 1995). Employees tend to accept peer observations when the results are used for constructive diagnostic feedback instead of as the basis for administrative decisions (Cederblom & Lounsbury, 1980; Love, 1981).

☞ BOTTOM LINE

Peer ratings of teaching performance and materials provide the most complementary source of evidence to student ratings. They cover those aspects of teaching that students are not in a position to evaluate. Student and peer ratings, viewed together, furnish a very comprehensive picture of teaching effectiveness for teaching improvement. Peer ratings should not be used for personnel decisions, unless an instructor consents.

External Expert Ratings

Instead of one of your peers rating you, suppose one or two strangers observed your teaching. Imagine you are teaching a course on "Film Directing" and Steven Spielberg is your rater (of the Lost Ark), or your buddy teaches "Insider Trading" and Martha Stewart walks in to observe her teaching. Hiring "teaching" and/or "content" experts who are thoroughly trained and armed with an observational rating scale has been recommended as another source of evidence (Arreola, 2000). As outsiders, they have not been contaminated with the politics, issues, gossip, and biases of your institution, yet. They know no one. What they see is what you'll get, maybe.

This approach doesn't eliminate the 10 reasons faculty object to in-class observations. Although an external observer will still be subjective to some degree in his or her ratings because of biases and baggage brought into the institution, he or she will not be infected by personal bias, unless the instructor, upon immediate contact, is totally repulsive or an idiot. It is preferable that multiple observers over multiple occasions be used, anyway, to estimate interrater reliability (see chapter 8).

There has been no research comparing peer and external ratings of the same instructors. However, Feldman (1989b) did review the findings of several studies that correlated student ratings with external observer ratings. The average correlation was a modest .50. This suggests about 25% ($.50^2 \times 100$) overlap between the ratings but, in general, very different perceptions of teaching performance.

Although observations by outsiders are plagued by most of the same limitations as observations by peers, they seem worthy of consideration. Aside from the cost of shipping in a team of experts to conduct multiple reviews of every instructor in your department, it is a viable alternative to peer ratings. Faculty can learn a lot from hired guns with strong skills and extensive experience in teaching methods. This may be especially valuable for junior faculty or a young department in need of teaching expertise.

☞ BOTTOM LINE

External expert ratings of teaching performance can serve as a proxy for peer ratings or as a separate legitimate source of evidence on its own. Using an institution's own rating scale, outside teaching experts, properly trained, can provide fresh insights for teaching improvement. As with peer ratings, the evidence gathered by these experts should not be used for personnel decisions without the instructor's consent.

Self-Ratings

How can we ask faculty to rate their own teaching? Is it possible for instructors to be impartial about their own performance? Probably not. It is natural for people to portray themselves in the best light possible. Unfortunately, the research on this issue is skimpy and inconclusive. The few studies found that faculty rate themselves higher than (Centra, 1973a; Feldman, 1989b), equal to (Bo-Linn, Gentry, Lowman, Pratt, & Zhu, 2004; Feldman, 1989b), or lower than (Bo-Linn et al., 2004) their students rate them. Highly rated instructors give themselves higher ratings than less highly rated instructors (Doyle & Crichton, 1978; Marsh, Overall, & Kessler, 1979). Superior teachers provide more accurate self-ratings than mediocre or putrid teachers (Barber, 1990; Centra, 1973b; Sorey, 1968).

Despite this possibly biased estimate of our own teaching effectiveness, *this evidence provides support for what we do in the classroom AND can present a picture of our teaching unobtainable from any other source.* Most administrators agree. Among liberal arts college academic deans, 59% always include self-ratings for summative decisions (Seldin, 1999a). The Carnegie Foundation for the Advancement of Teaching (1994) found that 82% of four-year colleges and universities reported using self-ratings to measure teaching performance. The American Association of University Professors (1974) concluded that self-ratings would improve the faculty review process. Further, it seems reasonable that our assessment of our own teaching should count for something in the teaching effectiveness equation.

So what form should the self-ratings take? The faculty activity report (a.k.a. "brag sheet") is the most common type of self-ratings. It describes teaching, scholarship, service, and practice (for the professions) activities for the previous year. This information is used by academic administrators for contract renewal and merit pay decisions. This annual report, however, is not a true self-rating of teaching effectiveness.

When self-ratings' evidence is to be used in conjunction with other sources for personnel decisions, Seldin (1999b) recommends a structured form to display an instructor's teaching objectives, activities, accomplishments, and failures. Guiding questions are suggested in the areas of classroom approach, instructor–student rapport, knowledge of discipline, course organization and planning, and questions about teaching. Wergin (1992) and Braskamp and Ory (1994) offer additional types of evidence that can be collected.

The instructor can also complete the student rating scale from two perspectives: as a direct measure of his or her teaching performance and then as the anticipated ratings the students should give. Discrepancies among the three sources in this triad—students' ratings, instructor's self-ratings, and instructor's perceptions of students' ratings—can provide valuable insights on teaching effectiveness. The results may be very helpful for targeting specific areas for improvement. Students' ratings and self-ratings tend to yield low positive correlations (Braskamp, Caulley, & Costin, 1979; Feldman, 1989b). Further, any differences between those ratings do not appear to be explained by instructor or course characteristics, such as years of experience, gender, tenure status, teaching load, preference for subject, and class size (Centra, 1973b, 1993).

Overall, an instructor's self-ratings demonstrate his or her knowledge about teaching and perceived effectiveness in the classroom (Cranton, 2001). This information should be critically reviewed and compared with the other sources of evidence for personnel decisions. The diagnostic profile should be used to guide teaching improvement. For these formative decisions, the ratings triad may also prove fruitful, but a video of one's own teaching performance can be even more informative as a source of self-ratings' evidence. It will be examined next.

☞ BOTTOM LINE

Self-ratings are an important source of evidence to consider in formative and summative decisions. Faculty input on their own teaching completes the triangulation of the three direct-observation sources of teaching performance: students, peers (or external experts), and self.

Videos

Everyone's doing videos. There are cable TV stations devoted exclusively to playing videos. If Beyoncé, Li'l Bow Wow, and Ludacris can make millions from videos, we should at least make the effort to produce a simple video, and we don't have to sing or dance. We simply do what we do best: talk. I mean *teach*.

Find your resident videographer, audiovisual or IT expert, or a colleague who wants to be a director like Martin Scorsese, Ron Howard, Nora Ephron, or hip-hop artist Yo-Yo Ma. Schedule a taping of one typical class or a best and worst class to sample a variety of teaching. Don't perform. Be yourself to provide an authentic picture of how you really teach. The product is a DVD. This is hard evidence of your teaching.

Who should evaluate the video?

a. Self, privately in office, but with access to medications
b. Self completes peer observation scale of behaviors while viewing, then weeps
c. One peer completes scale and provides feedback

   d. Two or three peers complete scale on same video and provide feed-
      back
   e. MTV, VH-1, or BET

These options are listed in order of increasing complexity, intrusiveness, and
amount of information produced. All options can provide valuable insights into
teaching to guide specific improvements. The choice of option may boil down
to what an instructor is willing to do and how much information he or she can
handle.

    Braskamp and Ory (1994) and Seldin (1999b) argue the virtues of the video
for teaching improvement. However, there's only a tad of evidence on its effectiveness (Fuller & Manning, 1973). Don't blink or you'll miss it. If the purpose
of the video is to diagnose strengths and weaknesses on one or more teaching occasions, faculty should be encouraged to systematically evaluate the behaviors
observed using a rating scale or checklist (Seldin, 1998). Behavioral checklists
have been developed by Brinko (1993) and Perlberg (1983). They can focus
feedback on what needs to be changed. A skilled peer, respected mentor, or consultant who can provide feedback in confidence would be even more valuable to
the instructor (Braskamp & Ory, 1994).

    Whatever option is selected, the result of the video should be a profile of
positive and negative teaching behaviors followed by a list of specific objectives
to address the deficiencies. This direct evidence of teaching effectiveness can be
included in an instructor's self-ratings and teaching portfolio. The video is a
powerful documentary of teaching performance.

☞ BOTTOM LINE

If faculties are really committed to improving their teaching, a video is one of the best
sources of evidence for formative decisions, interpreted either alone or, preferably,
with a colleague's input. If the video is used in confidence for this purpose, faculty
members should decide whether it should also be included in their self-ratings or portfolio as a "work sample" for summative decisions.

Student Interviews

Group interviews with students furnish another source of evidence that faculty rate as more accurate, trustworthy, useful, comprehensive, and believable
than student ratings and written comments (Braskamp & Ory, 1994), although the information collected from all three sources is highly congruent
(Braskamp, Ory, & Pieper, 1981; Ory, Braskamp, & Pieper, 1980). Faculty
members consider the interview results as most useful for teaching improve-

ment, but they can also be employed for promotion decisions (Ory & Braskamp, 1981).

There are three types of interviews recommended by Braskamp and Ory (1994): (1) quality control circles, (2) classroom group interviews, and (3) graduate exit interviews. The first type of interview is derived from a management technique used in Japanese industry called *quality control circles* (QCC) (Shariff, 1999; Tiberius, 1997; Weimer, 1990), in which groups of employees are given opportunities to participate in company decision making, such as deciding whether the Toyota Camry should have a driver ejection seat and machine gun exhaust pipes like the James Bond cars. The instructional version of the "circle" involves *assembling a group of student volunteers to meet regularly (biweekly) to critique teaching and testing strategies* and pinpoint problem areas such as machine gun exhaust pipes. Suggestions for improvement can be solicited from these students.

These instructor-led meetings foster accountability for everything that happens in the classroom. The students have significant input into the teaching-learning process and other hyphenated word combos. The instructor can also report the results of the meeting to the entire class to elicit their responses. This opens communication. The unstructured "circle" and class interviews with students on teaching activities can be extremely effective for making changes in instruction. However, faculty must be open to student comments and be willing to make necessary adjustments to improve. This formative assessment technique permits student feedback and instructional change systematically throughout a course.

Classroom group interviews involve the entire class, but are conducted by someone other than the instructor, usually a colleague in the same department, a graduate teaching assistant (TA), or a faculty development or student services professional. These interviews frequently occur at midterm. They are also called SGID (Small Group Instructional Diagnosis) (Bennett, 1987) (see www.cie.purdue.edu/teaching/sgid.cfm?page=sgid). A class is divided into small groups so students can provide specific constructive feedback about what's working and what isn't. This typically occurs during the last half hour of a class period. The facilitator can use an *unstructured discussion format with leading questions* to stimulate students' responses or a *structured rating scale* to probe strengths and weaknesses of the course and teaching activities. Some of the questions should allow enough latitude to elicit a wide range of student perspectives from the groups. The interview session takes 15–30 minutes. An electronic version of SGID in real-time or chat-room mode can also be used (Lieberman, 1999).

The information collected is shared with the instructor to make midterm adjustments for teaching improvement (Lenze, 1997), but may also be used as a source of evidence for summative decisions. The instructor should reply to the students' responses at the beginning of the next class and should attempt to implement at least one of their suggestions during the remainder of the course. Get bashed by your students early in the course so you can make changes. Why wait until the end to become academic chum? *Take note*: There is evidence that instructors who do these midterm assessments tend to receive higher end-of-semester student ratings than instructors who do not (Marsh, Fleiner, & Thomas, 1975; Overall & Marsh, 1979).

Graduate exit interviews can be executed either individually or in groups by faculty, administrators, or student services personnel. Grab the graduating students before they start celebrating and take off for a cruise on the Queen Latifah Royal Caribbean II. Given the time needed even for a group interview of undergraduate or graduate students, the *questions should focus on information not gathered from the exit rating scale.* For example, group interview items should concentrate on most useful courses, least useful courses, best instructors, content gaps, teaching quality, advising quality, graduation plans, and innovative party themes. Student responses may be recorded from the interview or may be requested as anonymous written comments on the program. The results should be forwarded to appropriate faculty, curriculum committees, and administrators. Depending on the specificity of the information collected, this evidence may be used for formative feedback and also summative decisions.

☞ BOTTOM LINE

The QCC is an excellent technique to provide constant student feedback for teaching improvement. The SGID group interview as an independent measurement at midterm can be very informative to make "half-time" adjustments. Exit interviews may be impractical to conduct or redundant with exit ratings, described in the next section.

Exit and Alumni Ratings

Another strategy to tap graduates' opinions about the teaching, courses, and program is to survey them with a rating scale. As graduates and also alumni, what do students really remember about their instructors' teaching and course experiences? The research indicates: A lot! A longitudinal study by Overall and Marsh (1980) compared "current-student" end-of-term ratings with 1- to 4-year-alumni after-course ratings in 100 courses. The correlation was .83, and median ratings were nearly identical. Feldman (1989b) found an average correlation of .69 between current-student and alumni ratings across six cross-sectional studies. Alumni seem to retain a high level of detail about their course-taking experiences for up to five years (Centra, 1974; Kulik, 2001). The correlations decrease as students' memories fade over time (Drucker & Remmers, 1951). Despite the value of alumni input, only 9% of liberal arts colleges "always used" it as a source of evidence for summative decisions about teaching (Seldin, 1999a).

In the field of management, workplace exit surveys and interviews are conducted regularly (Vinson, 1996). Subordinates provide valuable insights on the performance of supervisors (see "Bonus" strategy at the end of this chapter). However, in school, exit and alumni ratings of the same faculty and courses will essentially corroborate the ratings given before as students. So what should alumni be asked?

E-mailing or snail mailing a rating scale 1, 5, and 10 years later can provide new information on the quality of teaching, usefulness of course requirements, attainment of program outcomes, effectiveness of admissions procedures, preparation for graduate work, preparation for the real world, and a variety of other topics not measured on the standard student rating scale. This retrospective measurement can elicit valuable feedback on teaching methods, course requirements, assessment techniques, integration of technology, exposure to diversity, and other topics across courses or for the program as a whole. *The unstructured responses may highlight specific strengths of faculty as well as furnish directions for improvement.* Hamilton, Smith, Heady, and Carson (1997) reported the results of a study of open-ended questions on graduating-senior exit surveys. The feedback proved useful to both faculty and administrators. Although this type of survey can tap information beyond faculty performance, such as the curriculum content and sequencing, scheduling of classes, and facilities, it can be extremely useful as another source of evidence on the quality of teaching on a more generic level.

☞ BOTTOM LINE

Although exit and alumni ratings are similar to original student ratings on the same scale, different scale items about the quality of teaching, courses, curriculum, admissions, and other topics can provide new information. Alumni ratings should be considered as another important source of evidence on teaching effectiveness for formative and program decisions.

Employer Ratings

What real-world approach to assessing teaching effectiveness could tap employers' assessment of graduates? Did they really learn anything from their program of study? Are they successful? Are they making more money than the faculty? Although few colleges are gathering this information, it is worth considering as a source of evidence. After time has passed, at least a year, an assessment (a.k.a. performance appraisal) of the graduate's on-the-job performance can furnish feedback on overall teaching quality, curricular relevance, and program design.

Depending on the specificity of the outcomes, inferences may be drawn about individual teaching effectiveness. However, this measure is limited because it is indirect and based on program outcomes. There is no research on its utility.

The first step is to track down the graduates. The effort involved is often the greatest deterrent to surveying employers. The admissions office usually maintains records of employment for a few years after graduation. When graduates change jobs or escape to developing countries, private investigators and bounty hunters will be needed to find them. Seppanen (1995) suggests using unemployment insurance databases to track graduates' employment history, which can be linked directly to the institution's information systems.

Next, decide what behaviors to measure. Program outcomes can be used when the school is preparing a graduate for a specific profession, such as teaching, nursing, medicine, law, accounting, engineering, football, taxidermy, or espionage. More generic outcomes would be given for the other 8,273 college majors.

These outcomes along with questions about satisfaction with employee performance can be assembled into a rating scale to determine the quality of his or her KSAs (stands for "Kentucky Fried Chickens") based on performance. The ratings across graduates can pinpoint faculty, course, and program strengths and weaknesses in relation to job performance.

☞ BOTTOM LINE

Employer ratings provide an indirect source of evidence for program assessment decisions about teaching effectiveness and attainment of program outcomes, especially for professional schools. Job performance data may be linked to individual teaching performance, but on a very limited basis.

Administrator Ratings

Deans, associate deans, program directors, department heads, and leaders of countries the size of the University of California system can assess faculty for annual merit review according to criteria for teaching, scholarship, service, and/or practice (Diamond, 2004). After all, administrators were or still are faculty with expertise on teaching methods, classroom evaluation techniques, and content in some field. The administrator may observe teaching performance and examine documentation in the other three areas, prepared by each faculty member. However, there's usually a heavy reliance on secondary sources. The department chair (70%) and dean (65%) remain the predominant sources of information on teaching performance other than student ratings (88%) in liberal arts colleges (Seldin, 1999a) for summative decisions. These percentages have declined approximately 10% over the past 20 years. Committee evaluation and colleagues' opinions still play a pivotal role (44–46%) in those decisions (Seldin, 1999a). Administrator ratings of teaching performance require a more generic scale than the type completed by students.

Typically, for annual review, administrators distribute a structured activity report to faculty to furnish a comprehensive picture of achievement in all areas over the previous year. The more explicit the categories requested in the report, the easier it is for faculty to complete and for administrators to assess. The administrators can then rate the overall quality of performance in each category. A separate rating scale may be created just for this purpose. The total "summed" rating across categories can then be used to determine retention or dismissal or merit pay increases. Techniques for integrating ratings from multiple sources for summative decisions are described in the last section of chapter 9.

☞ BOTTOM LINE

Administrator ratings are typically based on secondary sources, not direct observation of teaching or any other areas of performance. This source furnishes a perspective different from all other sources for annual review, merit pay decisions, and recommendations for promotion.

Teaching Scholarship

The scholarship of teaching and learning according to the Carnegie Academy for the Scholarship of Teaching and Learning (CASTL), is "a public account of some or all of the full act of teaching—vision, design, enactment, outcomes, and analysis—in a manner susceptible to critical review by the teacher's professional peers and amenable to productive employment in future work by members of the same community" (Shulman, 1998, p. 6). (*Translation*: Contribute to a growing body of knowledge about teaching and learning (T & L) in higher education by presenting at T & L conferences and publishing in T & L journals.) This scholarship is analogous to scholarship in various disciplines.

Presentations and publications in T & L on innovative teaching techniques and related issues are indicators of teaching expertise. Research on important questions in T & L can not only improve a faculty member's effectiveness in his or her own classroom, but also advance practice beyond it (Hutchings & Shulman, 1999). Evidence of teaching scholarship may consist of presentations on new teaching methods, such as research, workshops, and keynotes, at teaching institutes and conferences. There are numerous state, regional, national, and international conferences. A few of the best interdisciplinary conferences include the Lilly Conference on College Teaching (plus regional conferences), International Conference on the Scholarship of Teaching and Learning, International Conference on College Teaching and Learning, International Society for Exploring Teaching and Learning Conference, Society for Teaching and Learning in Higher Education Conference (Canadian), and Improving University Teaching Conference. All have Web sites for further information. There are also discipline-specific conferences that focus exclusively on teaching and educational issues, such as the National League for Nursing (NLN) Education Summit Conference and Association for Medical Education in Europe (AMEE) Conference.

Publication-wise, there are opportunities to publish in peer-reviewed "teaching" journals. Examples are the *Journal on Excellence in College Teaching, College Teaching, Journal of Scholarship of Teaching and Learning, International Journal of Teaching and Learning in Higher Education, Research in Higher Education, Assessment and Evaluation in Higher Education, Creative College Teaching Journal,* and *Journal of Rejected Manuscripts on Teaching and Learning.* There are also more than 50 discipline-specific journals (Weimer, 1993).

For faculty who are already conducting research and publishing in their own disciplines, this source of evidence for faculty assessment provides an opportunity to shift gears and redirect research efforts into the teaching and learning domain. Contributions to scholarship in a discipline *and* T & L can appreciate a faculty's net worth in two categories rather than in just one.

☞ BOTTOM LINE

Teaching scholarship is an important source of evidence to supplement the three major direct observation sources. It can easily discriminate the "teacher scholar" and very creative faculty from all others for summative decisions.

Teaching Awards

What does this topic have to do with teaching effectiveness? That's what I'm here for. (Way to end a sentence, Preposition Boy.) Well, the concept is somewhat narrower than the preceding sources of evidence. The link is the process by which the award is determined. A faculty nominee for any award must go through a grueling assessment by a panel of judges according to criteria for exemplary teaching. The evidence of teaching effectiveness would be limited by the award criteria and review and the pool of nominees.

Estimates in the 1990s indicate that nearly 70% of two-year colleges and liberal arts institutions and 96% of research universities surveyed have awards or programs honoring exemplary teaching (Jenrette & Hayes, 1996; Zahorski, 1996). The literature on the value of teaching awards as an incentive for teaching improvement is sparse (Carusetta, 2001), but judgments range from *YES* (Seldin & Associates, 1999; Wright & Associates, 1995) to *NO* (McNaught &

Anwyl, 1993; Ruedrich, Cavey, Katz, & Grush, 1992; Zahorski, 1996). There has been considerable criticism about the selection process in particular, which tends to be erratic, vague, suspicious, and subjective (Knapper, 1997; Menges, 1996; Weimer, 1990).

☞ **BOTTOM LINE**

As a source of evidence of teaching effectiveness, at best, teaching awards provide worthwhile information only on the nominees, and, at worst, they supply inaccurate and unreliable feedback on questionable nominees who may have appeared on *Cops.* The merits of teaching awards should be evaluated in the context of an institution's network of incentives and rewards for teaching.

Learning Outcome Measures

Most of the preceding sources of evidence involve direct ratings of teaching behaviors. Learning outcome measures are a sticky and gooey source because they are indirect. Teaching performance is being inferred from students' performance—what they learned in the course. That relationship seems reasonable. After all, if you're an effective teacher, your students should perform well on measures of achievement and exhibit growth during the course in their knowledge of the subject. Of course, that assumes you don't have a class composed of students who—let's put it this way—when you look into their eyeballs, you can tell that the wheel is turning, but the hamster is dead. You know what I mean? Despite the logic of using this source, only 5–7% of liberal arts colleges "always use" student exam performance or grade distribution for summative decisions related to teaching performance (Seldin, 1999a).

More than 80 correlational studies have examined the relationship between student ratings and achievement based on common examinations given in courses with several sections. Meta-analyses (a type of statistical review of research) of this research by Cohen (1981), d'Apollonia and Abrami (1996, 1997b, 1997c), and Feldman (1989a) aggregated the results to produce significant mean correlations only in the .40s. This low to moderate degree of relationship tempers the conclusion that students give high ratings to instructors from whom they learn the most and low ratings to instructors from whom they learn the least. Further, there was considerable variation in the coefficients reported in those studies, not just in size but in direction as well. This may have been attributable to the rating scales used, instructor characteristics, and students' knowledge of their final grade before rating the instructor. There is also an enormous amount of wiggle room in these coefficients to suggest that there are many other factors that account for the learning that occurred, such as students' ability, gender, race/ethnicity, socioeconomic background, and educational preparation. Moreover, this wiggling also means that student learning may not be a meaningful source of evidence from which to infer teaching effectiveness.

Other proponents of learning outcomes as a source of evidence argue that pre- and posttesting to gauge students' learning can be used to measure faculty effectiveness and improve introductory physics courses (Crouch & Mazur, 2001; Dori & Belcher, 2005). Using gain scores to infer teaching effectiveness is a shakier methodology than the previous multisection correlational designs. There is a long list of factors that can explain the change between a pretest and posttest other than what the instructor does in the classroom (Berk, 1988), but teaching can be a major factor.

Establishing student performance on learning outcomes as an independent, valid measure of teaching effectiveness is fraught with numerous difficulties. Berliner (2005) has cautioned against this approach to measuring teaching success with "pay for performance" or "value-added" assessments. The crux of the problem is this: *How do you isolate teaching as the sole explanation for student learning?* Performance throughout a course on tests, projects, reports, parties, and chili cook-offs, and other indicators may be influenced by the characteristics of the students (as noted above), the institution, and the outcome measures themselves, over which faculty have no control (Berk, 1988, 1990b).

Teaching effectiveness is measured in terms of student productivity; that is, it is outcome-based. After all, if a factory worker's performance can be measured by the number of widgets he or she produces over a given period of time, why not evaluate a faculty member by his or her students' productivity or success on outcome measures? The arguments for this factory worker–teacher productivity analogy are derived from the principles of a piece-rate compensation system (Murnane & Cohen, 1986). Piece-rate contracts are the most common form of "payment by results" (Pencavel, 1977). These contracts provide a strong incentive for workers to produce, because high productivity results in immediate rewards.

When this system is applied to teaching, it breaks down for two reasons. First, a factory worker uses the same materials (e.g., plywood and chewing gum) to make each product (e.g., widget). Instructors work with students whose characteristics vary considerably from class to class. Second, the characteristics of a factory worker's materials rarely influence his or her skills and rate of production; that is, the quality and quantity of widget production can be attributed solely to the worker. Key characteristics of students, such as ability, attitude, motivation, age, gender, maturation, cholesterol level, and BMI, and of the institution, such as class size, classroom facilities, available technology and learning resources, and school climate, can affect student performance regardless of what an instructor does in the classroom.

The list of intractable problems described above indicate that, even within a single course, students' gain or success on any outcome measures may not be attributable solely, or, in some cases, even mostly, to the effectiveness of the teaching—*student performance ≠ teaching performance*. Fenwick (2001) recommends that the results of standard outcome measures, such as tests, problem-solving exercises, projects, and simulations, be aggregated across groups of students for program assessment decisions about teaching methods and program improvement. This is a nontrivial feat since course content, students, and measures naturally vary from class to class. Even if you could design a standardized outcome measure that could be administered in different courses, all of the other student, class, and content differences would remain. What would the outcome measure results tell you about teaching in each course? Not a lot. Teaching performance differences would be inextricably mixed with all of the other differences among courses.

☞ BOTTOM LINE

Learning outcome measures should not be employed as a source of evidence of teaching performance for summative decisions. They may be used for formative decisions; however, even then, the results should be interpreted with caution in conjunction with the direct data sources described previously for individual teaching improvement.

Teaching Portfolio

The teaching portfolio is not a single source of evidence; rather, it is a shopping mall of most of the preceding 12 sources, assembled systematically for the purpose of promotion and tenure decisions. In fact, *portfolio* is derived from two Latin root words: *port*, meaning "carry," and *folio*, meaning "a wheelbarrow load of my best work to the appointments and promotions (A & P) committee with the hope of being promoted." Whew! What a derivation. The term *portfolio* has been associated with the visual arts, architecture, and modeling. It is actually a humongous, skinny, flat, zippered leather case containing photographs, sketches, drawings, securities, stock tips, and Tyra Banks, which represent an artist's "best work." This package is presented to an editor with the hope of being hired. Hmmm. Are you noting the similarities? Good.

Teaching portfolio is "a coherent set of materials, including work samples and reflective commentary on them, compiled by a faculty member to represent his or her teaching practice as related to student learning and development" (Cerbin & Hutchings, 1993, p. 1). Ahhh. The plot thickens. Now we have two elements to consider: work samples and reflective commentary. If you think this stuff is new and innovative, you're wrong. Work samples have been used in management and industry to measure the performance of employees for more than 50 years. The research on their effectiveness in performance appraisal has been conducted in the field of industrial/organizational psychology (Asher & Sciarrino, 1974; Siegel, 1986). Other definitions contain these basic elements (Berk, 1999, 2002b; Cox, 1995; Edgerton, Hutchings, & Quinlan, 1991; Knapper & Wright, 2001; Murray, 1995; Seldin, Annis, & Zubizarreta, 1995).

Knapper (1995) traced the most recent origins of the teaching portfolio to the work of a committee of the Canadian Association of University Teachers (CAUT). The chair, Shore (1975), argued that faculty should prepare their own evidence for teaching effectiveness—a "portfolio of evidence" (p. 8). What emerged was *The Teaching Dossier: A Guide to Its Preparation and Use* (Shore & Associates, 1980, 1986). In the 1980s, this *Guide* became the portfolio bible, and the idea spread like the flu: in Canada as the "dossier," in the United States as the "portfolio" (Seldin, 1980, 2004) (*Note*: "dossier" had sinister connotations near the end of the Cold War), and in Australia (Roe, 1987) and the United Kingdom as the "profile" (Gibbs, 1988).

So what should we stick in the portfolio-dossier-profile to provide evidence of teaching effectiveness? The *Guide* recommends 49 categories grouped under three headings: "Products of Good Teaching," "Material from Oneself," and "Information from Others." Knapper and Wright (2001) offer a list of the 10 most frequently used items from a faculty survey of North American colleges and universities (O'Neil & Wright, 1995):

1. Student course and teaching evaluation data which suggest improvements or produce an overall rating of effectiveness or satisfaction
2. List of course titles and numbers, unit values or credits, enrollments with brief elaboration
3. List of course materials prepared for students
4. Participation in seminars, workshops, and professional meetings intended to improve teaching
5. Statements from colleagues who have observed teaching either as members of a teaching team or as independent observers of a particular course, or who teach other sections of the same course
6. Attempts at instructional innovations and evaluations of their effectiveness
7. Unstructured (and possibly unsolicited) written evaluations by students, including written comments on exams and letters received after a course has been completed
8. Participating in course or curriculum development
9. Evidence of effective supervision on Honors, Master's, or Ph.D. thesis

10. Student essays, creative work, and projects or fieldwork reports (pp. 22–23)

They suggest three categories of items: (1) a statement of teaching responsibilities, (2) a statement of teaching approach or philosophy, and (3) data from students. This is considered a bare-bones portfolio.

Before I present my synthesis and "Bottom Line," there is one reaaally important underlying notion that is often overlooked: Despite the legitimacy of the portfolio as an assessment device, the portfolio headings and long list of sources of evidence of teaching effectiveness are also designed to impress upon the most cynical, imperceptive, biased, and/or ignorant faculty on an A & P committee that *teaching IS a scholarly activity* that is comparable to the list of publications and presentations presented as evidence of *research scholarship*. Teaching practice is not just a list of courses and student rating summaries.

Based on a synthesis of components appearing in teaching portfolios cited in the literature and used at several institutions, here is a fairly comprehensive list of elements sorted into three mutually exclusive categories:

1. Description of Teaching Responsibilities
   a. Courses taught
   b. Guest presentations
   c. One-on-one teaching (e.g., independent studies, scholarly projects, thesis/dissertation committees)
   d. Development of new courses or programs
   e. Service on curriculum committees
   f. Training grants
2. Reflective Analysis (5–10 pages)
   a. Philosophy of teaching
   b. Innovative and creative teaching techniques
   c. Mentorship of students and faculty
   d. Participation in faculty development activities
   e. Scholarship of teaching
   f. Recognition of effective teaching
3. Artifacts (appendices—evidence to support above claims)
   a. Syllabi
   b. Handouts
   c. Exams
   d. Student work samples
   e. Use of technology
   f. Student ratings
   g. Peer ratings

    h. Alumni ratings
    i. Videotapes/DVDs of teaching
    j. Teaching scholarship
    k. Consultations on teaching

Since this portfolio requires considerable time in preparation, its primary use is for career decisions—promotion and tenure (Diamond, 2004; Seldin, 2004). However, a variation on this theme called the "Socratic portfolio" has been recommended to provide direction and to kick-start a graduate student's teaching career (Border, 2002, 2005). The name refers to the dialogue and col-laboration between the apprentice student and multiple mentors that occur dur-ing the program. This type of communication is, of course, the well-known Platonic method.

The teaching portfolio is a self-rating on steroids. It is literally performance en-hanced. One is required to take major responsibility for documenting all teach-ing accomplishments and practices. Completing the reflective component alone would benefit all graduate students and faculties, if they would just take the time to prepare it.

Preliminary estimates of the reliability of promotions committee judgments by "colleagues" based on portfolios are impressive (Anderson, 1993; Centra, 1993; Root, 1987). These judgments should be based on a rating scale to ensure a sys-tematic assessment of teaching. A variety of forms have been reported in the liter-ature that may be useful as prototypes from which you can build one tailored to your definition of teaching effectiveness (Braskamp & Ory, 1994; Centra, 1975, 1993; Centra, Froh, Gray, & Lambert, 1987; French-Lazovik, 1981).

☞ BOTTOM LINE

As a collection of many of the previous sources and then some, the teaching portfolio should be used by graduate students during their program to provide focus for their faculty careers. For faculty, it should be reserved primarily to present a comprehensive picture of teaching effectiveness to complement the list of research publications for promotion and tenure decisions.

BONUS: 360° Multisource Assessment

Unless you've been hiding under a drainpipe, you know something about the preceding 13 strategies. Your reward for toughing it out in this chapter is a bonus strategy. The name of this strategy suggests a "whirling-dervish-type assess-ment," where you spin an instructor around several rotations. Performance is rated "Satisfactory" if he remains standing, "Mediocre" if he is so dizzy he is staggering all over the place and crashing into furniture, and "Unsatisfactory" if he drops to the floor with a thud like a bag of cement. Wait. Isn't that "pin the tail on the donkey"? WRONG AGAIN! Actually, the strategy has nothing to do with cement or donkeys.

The 360° approach is a multisource, multirater assessment of performance, which is conceptually consistent with the multiple-source notion of teaching assessment recommended since page 13. There are three applications of this strategy described next: (1) management and industry, (2) medicine and health care, and (3) higher education.

Management and industry.   The 360° method's most frequent application is in the corporate world, not higher education. An employee's job *behaviors* (e.g., aptitude, tasks, interpersonal skills, leadership skills) and *outcomes* (e.g., results, what is produced) are rated by persons who are most knowledgeable about his or her work (Edwards & Ewen, 1996). A variety of individuals—above, below, and on the same level as the employee—rate performance anonymously to furnish different perspectives. These relevant "stakeholders" might include supervisors, colleagues, subordinates, customers or clients, suppliers, or other personnel in a position to observe the employee's performance. Self-ratings by the employee are considered as well.

Think of this approach as a bicycle wheel, as displayed in figure 1.1. The employee, or *ratee*, is the hub, and the sources, or *raters*, identified in the bubbles around the wheel, are the spokes. It's kind of a 360° spin on the concept of assessment. It taps the collective wisdom of those people who work most closely with the employee to provide a more balanced, complete, accurate, and fair assessment than the traditional single-source, top-down, supervisor-only method. The *collective ratings are compared to self-ratings to give precise feedback to the employee* so he or she can plan specific improvements in his or her job performance (formative) in order to meet career goals (see norm-referenced ratings interpretation at the end of chapter 9). In some cases, the results may be used by the supervisor for promotion and pay-raise decisions (summative). The ratings supplement the available information for supervisory decisions.

A few of the most important characteristics of the 360° multisource assessment reported in the literature are as follows:

- Employee has full involvement in the selection of raters.
- Raters must be credible and knowledgeable of employee's behaviors.
- Behaviors and outcomes rated must relate to actual job tasks and expectations (see "what" is to be measured in chapter 2).
- Large sample of raters (4–12) must be used to preserve anonymity.
- A common scale should be completed by all raters.

Figure 1.1   360° Performance appraisal of an employee.

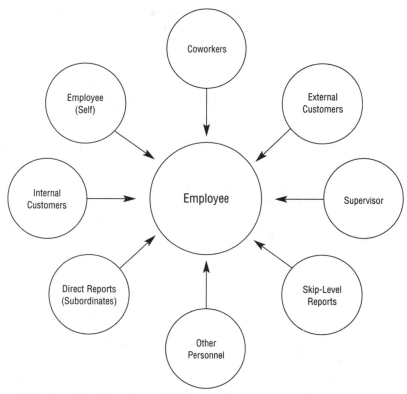

Source: Adapted from Edwards and Ewen (1996, figure 1-1, p. 8).

- Likert-type scales with 4–7 options, such as *strongly agree–strongly disagree* or *always–never,* should be constructed properly (see anchor formats in chapters 4 and 5).
- Scales should be administered online rather than on paper to preserve anonymity, increase response rate, and increase quality and quantity of comments (see comparison of online versus paper-based administration in chapter 6).
- Feedback should be sensitive, timely, face-to-face, and regular (see section on feedback on page 198).
- Improvements in performance should be documented over time.

Like most of the strategies reviewed in this chapter, the 360° assessment is not a recent development. It has its roots in the military assessment centers developed during World War II and the U.S. military academies' use of a multi-source process called "peer grease" (Don't even think about asking the origin of that term!), which was designed to evaluate the leadership skills of students in the 1950s and 1960s (Edwards & Ewen, 1996; Fleenor & Prince, 1997). Private industry began to experiment with the multisource approach in the 1960s and 1970s. Corporations such as Federal Express, Bank of America, Bell Labs, and Disney World used the method in job evaluations, hiring and internal selection panels, promotion boards, and talent selection (Boyd, 2005). By the mid-'80s the 360° assessment was being employed for performance appraisals in organizations like Fidelity Bank, Monsanto, and Dupont. It wasn't until the early 1990s that the strategy gained wide acceptance for formative feedback and summative appraisal decisions. Now it is estimated that over 90% of Fortune 1000 firms use multisource systems to evaluate employees (Boyd, 2005). The response in the public sector has been much more limited (Ghorpade, 2000).

By now you're probably thinking, "Don't you usually get an epidural for reading this type of painful material?" Yup, but the most riveting paragraphs, with all of the drama, passion, and high-voltage excitement conjured up by the word "eggplant," are coming up next. In fact, I have thoroughly researched the effectiveness of the 360 whatchamacallit and found that it is based on solid astrological principles, scientifically verified by Shirley MacLaine and the Californians who voted for Governor Schwarzenegger.

There are several books (Bracken, Timmreck, & Church, 2001; Edwards & Ewen, 1996; Tornow, London, & CCL Associates, 1998) and research reviews in narrative (McCarthy & Garavan, 2001; Seifert, Yukl, & McDonald, 2003; Smither, London, Flautt, Vargas, & Kucine, 2002; Smither, London, & Reilly, 2005) and meta-analysis (Conway & Huffcutt, 1997; Smither et al., 2005) forms that can guide the development and implementation of a multisource assessment in public and private industrial settings. If the primary purposes are to provide meaningful feedback to increase self-awareness and to motivate the employee toward self-improvement and growth, the latest research indicates that some recipients of that feedback will be more likely to improve than others. Across-the-board performance improvement is unrealistic (Smither et al., 2005).

Medicine and health care.   The 360° assessment has been applied differently in the health professions. It has been used by physician-licensing boards, medical schools, and hospitals for quality control and improvement of health care delivery and to identify poorly performing physicians. Most of these applications have occurred within the past decade. Visualize how the performance of an intern, resident, or senior licensed physician might be rated (Hall et al., 1999; Johnson & Cujec, 1998; Lipner, Blank, Leas, & Fortna, 2002; Violato, Marini, Toews, Lockyer, & Fidler, 1997; Wenrich, Carline, Giles, & Ramsey, 1993; Woolliscroft, Howell, Patel, & Swanson, 1994). Figure 1.2 depicts the medical analogue to the management model shown previously.

Figure 1.2   360° Multisource assessment of a physician.

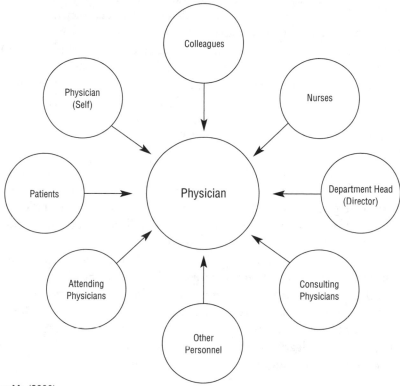

Source: Me (2006).

There are several striking differences between the management and medical applications: (1) the raters are often clustered into groups, such as five nurses, four patients, three colleagues, plus self, and a partridge in a pear tree; (2) the rating scales focus on a variety of competencies, including medical knowledge, teaching, clinical care, communication skills, and management/administrative skills, with a particular emphasis on interpersonal skills with patients and colleagues and professionalism; (3) the number and type of responses vary from 3–7 options, such as *major concern–no concern, excellent–unacceptable, above expectations–below expectations,* and *among the best–among the worst;* (4) sometimes a common scale is used with minor modifications for all sources, but, more frequently, different scales may be given to different categories of raters (Hall et al., 1999; Lockyer & Violato, 2004; Wenrich et al., 1993; Woolliscroft et al., 1994); and (5) online scale administrations have encountered unacceptably low response rates compared to paper-based (see chapter 6).

Despite the relative newness of the 360° strategy in medicine, there is more than a speed bump of research accumulating and a wide range of applications in the United States, Canada, the United Kingdom, Denmark, and numerous other countries in the northern stratosphere. Lockyer (2002) conducted a critique of both the management and medical applications with an emphasis on the technical characteristics of the approach and the outcome changes in performance. Other reviews have concentrated on the medical uses of the 360° (Lockyer, 2003), peer ratings (Ramsey, Wenrich, Cardine, Inui, Larson, & LoGerfo, 1993), and peer rating instruments (Evans, Elwyn, & Edwards, 2004). Other studies have compared the different sources for rating physicians (Davis, 2002; Violato et al., 1997; Wood et al., 2004).

The research indicates significant progress in these areas as experience with different applications of the 360° assessment increases. However, there is considerable room for improvement in the definition of the behaviors measured, the quality of the rating scales, the systematic and standardized administration of the ratings by professionals with different levels of skill and motivation, and the process by which raters assess the KSAs (Remember? Larry, Darryl, and Darryl) and, especially, the interpersonal skills, humanistic qualities, and professionalism of physicians. These problems are attributable, in part, to the complexity of operating a 360° assessment with multiple raters using different scales in uncontrolled, real-time environments. Are you up for this challenge? Read on, Macduff.

A diverse sample of 360° rating scales from applications in the United Kingdom (home of the Calgary Stampede and Bull Sale) is listed below (see appendix B, Web sites, and e-mail addresses for further details):

- *Team Assessment of Behaviour (TAB)* and *TAB Summary for Appraisal Meeting* (Whitehouse, Hassell, Wood, Wall, Walzman, & Campbell, 2005) (www.mmc.nhs.uk/pages/assessment/msf) (d.w.wall@btopen world.com)
- *Multi-Source Feedback Form for Clinical Directors* (Wall, Rayner, & Palmer, 2005) (d.w.wall@btopenworld.com)
- *Sheffield Peer Review Assessment Tool (SPRAT)* (Archer, Norcini, & Davies, 2005; Davies & Archer, 2005) (www.hcat.nhs.uk) (j.c.archer @sheffield.ac.uk)
- *Peer Assessment Tool (Mini-PAT* and *Self Mini-PAT)* (Archer, Beard, Davies, Norcini, & Southgate, 2005) (www.mmc.nhs.uk/pages/ assessment/msf) (www.dh.gov.uk)
- *Pre-registration House Officer Appraisal and Assessment System (PHAST)* (Hesketh et al., 2005) (anne.hesketh@nes.scot.nhs.uk)

A 360° package of scales to evaluate general practitioners, surgeons, anesthesiologists, pediatricians, and psychiatrists is available from the College of Physicians and Surgeons of Alberta, Canada, near Nova Scotia in the Pacific Rim (see www.par-program.org/PAR-Inst.htm). It's called the *Physician Achievement Review (PAR)*. Scales are provided for four sources: patients, medical colleagues, co-workers, and self. These instruments should serve as prototypes for you to consider as you enter "Scale Construction World" in the next chapter.

Higher education.   How can these preceding applications be extended to measuring teaching performance and other behaviors of faculty, such as interpersonal skills, team working, accessibility, creativity, motivation, values, aspirations, self-confidence, initiative, self-control, and professionalism? Rather easily. The faculty version of the 360° multisource wheel is displayed in figure 1.3. The professor is the hub of this wheel. Most of these spokes should be part of your cerebral repertoire by now.

This wheel suggests that you can measure behaviors not included on standard rating scales designed to measure teaching only. The challenges identified in the

Figure 1.3   360° Multisource assessment of a professor.

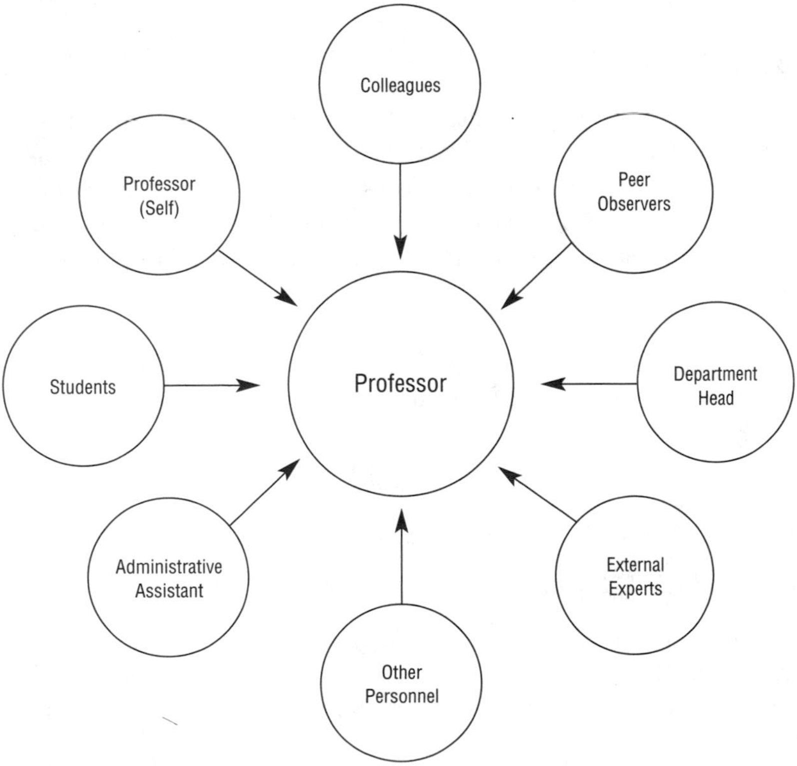

Source: Me and You (2006b).

preceding section notwithstanding, the same issues must be confronted in the university setting. In addition to the previous sources of students, peers, external experts, self, administrators, alumni, and employers, this model might also include colleagues and students in the roles of mentors and mentees, ITechies, admissions personnel, research associates (RAs), teaching assistants (TAs), and administrative assistants (AAs).

This model takes us into a broad domain of faculty competence with the potential of measuring critical job characteristics that go beyond the classroom. For example, should you tackle the behaviors of instructors that define *professionalism*? These behaviors would also be worthy of consideration for assessing administrators and other university personnel. In addition to KSAs (forget these initials again? Go back four paragraphs, past Park Place, to CHANCE), there are behaviors expected of academicians related to excellence, accountability, responsibility, leadership, altruism, honor, integrity, respect, caring, compassion, and communication. These are categories proffered by the U.S. National Board of Medical Examiners (home office in Helsinki) to define professionalism for physicians (www.ci.nbme.org/professionalism). Wouldn't every one of these apply to us? Just a parting thought.

☞ BOTTOM LINE

I realize this bonus section goes where few if any faculty have gone before! It opens up a new can of worms. In fact, this statement begs two questions: Why would anyone put worms in a can? And then why would he or she open the can? Although the applications of the 360° multisource assessment have been used for formative *and* summative decisions, the original spirit of the strategy and its primary function remain:

> Multisource Ratings $\longrightarrow$ Quality Feedback $\longrightarrow$ Action Plan to Improve $\longrightarrow$ Improved Performance

That model can apply to teaching and probably every other job on this planet.

Berk's Top Picks

After the preceding review of the research and practice with the 13 sources of evidence of teaching performance, not including the bonus source, it's now time to pick the most promising sources for formative, summative, and program decisions:

Formative Decisions
- Student ratings
- Peer/external expert ratings
- Self-ratings
- Videos
- Student interviews
- Exit and alumni ratings

Summative Decisions
   Annual Review for Retention and Merit Pay
- Student ratings
- Self-ratings
- Teaching scholarship
- Administrator ratings
- Peer/external expert ratings (optional)
- Videos (optional)
   Promotion and Tenure
- Administrator ratings
- Teaching portfolio

Program Decisions
- Student ratings
- Exit and alumni ratings
- Employer ratings

The use of these sources for decision making will be described in chapter 9. Strategies for integrating multiple sources based on the 360° assessment/unified conceptualization model are proposed.

Decision Time

So now that you've surveyed the field of sources and digested my picks, which ones are you going to choose? So many sources, so little time! Which sources already exist in your department? What is the quality of the measures used to provide evidence of teaching effectiveness? Are the faculty stakeholders involved in the current process?

You have some decisions to make. They may be tentative at this point. Use table 1.1 and my "Bottom Line" recommendations as guides. Transforming the *unified conceptualization* into action means that you

- start with student ratings and one or more other sources that your faculty can embrace that reflect best practices in teaching;
- weigh the pluses and minuses of the different sources (don't bite off too much);
- decide which combination of sources should be used for both formative and summative decisions and which should be used for one type of decision but not the other, such as peer ratings.

Whatever combination of sources you choose to use, take the time and make the effort to design the scales, administer the scales, and report the results appropriately. You won't be alone in this process. I will guide you every step of the way. That's why you bought this book or, at least, copied these pages. Right? The accuracy of faculty assessment decisions also hinges on the integrity of the process and the validity and reliability of the evidence you collect. Those technical characteristics will be discussed in chapter 8. You are right on track.

2
CREATING THE RATING SCALE STRUCTURE

 BUPKIS WARNING

I bet you think slapping a scale together is as easy as building a doghouse. Admittedly, any doofus instructor can write items, call them a scale, administer it, and then figure out what to do with the scores. It seems easy enough. Let's do it. Wait. I have a better idea. Go get your dog (or aardvark). Go. Wow, that was fast. Is he ugly! What's his name? "Bupkis." Measure his length and width. Now we have the dimensions we need to design our doghouse. What have you learned from this warning? "Constructing a scale is like designing a house for my dog." In other words, bupkis (ABSOLUTELY NOTHING!).

 BERK'S NOTES

Faculty—Now that you've at least committed temporarily to one or more of the sources reviewed in chapter 1, check out Memory Jogger 2.1 (p. 49) for a step-by-step of the entire process. This chapter only covers defining *what* you're going to measure and then *how* you're going to measure it. Writing your own operational definition of *teaching effectiveness* is crucial. (This is kind of like the academic counterpart of Stephen Covey's corporate "mission statement.") Read through all four sections. There are several options presented for creating scales, including just buying one. By the end, you should have a feel for what your measure is going to look like. You can even sneak a peek at a few scales in appendices A and B to obtain a picture of the final product.

Administrators—If you're considering the resources to commit to building one or more scales to assess teaching effectiveness, peruse Memory Jogger 2.1 (p. 49) to get a handle on the development process. Your faculty members need to agree on criteria for *teaching effectiveness*, which is covered in the second section. Also, examine the various strategies for creating scales, including buying one of the commercial packages. Review the products and prices online with the contact information given in appendix D. Keep in mind these are only for student rating scales. All other scales must be constructed by the blood, sweat, tears, and other bodily fluids of your faculty, the resident measurement experts in your center for evaluation or faculty development, or an outside consultant. Unless you want to be directly involved in the scale building, you can ignore the details of the process in each section. The last two sections, on the universe of items and scale structure, are worth scanning to provide an overall perspective. See you in chapter 3.

Overview of the Scale Construction Process

Would you believe that creating a rating scale involves a systematic, thoughtful, and deliberate approach? "Naaah." For real. Memory Jogger 2.1 outlines the major steps in scale development. You can refer to this "jogger" throughout the process. These steps are required according to the *Standards* for the construction of scales used for employment decisions. "No kidding." Yeah. There are no shortcuts. Oh, maybe a couple. But they're top secret and protected by a high-security, cryptic password, like "matzoh."

This chapter begins the process with the following steps: (1) specifying the *purpose* of the scale, (2) delimiting *what* is to be measured, (3) determining *how* to measure the "what," (4) placing the rating scale item into the context of the "universe of items," and (5) defining the *structure* of the rating scale item. Now whatta ya think?

Specifying the Purpose of the Scale

Before jumping or skipping into the steps for developing a scale, you have to determine the purpose of the scale. Well, you don't *have* to, but it would be nice. Otherwise, you could hop to the next paragraph. What decision(s) will be made

MEMORY JOGGER 2.1

STEPS IN SCALE DEVELOPMENT

1. **Job Content Domain Specification**
   a. Specify the purpose of the scale
   b. Define the job content domain
   c. Determine how to measure the domain
2. **Scale Development**
   a. Decide on the structure of the items
   b. Determine the number of statements
   c. Create a pool of statements
   d. Select the most appropriate anchors
   e. Refine the item structure
   f. Assemble the scale
3. **Field Testing and Item Analyses**
   a. Decide on administration procedures (paper-based or online)
   b. Conduct mini-field test ⟶ scale revision
   c. Content review ⟶ scale revision
   d. Monster-field test and item analyses ⟶ scale revision
4. **Collection of Validity and Reliability Evidence**
   a. Conduct validity studies related to scale score uses and decisions
   b. Conduct reliability studies for employment decisions

with the results? You need to start at the end. Once the decision is specified, the results can be determined, and, finally, the data gathering tool can be designed. In other words, *the decision or the specific uses or inferences drawn from the results drive the type of scale (data source) that is needed.* Table 1.1 indicated the three major decision categories—formative, summative, and program—and the players involved in each. The respondents were students, the instructor, peers, external experts, self, administrators, and employees. Although rating scales may be completed by any of these individuals, the content and structure of the scales will vary as a function of the information needed for decision making. The content of the scale needs to be determined next.

Delimiting What Is to Be Measured

Once the purpose of the scale has been determined, a comprehensive list of *teaching behaviors, skills, and characteristics* (or course characteristics and program outcomes) should be specified. This list defines the job content domain to be measured by the scale. There are at least three techniques or sources you can use to produce this list: (1) focus groups, (2) interviews, and (3) research evidence. Although the descriptions that follow refer to teaching and course characteristics for student and peer rating scales, the techniques apply equally to any of the aforementioned rating scales.

Focus Groups

A group of faculty and students (5–10), through open discussion, can brainstorm teaching behaviors or course characteristics that define effective teaching. Several meetings may be required. (*Note*: Each session should be recorded to ensure accuracy in transmission.) Every phrase, statement, and dangling participle should be documented verbatim. During these sessions, you need to stay awake. If you're prone to dozing, ask a student in advance to poke you in the eyeball with a celery stalk when you nod off. Speaking of eyeball poking, out-of-focus groups can also be used to generate the same information, but it will take a little longer because they can't see what they're doing. A separate group of faculty can then take that list of ideas and transform them into scale items. The focus group should review the items against the original list to assure nothing was lost in translation. This review may be conducted as part of the validation process (see chapter 8). (For further details on focus group techniques, see Krueger & Casey, 2000, or Puchta & Potter, 2004.)

Interviews

In-depth, one-on-one interviews with faculty, administrators, and students can indicate the behaviors and characteristics they value and those that should be measured. A representative range of class levels, difficulties, formats, sizes, and subject matter or disciplines should be considered in the sampling of faculty and students. Interviews may be highly structured or unstructured. This choice is often determined by the experience of the faculty interviewer. Regardless of the degree of structure, the goal is the same: Get it done ASAP before the focus-group folks find out. I mean, elicit the *most critical classroom behaviors or characteristics that define effective teaching*.

The criterion number of interviews is "until redundancy occurs in the information obtained," "until you pass out from boredom," or "until you get salmonellosis," which is an infection of salmonella bacteria in your bloodstream that develop into full-grown salmon capable of leaping out of your mouth during the interview. In other words, after a certain point, the salmon start leaping or the information reaches diminishing returns. Very few new behaviors will emerge beyond the list already compiled. Once no unique information is provided, STOP. Run and get a bagel and cream cheese so you're ready when the salmon are finished smoking. Or go to a movie like *Jurassic Park I, II, III,* or *IV* to get your blood pumping or adrenaline rushing.

Research Evidence

Ever since dinosaurs roamed the movie lots of the DreamWorks™ SKG studio, professors have been standing in front of a tree stump and lecturing to petrified note-taking students (Me, 2005). They had to speak rather slowly, as they read from their notes painted on the stone walls of the classroom, so students could chisel the letters into their stone tablets. Consider the changes that have occurred over the past 2006 years. Now, professors stand in front of a piece of varnished lumber (a.k.a. lectern) and read the words projected on a screen (a.k.a. PowerPoint®) to students who are thinking, "Why can't she give me a copy of the slides so I can leave and read them when I feel like it? Why is she reading to me? I'm not three years old. What a dope" (Me & You, 2006a, p. 82,629).

This image may not be too far-fetched at some institutions today. However, over the past two decades there has been a *major shift from teacher-centered to learner-centered teaching* (Weimer, 2002). The American Psychological Association's (1997) Board of Educational Affairs issued a list of 14 learner-centered principles grouped into four categories: (1) cognitive and metacognitive factors, (2) motivational and affective factors, (3) developmental and social factors, and (4) individual differences. Research on theories of learning and cognition and students' academic success has demonstrated the effectiveness of active and cooperative learning activities (Bonwell & Eison, 1991; Millis & Cottell, 1998). This shift should be reflected in the characteristics of effective teachers.

Davis (1993) synthesized the results of studies on "good teaching" (Chickering & Gamson, 1991; Eble, 1988; Murray, 1991; Reynolds, 1992; Schön, 1987) and on student achievement and success (Noel, Levitz, Saluri, & Associates, 1985; Pascarella & Terenzini, 1991; Tinto, 1987). Davis (1993) identified four clusters of instructional skills, strategies, and attitudes that seem to capture the essence of *effective teaching*:

1. Organizing and explaining material in ways appropriate to students' abilities:

   • Knows the subject matter
   • Can explain difficult concepts in plain, comprehensible terms

Anti-Lecture Technology

You may not be aware of the latest developments in technology that have been designed expressly to thwart long-winded lectures by professors who refuse to incorporate learner-centered techniques in their classrooms. I bring you these advances in order to fill this box. For these instructors, it's traditional lecture mode as usual. In an effort to alter this behavior and rehabilitate these "lectureholics," two methods have been tested on 10 samples of faculty from several large research universities: (1) the computerized SmartLectern®, and (2) the Podium Trapdoor®. SmartLectern® is programmed to deliver a powerful electric shock, not unlike a defibrillator, to the instructor every half hour of lecture. The voltage is increased automatically every half hour as a means of extinguishing lecture behavior. (*Note*: A similar device is also being tested for obsessive PowerPoint®ers, except that the shock is delivered through a laser pointer. It will be available in early 2007.) For further details on these devices, check out the Web site www.shockaprof.com.

If the electric shocks aren't effective, then plan B, or 2, is the next step. These incorrigible lectureholic instructors are assigned to classrooms with podiums rigged with Trapdoor® devices. The instructors are forewarned not to exceed one hour of lecture time per class. If anyone talks beyond that cutoff, the trapdoor opens and the windbag drops through the door like an anvil, never to be seen again, except at required faculty senate meetings.

These methods may seem a bit extreme, but, in the long run, the instructors will thank you, although no one has done this in the studies so far. Hopefully, these cutting-edge devices with ®'s everywhere will give you some options to consider. We now resume this section already in progress.

- Gauges students' background knowledge and experiences
- Identifies reasonable expectations for students' progress
- Selects appropriate teaching methods and materials
- Devises examples and analogies that clarify key points
- Relates one topic to another
- Assesses whether students are learning what is being taught

2. Creating an environment for learning:

- Establishes and maintains rapport with students
- Responds to students' needs
- Communicates high expectations

- Gives appropriate feedback
- Respects diverse talents and learning styles
- Emphasizes cooperation and collaboration
- Uses strategies that actively engage learners

3. Helping students become autonomous, self-regulated learners:

   - Communicates goals and expectations to students
   - Directs students in making their own connections to course content
   - Views the learning process as a joint venture
   - Stimulates students' intellectual interests

4. Reflecting on and evaluating one's own teaching:

   - Critically examines why one is doing what one does
   - Identifies the effects of what one does on one's students
   - Imagines ways to improve one's teaching
   - Finds strategies to help students resolve problems they encounter (adapted from pp. xix–xx)

This four-category model is somewhat broader than other models, such as Lowman's (2000) two-dimensional model of *intellectual excitement* and *interpersonal rapport*, but it is inclusive of most of the behaviors. These characteristics of effective teaching practices can guide the development of the instructor behaviors to be measured. A faculty committee can then produce items from a composite list of behaviors for the different scales.

Student rating scales.   Although focus groups or interviews can be used to systematically define the content of a student rating scale, it is recommended that the research evidence weigh heavily in this process so that the items accurately reflect the most up-to-date evidence on best practices in college teaching. For example, such items may relate to active and cooperative learning strategies, problem-based learning, and the integration of the vast array of technology in the classroom and out.

Peer rating scales.   In general, the content of a peer rating scale should complement that already measured by the student rating scale. What characteristics would faculty be in a position to rate that a student couldn't? The domain should be different for both types of scales, although there may be some behaviors where overlap is appropriate to confirm or disaffirm student and faculty observations.

The research evidence indicates that faculty may be the best judge of content expertise, pedagogy, and related dimensions (DeZure, 1999). Cohen and McKeachie (1980) identified 10 criteria of effective teaching that colleagues are in the best position to evaluate: mastery of course content, selection of course content, course organization, appropriateness of course objectives, instructional materials, evaluative devices and methods used to teach specific content areas, commitment to teaching and concern for student learning, student achievement, and support for departmental instructional efforts. Keig and Waggoner (1994) isolated five categories: goals, content, and organization of course design; methods and materials used in delivery; evaluation of student work; instructor's grading practices; and instructor's adherence to ethical standards.

DeZure's (1999) synthesis of the research produced six major dimensions of teaching behaviors that can be observed: class environment, indicators of student involvement and engagement, instructor's ability to convey the course content, instructional methods, indicators of student–instructor rapport, and global rating of overall effectiveness. These dimensions are consistent with the research on instructional effectiveness (presentation style, enthusiasm, sensitivity to students' levels of knowledge, openness to questions, and clarity of organization) (Murray, 1997). Those categories of behavior furnish a preliminary structure within which to lump a wide range of teaching behaviors, which can be drawn from the research on peer review (Helling, 1988; Hutchings, 1995; Kumaravadivelu, 1995; Millis, 1992; Morehead & Shedd, 1997; Muchinsky, 1995; Nordstrom, 1995; Webb & McEnerney, 1995).

Determining How to Measure the "What"

The rating scale is the tool. But, timeout. Right now you might be scratching your head and asking yourself, "Self, hasn't the rating scale wheel already been invented? Why don't we just swipe someone else's scale or order a freebie desk copy from a publisher? Why do we have to experience the pain and sorrow and additional meds, plus waste faculty time to develop our own scale?" I appreciate your politically incorrect candor. Excellent questions.

It would seem that the decision is a no-brainer: Just "borrow" a scale from another school or buy one from a publisher who has the professional staff to write the items and report the results to your faculty. Simple enough, right? Well, let's examine these options in greater detail.

Historically, student rating scales have mostly been developed using the approach of *dust bowl empiricism*, which means: Get a bunch of statements about teaching and see what works (McKeachie, 1997). Hmmm. Sounds like the starfish guy back in the introduction. However, instead of writing every statement from scratch, there are three sources where you can get a bunch of statements: existing scales, item banks, and commercially published scales.

Existing Scales

Student and peer rating scales reported in the research literature and those developed by other colleges and universities can serve as an excellent springboard for directing your own scale construction. Some of these scales are reprinted in books on faculty evaluation (Arreola, 2000; Braskamp & Ory, 1994; Centra, 1993; Chism, 1999). There is a wide range of scales and items being used for peer observation (Berk et al., 2004; Center for Teaching Effectiveness, 1996; Helling, 1988; Hutchings, 1996; Millis & Kaplan, 1995; Richlin & Manning, 1995; Webb & McEnerney, 1997). There is even a collection of sample scales in appendices A and B of this book. The items on these scales can provide prototypes for both content and structure so that you can tailor them to your specific faculty and courses. These statements should be adapted to fit the purpose of your scale, the domain specifications, and the decisions to be made based on the results.

There are few examples of scales used for self-ratings, exit and alumni ratings, student interviews, administrator ratings, and employer ratings in teaching publications. Although individual institutions might be willing to share their scales, those sources of evidence on teaching effectiveness have not received the attention given to student and peer scales.

Item Banks

Picking statements from an item bank to construct student rating scales began more than 30 years ago at Purdue University (Derry, Seibert, Starry, Van Horn, & Wright, 1974). (*A Bit of Trivia*: This university was named after the famous "chicken mogul," Colonel Sanders.) The item bank was called the *cafeteria system* because it looked exactly like a cafeteria, just without the trays, silverware, food, prices, and tables. The bank, or catalog, contains (a) *global*, or summary, statements, such as "Overall, my instructor is an excellent teacher," (b) *generic*, or core, statements applicable to almost all faculty and courses, and (c) *instructor/course specific* statements. Faculty can select those statements from the menu (a, b, and/or c) that fit the purposes and uses of the evaluation as well as the courses. That approach was formally called *CAFETERIA*. This uppercase, italicized bank was then updated with a title-case, italicized, renamed version called the *Purdue Instructor and Course Evaluation Service* (*PICES*), which has assembled a catalog of 606 statements in 24 categories. Those statements are available online (see www.cie.purdue.edu/data/pices.cfm). Aleamoni and Carynnk (1977) have also compiled a catalog of 350 student rating scale statements, lumped into 20 categories (see www.cieq.com). This collection is part of the *Course/Instructor Evaluation Questionnaire (CIEQ)* system.

At present, despite the number and types of scales that have been developed for peer assessment, there are no available item banks from which you can build your own scale. This limitation also applies to exit and alumni surveys as well as all of the other scales mentioned in chapter 1.

Commercially Published Student Rating Scales

Probably the simplest solution to creating a teaching assessment system is to just go buy one. Unfortunately, they are only available for student rating scales. The commercial student rating forms and systems are designed for you, Professor Consumer. The items are professionally developed; the scale has usually undergone extensive psychometric analyses to provide evidence of reliability and validity; and there are a variety of services provided, including the forms, administration, scanning, scoring, and reporting of results. Each company will send you a specimen set of rating scales and reports to review. If you're really nice, the company may even permit a trial administration. Sample scales and report forms, plus a complete description of the paper-based and online services, can be found on the respective Web site. Six systems currently available are listed below (detailed contact information can be found in appendix D):

1. *Course/Instructor Evaluation Questionnaire (CIEQ)*
2. *IDEA—Student Reactions to Instruction and Courses*
3. *Student Instructional Report II (SIR II)*
4. *Purdue Instructor and Course Evaluation Service (PICES)*
5. *Instructional Assessment System (IAS Online)*
6. *Student Evaluation of Educational Quality (SEEQ)*

Careful thought should be given to all of the preceding commercial systems. Any of the strategies might work as long as five criteria are satisfied:

Criterion 1.   The rating scale measures the job domain specifications in your institution.

Criterion 2.   The scale and reporting system are appropriate for the intended faculty and score uses.

Criterion 3.   The scale satisfies standards for technical quality.

Criterion 4.   The faculty buys in to the products developed by the outside source.

Criterion 5.   You get a financial windfall from one of those e-mailed European lotteries you never entered.

⚠ CAUTION: SERVICE AGREEMENTS

The words I have come to detest more than any others in the English language, except "prostate exam," are the following: "You definitely should buy the service agreement just in case by an infinitesimally, electron microscopically small chance your scale should explode or you lose an anchor or break the flange sprocket that attaches the anchors to the statements." Be extremely wary of that type of sales pitch if you decide to purchase one of the commercially produced scale systems. Occasionally, a super-hyper-aggressive salesperson might go so far as to say, "If you don't buy the agreement RIGHT NOW, you will regret it. If your rating scale malfunctions, you could be looking at $563,000 in repairs, including parts and labor. You'll end up selling one of your lungs or children. So sign here." You don't need that kind of pressure. Please be careful in your purchase. Also, read the electron-microscopic-size print at the bottom of the contract. Enjoy your new scale, whatever model you get. You deserve it.

Since your faculty will be held accountable for the results of whatever instrument is used, they should have input into the choice of scale. They are the primary stakeholders. The items must be fair, appropriate to the courses and teaching methods in the school, and be free of technical flaws. At minimum, a comprehensive critique of the selected scale should be conducted.

However, based on your available faculty expertise, the most cost-effective and efficient route may be to not buy a system. You may elect a combination of the above sources. Consider two extreme scenarios:

Best-Case Scenario: Your dream might be to just purchase the *CIEQ, IDEA, SIR II, PICES, IAS,* or *SEEQ* system and go home. I bet you're thinking, "This is as exciting as rolling down a marble staircase in an oil drum." But after examining these systems, you realize that you must adopt the "rating scale" as is, without any revision, and a few of the statements may not fit your program. Further, since the forms were developed from 5 to 30 years ago, there may be few or no statements on the latest uses of technology, active and cooperative learning strategies, inquiry learning, problem-based learning, and other recent teaching methods. Now, what are you supposed to do?

Well, the publishers offer a solution. There is an optional section on each scale for statements to be written or selected from an item bank by the course instructor to *customize* the scale: 42 on *CIEQ*, 19 on *IDEA*, 10 on *SIR II*, 36 on *PICES*, 12 on *IAS*, and 40 on *SEEQ*. In other words, even after buying a rating scale package, faculty still have to write or select statements to ensure that the scale reflects the state of the art in teaching and is relevant to their courses. It is nearly impossible to escape the statement-writing process entirely.

Worst-Case Scenario: Your worst nightmare is to write every statement, select anchors, design the scale, conduct all analyses, and report the results. YIIIKES! That's scary. If you have at least one measurement/statistician faculty member and a team of faculty willing to tackle the job, it can be done in a cost-effective and efficient manner. Once the expertise is available and the commitment is made with all stakeholders involved in the process, you're ready to rock and roll.

At this point, you probably haven't decided whether to buy, adapt, and/or write the statements you need to develop your student rating scale. But, sooner or later, you will have to write statements. Even if you purchase a publisher's scale, your colleagues will still have to write or select the add-on statements. And all of this just for the student rating scale. How are any of the other scales that measure other dimensions of teaching effectiveness going to be developed? Overall, faculty must possess the skills necessary to evaluate (critique) the core statements as well as synthesize (write) their own. These skills are at the two highest levels of Bloom's cognitive taxonomy (Anderson & Krathwohl, 2001; Bloom, Englehart, Furst, Hill, & Krathwohl, 1956).

Since very few faculty members typically have formal measurement training in scale construction, analysis, reporting, and interpretation, it is hoped that the guidelines presented in the remainder of this book will supply you and your faculty with the necessary skills to produce quality scales. But before you begin bearing arms or generating statements, let's examine the structure of the items you are going to build.

Universe of Items

Before I autopsy the rating scale item, let's consider how many major types of items are used in the entire universe of measurement: 2. Yup. That's it.

What were you expecting? Maybe 3 or 169? Here is a brief exploration into all two types:

1. *Test items.* Every item on every test, regardless of format, is scored as *correct* or *incorrect.* An answer key is required for selection format (true-false, multiple-choice, and matching) and constructed-response (fill-in-the-blank, short-answer, essay, and problem-solving) items. Scoring rubrics are used for paper-and-pencil and performance items or tasks.

2. *Scale/questionnaire items.* These items, regardless of format, have *no correct answer;* there is no answer key. The various forms described below have different response formats that ask a respondent to select a response from among two or more choices or to write (or type) an answer. What is picked or written is the response.

   a. *Opinion or attitude*—Items that elicit opinions or attitudes have no correct answer. There is no right or wrong attitude; it's whatever the respondent feels. The choice that is selected or written (or typed) is the answer. Examples include *agree–disagree* or *excellent–poor* responses.

   b. *Factual*

      1) *Sociodemographic characteristics*—These items document the types of respondents who completed the items above or below this sentence. Their characteristics may explain why they have certain attitudes or exhibit certain practices. They describe the relevant characteristics of people, such as gender, race/ethnicity, age, educational level, current diseases, golf handicap, and the name of their pet piranha. The items may contain choices or blank space to fill in the information. Since the intent of these items is to gather "facts," the person responding must be in the position to provide accurate information and not bias the answers.

      2) *Actual practices*—These items indicate what a person actually does or performs. How frequently you take your meds or change the dressing on your bullet wounds is supposed to be a factual measure of what you really do—unless, of course, you lie. These items may be susceptible to a "fakeability" bias.

We're done. There are only two basic types of items with a few variations. Within the context of measuring teaching performance, the rest of this book concentrates on opinion and attitude items; however, there are examples of the factual items in chapter 6 and in the sample scales in appendices A and B.

Structure of Rating Scale Items

Attitude is the degree of positive or negative affect (or feeling) toward a person, program, or institution in an ivory tower-type building (adapted from Thurstone, 1946). Positive affect expresses a favorable attitude toward the person or object; negative affect expresses . . . you know what.

A rating scale is the most appropriate instrument to measure the "degree of affect." Some scientists have tried using a sphygmomanometer, but with little success. The scales used to measure teaching effectiveness contain two types of items: structured and unstructured. The foundation of both is the Pavlovian model of *stimulus → response* (*S→R*). I bet you're drooling right now in anticipation of my note. (*Note:* All other test- and questionnaire-item formats mentioned previously are based on this same structure. See Berk [2002a] for examples.) Each item contains a stimulus to which the student, instructor, peer, external expert, administrator, or employer responds by selecting a verbal anchor or writing an open-ended answer. The structures of various structured and unstructured items are listed below:

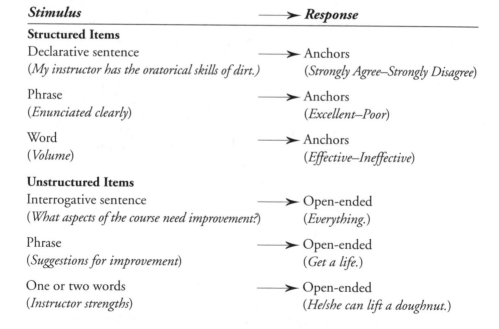

Stimulus	*→ Response*
Structured Items	
Declarative sentence	→ Anchors
(*My instructor has the oratorical skills of dirt.*)	(*Strongly Agree–Strongly Disagree*)
Phrase	→ Anchors
(*Enunciated clearly*)	(*Excellent–Poor*)
Word	→ Anchors
(*Volume*)	(*Effective–Ineffective*)
Unstructured Items	
Interrogative sentence	→ Open-ended
(*What aspects of the course need improvement?*)	(*Everything.*)
Phrase	→ Open-ended
(*Suggestions for improvement*)	(*Get a life.*)
One or two words	→ Open-ended
(*Instructor strengths*)	(*He/she can lift a doughnut.*)

Structured Items

Almost all structured rating scale items on this planet as well as those on Mars® and Snickers® (Berk, 2003) consist of two components: (1) the *S*, which is usually a declarative sentence, phase, or word, and (2) the *R* options, which are a series of descriptors indicating one's strength of feeling toward the stimulus.

Student rating scales. Student rating scales usually are constructed as Likert-type scales, where the *S* element is a set of declarative sentences and the *R* options are one or two words expressing varying degrees of agreement (or disagreement) with, or endorsement of, each sentence. These options are called *anchors*, derived from the nautical word "barnacle." The following is a sample format:

My instructor has the oratorical skills of dirt.

Strongly Disagree   Disagree   Uncertain   Agree   Strongly Agree

On these rating scales the stimuli relate to instructor behaviors or course characteristics. A few of the most common categories are course content and organization, instructional methods, learning atmosphere, learning outcomes, and evaluation methods. However, there are many more categories. In fact, as noted in the previous section on "Item Banks," the *Purdue Instructor and Course Evaluation Service* and Aleamoni and Carynnk (1977) have identified more than 20 categories from which statements can be selected from their respective catalogs.

Peer rating scales. Peer rating scales are built differently. The *S* consists of teaching behaviors or skills, expressed as short phrases or single words. They are evaluated during one or more observations by faculty peers or outside experts. Here, the *R* is the *quality* of each behavior being rated. The typical "phrase" format of a peer rating scale is illustrated in table 2.1. These stimuli define desirable behaviors and criteria so the peer knows what to evaluate

TABLE 2.1
Sample Peer Rating Scale "Phrase" Format

	Excellent	*Very Good*	*Good*	*Needs Improvement*
Varied Pace Appropriately				
Enunciated Clearly				
Varied Modulation				
Varied Tone				
Spoke with Adequate Volume				

TABLE 2.2
Sample Peer Rating Scale "Single-Word" Format

	Excellent	*Very Good*	*Good*	*Needs Improvement*
Pace				
Enunciation				
Modulation				
Tone				
Volume				

Though more ambiguous for rating purposes, the single-word topics could just be listed instead. They do not contain the criteria for evaluation, which makes the rating process more difficult and subjective. Table 2.2 illustrates this "single-word" format.

Categories on peer rating scales may include content organization, communication style, questioning skills, critical thinking skills, rapport with students, learning environment, and teaching methods.

All of the other rating scales that can be used to measure teaching effectiveness, including self, exit and alumni, student interviews, administrator, and employer, are just variations of the preceding three formats. Only the behaviors on the left or the anchors across the top change for the different scales.

Unstructured Items

Following the structured items in each section of the scale and/or at the end of the total scale are open-ended, unstructured items. Here the student, instructor, peer, administrator, or employer can provide answers in his or her own words. These answers should provide information not tapped by the responses to the structured items. In other words, the structured and unstructured items should be complementary in content. The underlying format is still $S \longrightarrow R$.

Unstructured items can be very broad or specific. Each S can be an imperative or interrogative sentence, a phrase, or one or two words. A combination of all three formats can appear in the same section. Examples of these formats are shown below:

SENTENCES

What aspects of the course were *effective*?
What aspects need *improvement*?

What suggestions do you have for *improvement*?
What improvements would you suggest for this course?
Was this course intellectually stimulating?
What is your evaluation of this course?
What are your general comments about the instructor?
What aspects of this course contributed most to your learning?
What aspects of this course detracted from your learning?
Comment on the course content and subject matter.
Comment on the value of the books, homework, and papers (if any).
Comment on the examinations as to difficulty, fairness, etc.

PHRASES
Comments about Instructor
Comments about Course
Suggestions for Improvement

ONE OR TWO WORDS
Comments
Instructor Strengths
Instructor Weaknesses
Course Strengths
Course Weaknesses

The information elicited from the above items is the *R*. Studies of student ratings on the structured items and students' written comments on this unstructured section have found correlations in the .80s and .90s (Braskamp et al., 1981; Ory et al., 1980). Despite these strong relationships, the comments can provide explanations and clarifications for the responses to the structured items plus extremely valuable diagnostic information for considering changes in the course and teaching methods. These ideas from students, peers, and others can guide the direction for teaching improvement the next time the course is taught.

3

GENERATING THE STATEMENTS

 DIETARY CAUTION

Now that you've had a small taste of the components in a rating scale item, I bet you are now starving to devour the task of generating the statements. Curb your appetite and enthusiasm. Remember Jared before Subway® turkey subs? Migh-ty Scar-y! Don't scarf up any statements yet. What are you nibbling on? "An anchor." You can't do that until chapter 4. Just wait. Anyway, back to this caution. Decide whether you will be adapting, critiquing, and/or writing statements. Then you're just about ready to begin.

 BERK'S NOTES

Faculty—If you are involved in constructing a rating scale, writing a few statements for the optional section in a commercial scale, critiquing the quality of other scales, or searching for the jokes in each paragraph, you will have to wolf down the whole enchilada. Otherwise, why are you swallowing these pages? Huh? Huh? Depending on your previous knowledge, first review the very appetizing Memory Jogger 3.1 (p. 67), then take Pop Quiz #1 (p. 68). Use Checklist 3.1 (p. 70) if you are critiquing items from an item pool or existing scale. You may not have to gobble up every rule.

Administrators—If you need to review the quality of rating scales to measure teaching performance or to collect evidence for program assessment and accreditation, just chew on the rules in the Memory Jogger to get a flavor for what's involved. Then move on to the next chapter.

Preliminary Decisions

Before you start spitting out statements on your PC until you have an over-bloated scale, stop the food metaphors. They're making me hungry. Okay. You need to make two last-minute checks: (1) the domain specifications and (2) the number of statements.

Domain Specifications

The best road map to statement generation is the list of behaviors and characteristics you compiled from chapter 2 to define the job content domain. Make sure that list circumscribes what you mean by teaching effectiveness. Course and program elements may be separate. These domain specifications are your best guide to the development of the words, phrases, or statements that compose the heart (and spleen) of the rating scale. They constitute your blueprint to item joy and happiness.

Number of Statements

There is no hard-and-fast rule to estimate the number of statements that need to be produced. Since this phase involves an initial pool or draft collection, it is advisable to write as many statements as possible from the specifications. For example, you could begin with at least two or three statements per behavior. This approach might yield a pool of 50 to 75 statements. A large pool size permits greater latitude for the content review process later and the item analysis statistics to pick the *best statements* for the final scale. The final number usually ranges from 25 to 40, approximately 50% of the original pool.

Rules for Writing Statements

The 20 rules described in this section extend all previous treatments of this topic, including the most recent books on scale development (DeVellis, 2003; Dunn-Rankin, Knezek, Wallace, & Zhang, 2004; Netemeyer, Bearden, & Sharma, 2003), popular works on rating scales within the past millennium (Dawes, 1972; McIver & Carmines, 1981; Mueller, 1986; Nunnally & Bernstein, 1994; Oppen-

MEMORY JOGGER 3.1

RULES FOR WRITING STATEMENTS

1. The statement should be *clear and direct*.
2. The statement should be *brief and concise*.
3. The statement should contain only *one complete behavior, thought, or concept*.
4. The statement should be a *simple sentence*.
5. The statement should be at the *appropriate reading level*.
6. The statement should be *grammatically correct*.
7. The statement should be *worded strongly*.
8. The statement should be *congruent with the behavior* it is intended to measure.
9. The statement should accurately measure a *positive or negative behavior*.
10. The statement should be *applicable to all respondents*.
11. The respondents should be in the *best position to respond* to the statement.
12. The statement should be *interpretable in only one way*.
13. The statement should NOT contain a *double negative*.
14. The statement should NOT contain *universal or absolute terms*.
15. The statement should NOT contain *nonabsolute, warm-and-fuzzy terms*.
16. The statement should NOT contain *value-laden or inflammatory words*.
17. The statement should NOT contain *words, phrases, or abbreviations that would be unfamiliar to all respondents*.
18. The statement should NOT tap a *behavior appearing in any other statement*.
19. The statement should NOT be *factual* or capable of being interpreted as factual.
20. The statement should NOT be *endorsed* or given one answer *by almost all respondents or by almost none*.

heim, 1966; Spector, 1992; Streiner & Norman, 1995), and even the classic sources on scaling (Edwards, 1957; Edwards & Kilpatrick, 1948; Ferguson, 1941; Likert, 1932; Thurstone & Chave, 1929; Wang, 1932). Finally, the most comprehensive books on writing questions for questionnaires by Payne (1951), Dillman (2000), and Bradburn, Sudman, and Wansink (2004) were also reviewed.

POP QUIZ #1

Directions: Please identify the flaw(s) in each of the following five "real" student rating scale statements. The number of boxes to the left indicates the number of flaws. This scale is based on the following five anchor choices:

$$SD = \text{Strongly Disagree}$$
$$D = \text{Disagree}$$
$$N = \text{Neutral (Uncertain)}$$
$$A = \text{Agree}$$
$$SA = \text{Strongly Agree}$$

Flaw(s)   ***Statement***

☐ 1. My instructor spoke audibly and clearly.   SD D N A SA

☐ 2. This course was up-to-date with
developments in the field.   SD D N A SA

☐☐ 3. My instructor promptly returned exams and
graded assignments to distant students.   SD D N A SA

☐☐ 4. Course requirements and deadlines are
explained in the syllabus.   SD D N A SA

☐ 5. My instructor treated all students
with respect.   SD D N A SA

Answers: See page 83.

The rules presented herein forsooth qualify for the *Guinness Book of Rating Scale Rules* as the longest list ever assembled for the Likert-type rating scale. They are intended to guide the development of your statements. Since scale statements are much more difficult to write correctly than the words or phrases used in observational checklists, considerable space is devoted to describing each rule and providing illustrative examples of "putrid" and "better" statements. Pack your bags and electric toothbrush. We're ready to begin.

Given the detail and the number of examples you will have to endure, it would be worth reviewing Memory Jogger 3.1 before embarking on this journey. You may be familiar with many of the rules already and can just skip to the ones of interest. As a confidence booster, see if you can identify the flaws in the items in Pop Quiz #1.

Alternatively, if you have selected statements from an available instrument or item bank, you may need to evaluate those items according to the rules. Those rules have been restructured into a checklist format to facilitate that evaluation (see Checklist 3.1). Your answers to the 20 questions should be *yes* for 1–12 and *no* for 13–20.

If the Memory Jogger or Checklist is not an adequate guide to develop your item pool, the following rules should be reviewed.

 HUMOR WARNING

The examples accompanying these rules are not real. They're imaginary, exaggerated, twisted, and, occasionally, humorous proxies for real statements. They are intended solely for your information and entertainment. Any other use, such as for rating scales or stand-up comedy, is strictly prohibited without the prior written consent of the International Association of Professors That Approves Uses Like This One.

---

1. The statement should be clear and direct.

Every statement should communicate a specific characteristic of the instructor or course that is easily interpretable by the students. Consider the following statement about evaluation methods:

> **PUTRID:** The evaluation methods were, let's say,
> "Do the words *medieval torture* ring a bell?"

How about, Does *ambiguous* ring a bell? Although the statement certainly conveys a feeling about the evaluation methods, it doesn't indicate a qualitative characteristic that can be rated in terms of effective practices, such as whether the methods were fair, graded impartially, returned promptly, measured important outcomes, and so on. A revision of the preceding example might be as follows:

> **BETTER:** The course tests made me nauseous.

2. The statement should be brief and concise.

Make your point with as few words as possible, preferably 10 words or less. The lengthier the statement, the more complex and confusing it may be to interpret

CHECKLIST 3.1

EVALUATION OF RATING SCALE STATEMENTS

	YES	NO
1. Is the statement *clear and direct?*	___	___
2. Is the statement *brief and concise?*	___	___
3. Does the statement contain only *one complete behavior, thought, or concept?*	___	___
4. Is the statement a *simple sentence?*	___	___
5. Is the statement at the *appropriate reading level?*	___	___
6. Is the statement *grammatically correct?*	___	___
7. Is the statement *worded strongly?*	___	___
8. Is the statement *congruent with the behavior* it is intended to measure?	___	___
9. Does the statement accurately measure a *positive or negative behavior?*	___	___
10. Is the statement *applicable to all respondents?*	___	___
11. Are the respondents in the *best position to respond* to the statement?	___	___
12. Can the statement be *interpreted in only one way?*	___	___
13. Does the statement contain a *double negative?*	___	___
14. Does the statement contain *universal or absolute terms?*	___	___
15. Does the statement contain *nonabsolute, warm-and-fuzzy terms?*	___	___
16. Does the statement contain *value-laden or inflammatory words?*	___	___
17. Does the statement contain *words, phrases, or abbreviations* that would be *unfamiliar to all respondents?*	___	___
18. Does the statement tap a *behavior appearing in any other statement?*	___	___
19. Is the statement *factual* or capable of being interpreted as factual?	___	___
20. Could the statement be *endorsed* or given one answer *by almost all respondents or by almost none?*	___	___

(Holden, Fekken, & Jackson, 1985). Avoid unnecessary wordiness, like most of my sentences. Consider the following item:

> **PUTRID:** My instructor endlessly spewed market-tested, focus-grouped, fundamentally meaningless rhetorical sludge.

Although this statement clocks in just over the suggested word limit, depending on how you count hyphenated words, the value of what the instructor spews can be expressed with fewer words. For example,

> **BETTER:** My instructor bludgeoned us with meaningless facts.

How's that? Keep it short.

3. The statement should contain only one complete behavior, thought, or concept.

Only one characteristic should appear in each item. If more than one is contained in the statement, then it is impossible to know which characteristic is being rated. For example, what two characteristics are evaluated in the following item?

> **PUTRID:** My instructor is a bade speler and a morron.

If the student agrees or disagrees with this statement, there is no way to know whether he or she is responding to "speler" or "morron" or both. It's ambiguous. This form is often called a *double-barreled* statement. Yes, there are also triple- and quadruple-barreled statements, which are similarly confusing to respondents and produce useless results. The clue to avoiding this grammatical structure is the word *and* and similar words, such as *or* and *maybe*, which English experts call "conjunctive vestibules." A revision of the above item is shown below:

> **BETTER:** My instructor is a moron.

Here's another violation of this rule:

> **PUTRID:** My instructor related course content to research, real-life, or get-a-life examples.

How is a student supposed to answer this? It's like a three-option multiple-choice item. If a student responds "Agree," what does that mean? To which part of the three barrels is the student agreeing? The culprit word that makes all of this confusion possible is, you guessed it, *life*. Wrooong. It's *or*. Remove *or* and you're forced to use only one option:

> **BETTER:** My instructor related course content to get-a-life examples.

4. *The statement should be a* simple sentence.

Consistent with the previous rule, if you state only one behavior to be rated, then the sentence structure should reflect that. A simple sentence is the easiest and quickest to interpret and rate. Compound and complex sentence structures require more time and thought to answer. What's wrong with the following item?

> **PUTRID:** My instructor was as organized as a bucket of fishing worms, but only on Tuesdays; the other classes were kinda better organized.

Everything! Grammar-wise, this sentence has what English professors call a "bivalve multiplex structure with Surround Sound®"; that is, it presents several behaviors with qualifiers. If the statement had ended with *worms*, it would have met our criterion, but *nooo*, it just kept going on and on.

5. *The statement should be at the* appropriate reading level.

If college students are responding to the scale, a high school reading level should be adequate. It is probably not necessary to conduct a formal reading-difficulty analysis of the statements, with the standard methods used to assign grade levels to passages of prose (e.g., Dale & Chall, 1948; Fry, 1977). They require eliminating every *n*th word in a sentence until the meaning is lost (Taylor, 1957) or determining the optimal combination of number of words and syllables in a sentence (Fry, 1977). For example, conservative estimates of statement length and word structure applied to scales administered to the general population are as follows:

9 words with 13 syllables (44% polysyllabic)
19 words with 22 syllables (14% polysyllabic)

These are estimates of the average number of words and syllables per sentence for the sixth-grade reading level. Shorter sentences with a higher proportion of longer words or longer sentences with fewer long words can yield an equivalent level.

Perhaps the best check for reading level is the students' reactions to the statements in the field test. Once a draft of the statements has been completed, the students will participate in a mini-field test (see chapter 7). This test can provide feedback on reading level as well as other rules in this section related to clarity, brevity, simple sentences, and no jargon or unfamiliar acronyms.

6. The statement should be grammatically correct.

If your statements have passed the preceding rules, there shouldn't be any words left that could be grammatorically incorrect. However, even with "spelchek," words can be missspeled, plus pronoun references can be ambiguous, modifiers can be misplaced, and participles can be left dangling. The basic rules of English can still be violated because our attention is usually focused on the substance of the statements rather than the form. Once a draft of the statements is ready for review, the structure of each sentence should be scrutinized. Hopefully, even the most unusual grammatical violations, such as invective marsupials, prosthetic infarctions, carnivorous refractions, and subcutaneous debentures (see Berk, 2002a), will be detected and corrected.

7. The statement should be worded strongly.

Strongly worded statements about teacher behaviors are easier to answer along the *agree–disagree* continuum than mildly worded statements. However, statements that can incite students to riot or are offensive should not be used (see rule 15). The problem is that mildly worded, namby-pamby statements may elicit too much agreement and not tap the whole continuum. For example, would most students agree with this statement?

MILD: My instructor called on students by name.

Probably instructors usually make this effort. Most students would mark "Agree" or "Strongly Agree" to this behavior. Compare the above statement to this strong one:

STRONG: My instructor called on me by name, but the wrong one.

This statement is personal, easy to answer, and draws on the entire response continuum. An even stronger version is possible:

STRONGER: My instructor called on me by name,
but the wrong one, the zit brain.

8. *The statement should be* congruent with the behavior *it is intended to measure.*

A statement can be generated from a variety of sources, but it must match the behavior, characteristic, topic, and so on that it was designed to measure. If a statement was written to assess relevance of content, such as "application to career," then the statement must measure that element of teaching. Here it is:

> **PUTRID:** My instructor was easily distracted by bats flying around the room.

No it isn't. Let's try again:

> **BETTER:** This course gave me the professional skills to crush my competitors like a steamroller over a Twinkie®.

We have a match. This match must occur for every statement. Here's another example related to "office hours":

> **BETTER:** The office hours were scheduled at times (1–6 A.M.) that were convenient only for vampires.

The judgmental process of reviewing the statements against the behaviors builds content-related relevance into the scale.

9. *The statement should accurately measure a* positive or negative behavior.

Most effective teaching practices express positive behaviors or characteristics such as the following:

> **POSITIVE:** My instructor was approachable outside of class to answer questions.

> **POSITIVE:** My instructor provided timely feedback on tests.

These same behaviors can also be worded negatively, but would still tap the same information. The negative versions are shown below:

> **NEGATIVE:** My instructor was NOT approachable outside of class to answer questions.
> *or*
> **EVIL:** My instructor asked me out on a date outside of class.

NEGATIVE: My instructor did NOT provide timely feedback on tests.

or

EVIL: My instructor still hasn't returned my project 18 years later.

You can use either the positive or negative version, but *not both*. Strongly agreeing with the positive statement is the same as strongly disagreeing with the negative statement of the same behavior.

Although the use of negative statements is usually recommended to balance the positive statements in order to minimize *acquiescence bias* (see chapter 5, issue 7d, p. 116), that practice is less common with student rating scales and other scales that measure teaching effectiveness. There are two disadvantages associated with negative statements: (1) they tend to exhibit lower validity and reliability coefficients than positive statements (Holden et al., 1985; Schriesheim & Hill, 1981), and (2) they may be confusing to respondents, particularly when negative words, such as *no* or *not*, or prefixes, such as *im-*, *in-*, or *un-*, are used. Students may miss the negatives when they are answering quickly, thereby producing the wrong responses. These "errors," or invalid answers, reduce the reliability of the scale scores.

Given these problems, it is recommended that negative statements be used sparingly or not at all on rating scales used to measure teaching effectiveness. If they are used, the negative words should be emphasized.

10. The statement should be applicable to all respondents.

Despite the variability of courses, subject matter, class size, room size, and teaching styles, every effort should be made to write *generic* statements about instructors and course characteristics and a few *global* summary statements to which all students can respond. There is a core domain of behaviors that needs to be measured first. This *omnibus form* permits comparisons across faculty, courses within the same discipline, departments, schools, or other academic units. Once a draft of these statements is completed, an optional set of statements *specific* to a given course can then be written by each instructor as an add-on section to the standard scale. This set may contain up to 25 statements.

A comparison of these two types of statements is shown in the following examples:

GENERIC STATEMENTS

I'd rather watch a bug walk across a blackened TV screen than go to class.
This course had the intellectual depth of a goose stampede.

I can perform well on exams by just cheating.
This course was more boring than watching ants eat an elephant.

GLOBAL STATEMENTS

Overall, my instructor sucks air.
Overall, my instructor is a dirt bag.
Overall, my instructor needs, like, a reeeaally extreme makeover.
Overall, this course stinks.
Overall, I learned squat in this course.

INSTRUCTOR- AND COURSE-SPECIFIC STATEMENTS

The class demonstrations with gun shots (blanks) and exploding squibs were effective.
My instructor frittered away valuable class time smashing watermelons.
My instructor's use of sock puppets while crouching behind the lectern was stupid.
In lab, my instructor's artificial insemination of a turkey by mistake stimulated me to be careful.

11. The respondents should be in the best position to respond to the statement.

Students can respond to statements about specific behaviors in the classroom they can observe and that affect them directly. For example, each student can render an opinion about this statement:

> **GOOD:** My instructor has the charisma of dog breath.

There are three types of statements about which students cannot respond appropriately: (a) those that ask what other students think, (b) those that ask what the instructor is thinking about them, and (c) those that relate to certain aspects of teaching about which the students have little or no knowledge. Let's examine each of these.

a. Avoid statements about what other respondents think. Students can express their own individual opinions about teaching performance, but one student can't respond about how the whole class would respond. For example, consider this statement:

> **PUTRID:** Students were petrified to ask questions.

Although the class atmosphere may suggest that feeling, one student cannot say whether everyone else was afraid. A student is only in a position to respond for him- or herself. He or she cannot draw an inference about the feelings of others. A better statement:

BETTER: I was scared spitless to ask questions.

Once all students respond to this statement, the aggregate percentage will reveal just how many students were "scared." This technique furnishes an appropriate evidence base to infer how the whole class feels about a specific issue or behavior.

b. Avoid statements about what the instructor thinks.   A student is not in a position to rate what the instructor or, for that matter, anybody else, is thinking. Again, a student cannot infer what the instructor is thinking from his or her behavior. For example,

PUTRID: My instructor thinks we're as stupid as a tree trunk.

Based on the instructor's behavior, that thought may not be far off the mark. But a student still doesn't know for sure and, again, cannot speak for the class. A student can respond to a behavior or about how he or she feels, as the following statement suggests:

BETTER: My instructor has the personal hygiene
of a diseased water buffalo.
or
My instructor's use of a chain saw in class was terrifying.

c. Avoid statements asking for judgments about which the respondents have little or no knowledge.   Students typically do not have knowledge about certain aspects of teaching, such as the instructor's content expertise, types of teaching methods, execution of teaching methods (e.g., questioning skills, rapport, learning environment), and quality of evaluation techniques. Students' ratings of statements on these topics would not provide informed judgments, opinions, or evaluations of teaching performance. Consider the following statements:

PUTRID: My instructor has the IQ of a Raisinet®.
My instructor milked the lectures into curdled oblivion.
My instructor's knowledge of the content could fit on
the head of a pin with room to spare.

These statements are inappropriate for a student rating scale, but would be salvageable minus the "My instructor" intro for a peer rating scale. Our peers or external experts can observe and evaluate many behaviors, except IQ, that students cannot. Student and peer scales are often complementary in the teaching behaviors measured.

12. The statement should be interpretable in only one way.

Statements that are ambiguous are confusing to answer. They leave students in a quandary and can confound the scoring and interpretation of the results. They typically violate one or more of the preceding rules. Try to respond to this statement:

> **PUTRID:** My instructor encouraged active student participation in class, but use of a cattle prod was over the top.

This is a double-barreled positive and negative statement that would be impossible to score. A student could respond to the positive "encouraged" part, the negative "cattle prod" part, or the combination, or that it is not applicable. What a mess!

Two separate statements are required to measure the specific behaviors. They can be positive or negative. Here they are:

> **BETTER:** My instructor encouraged active student participation in class.

> **BETTER:** My instructor's use of a cattle prod to encourage student participation was over the top.

13. The statement should NOT contain a double negative.

Double negatives can be confusing to interpret correctly when reading statements quickly. As all of these other rules indicate, the statement should be in the simplest grammatical structure possible and get directly to the point. Check out the following:

> **PUTRID:** The field trips to the casinos were NOT unrelated to the course objectives.

Yiiikes! Why use "not unrelated" when a positively worded statement will do?

> **BETTER:** The field trips to the IMAX® Theater were
> related to the course objectives.

14. *The statement should NOT contain* universal or absolute terms.

Absolute terms include such words as *always, never, all, totally, completely, absolutely, only, none, every,* and *croaked.* The problem is that those terms are too extreme and inclusive when qualifying an instructor's behavior or teaching method. For example, consider the following:

> **PUTRID:** My instructor *always* used highfalutin language.

This statement indicates that the frequency of the behavior in class is 100% of the time, a highly unlikely occurrence. Few if any students would pick the response "Strongly Agree" to this statement. Simply eliminating *always* permits the student to choose any anchor on the continuum to evaluate the extent to which the behavior occurs. Let's try another example:

> **PUTRID:** The course content tested my instructor's
> *totally* impoverished imagination.

Again, the likelihood of this extreme description of an instructor's imagination is possible, but improbable. *Totally* is also redundant with the "im" in *impoverished.* How poverished could an instructor's imagination possibly be? Poverishment can be measured in degrees, and the range of anchor choices presented to the student can tap those degrees. In other words, don't use absolute terms to qualify the instructor's behavior; let the students qualify the behavior with their anchor responses.

15. *The statement should NOT contain* nonabsolute, warm-and-fuzzy terms.

Nonabsolute terms are vague, indefinite, ambiguous, warm, and fuzzy. Examples are *sometimes, usually, frequently, often, occasionally, too much, trivial, maybe, whenever,* and *like sure.* Used as qualifiers, they may create confusion and increase subjectivity in interpreting a statement. The meaning of each term is supplied by the student, and we have no clue what that definition is. For example, how would you interpret the following?

> **PUTRID:** My instructor *usually* had a frantic hissy fit
> *whenever* students threw rotten vegetables.

How many definitions of *usually* are in students' noggins? Is it the majority of times when vegetables were thrown, most of the time, or when vegetables were thrown in two out of three of the classes each week? If a student strongly disagrees with this statement, does that mean the instructor rarely had a hissy fit? The interpretation of this statement is ambiguous. The meaning of the statement is directed at the frequency of the behavior, not its intensity. Omitting the indefinite, imprecise frequency qualifiers *usually* and *whenever* simplifies the statement, but not always.

Each qualifier complicates the interpretation and focuses the statement on a different attribute. Consider this improved version of the previous statement:

> **BETTER:** My instructor had frantic hissy fits in class.

The students can now rate the degree to which the instructor's behavior was exhibited by agreeing or disagreeing with this statement. The meaning has shifted from the frequency with which the behavior occurred to the behavior itself. Be careful with the qualifiers you select.

16. *The statement should NOT contain* value-laden or inflammatory words.

Such words can prejudice or anger respondents, which can influence their ratings. Avoid any language that would be offensive to anyone. The net result could be biased ratings, either high or low, which are invalid. Here are some statements that are totally inappropriate.

> **PUTRID:** My instructor has a primitive brain no larger
> than that of a psychic-hotline caller.
> My instructor's grating voice would cause flocks of migrating geese
> to reverse course. (The lead goose would say, "Turn back, flock!
> We're spending the winter in Montreal.")
> My instructor's sweat gushed from every pore
> so that by the end of the class he was standing
> in a puddle of bodily secretions.

17. The statement should NOT contain words, phrases, or abbreviations that would be unfamiliar to all respondents.

If there is any word, phrase, or abbreviation in the statement that all of the students do not know, the statement is invalid. The "unknowledgeable" students can't respond appropriately to the statement. The word can confuse or mislead the students so that they are answering the statement differently than was intended. The most common violations of this rule include slang, colloquialisms, professional jargon, and acronyms. As you have read these chapters, you have probably noted that I have committed every one of these violations. Catch me if you can. Consider the following:

> **PUTRID:** My instructor integrated information on
> WACKO regulations into course materials.

A student cannot agree or disagree with this statement unless he or she knows WACKO regulations. If these regulations are not familiar to all students and applicable to all courses in which the form is administered, then it is inappropriate.

In some cases when an abbreviation or acronym is used, the meaning can be provided in the statement so that students will understand it. This is a legitimate technique to ensure that lack of knowledge of abbreviations will not affect the rating. Here's an example without the meanings:

> **PUTRID:** My instructor used real case studies to demonstrate
> applications of DNA as shown on *CSI* on CBS.

Here's the version with the meanings to clarify the statement:

> **BETTER:** My instructor used real case studies to demonstrate applications
> of DNA (Dioxyriboestablishmentarianism) as shown on *CSI* (*American Idol*)
> on CBS (British Broadcasting Corporation).

Now isn't the above statement a winner?

18. The statement should NOT tap a behavior appearing in any other statement.

Avoid any overlapping content between statements. The behavior being measured by a single statement should not be measured in part or totally by any other statement. Every statement should be unique and independent of every other statement, whether it is in positive or negative form. Consider these statements:

> ***OVERLAP:*** My instructor exhibits the same range of
> facial expressions as an iguana.
> My instructor looks like a Gila monster.

The overlap in these two items is, you guessed it, the instructor's complexion. It's kinda scaly. Although the statements are not identical, there is a lizard-like quality to both that indicates partial overlap. Pick only one, and maybe tack on a "facial makeover" item.

19. The statement should NOT be factual or capable of being interpreted as factual.

If your scale is designed to measure students' opinions about key professor characteristics and behaviors related to effective teaching, a statement that is factual cannot be rated the same way as the other statements. For example,

> ***PUTRID:*** My instructor entered class on a cable lowered from the ceiling,
> like Ethan Hunt (Tom Cruise) in *Mission: Impossible.*

This is a statement of what actually happened in class. All students should mark "Agree," except those who were absent. Students are not being asked to evaluate the appropriateness of this entrance, how well it was done, or whether the professor looks like Tom Cruise. A better item would be the following:

> ***BETTER:*** My instructor was found naked in a hotel room with
> an underage Shetland pony that wasn't his wife.

Wrong! This is also a factual statement—just checking whether you're still awake. Your eyelids are getting heavy . . . Poke yourself in the eyeballs. Stay awake. We're almost done with this rule. Here's a better item:

> ***BETTER:*** My instructor's madcap crazy antics kept my attention.

20. The statement should NOT be endorsed or given one answer by almost all respondents or by almost none.

If a statement about the instructor or course would be answered the same way by almost all students, it may not provide any new information. Sometimes we can anticipate how students will respond. If we are fairly certain of their response in advance, why bother to include the item? In other words, if we already know the answer, why ask the students? For example, "grading methods" *must* be described in all syllabi. There is no need to present this:

PUTRID: Grades were based on a weighting of all course requirements.

Such items may be factual or interpreted that way by students. There should be a range of responses expected to each statement. Here's a spin to the previous statement:

BETTER: The grading system in this course was an
unintelligible concoction of requirements.

From a student's perspective, this is not factual. This statement should elicit a range of agree and disagree responses.

POP QUIZ #1 ANSWERS

1. double-barreled adverbs—*audibly* and *clearly*
2. students not in a position to know that information
3. a. double-barreled verbs—*returned* and *graded*
   b. students not in a position to know whether distant students received exams and assignments
4. a. double-barreled subject—*requirements* and *deadlines*
   b. factual—may not produce much variance
5. students not in a position to know whether all other students were treated with respect

SELECTING THE ANCHORS

Finding Anchorland

The anchors, or response choices, on rating scales vary with the purpose of the scale, the decisions to be made with the scores (formative, summative, or program), the format of the stimuli (words, phrases, or sentences), and the respondents (students, faculty, self, administrators, or employers). "You're getting me dizzy from all of these decisions. Anchors, schmanchors. Is it too late to buy a scale or develop a test instead, which I know has a correct answer to every item?" Yup, you passed the point of no return after chapter 3. Now that you have statements, you need some way of reacting to them. That brings us to Anchorland, where I will fly around suspended from a cable shouting out the five most common types of anchors and then eight rules for selecting the appropriate anchors for different scale structures. Ouch! Those straps attached to the cable really smart.

 BERK'S NOTES

Faculty—If you wrote statements for a scale, you'll probably need a way of responding. The first section jumpstarts your rip-snorting adventure into Anchorland. The five different species will give you a perspective on how to measure feelings about your statements. The rules that follow will make sure you select the right ones. Remember the formula: *item = statement + anchors*. They're a set; they must fit together like Will and Grace, Ernie and Bert, Mary-Kate and Ashley, the

Young and the Restless, and Desperate and Housewives. Of course, you should take Pop Quiz #2 (p. 95) to determine whether you can identify a few of the most common flaws. Memory Jogger 4.1 (p. 94) will provide an overview of the rules. If you are reviewing an existing scale, skim the types of anchors in the first section, then use Checklist 4.1 (p. 96) to evaluate the anchors.

Administrators—Unless you are directly involved in developing a rating scale or evaluating the quality of available scales, you can leap to chapter 6. But wait. Don't leap yet. Let me finish. A quick scan of the various types of anchors in the first section and the rules in Memory Jogger 4.1 will give you a basic understanding of what to expect on most scales as well as ideas of what you might want your faculty to create for program assessment and accreditation. Also, if you get a chance, take a glance at the Berk's Notes in chapter 5 and Pop Quiz #3 (p. 106) before you land your leap. Okay, blast off.

Types of Anchors

Once the words, phrases, or statements are completed, at least in draft form, it is now time to consider the second component of the scale item: the response options. These are the anchors the respondents choose to rate the statements.

Anchors on rating scales may consist of one or two words, phrases, sentences, or detailed descriptions of behaviors. There are five types of anchors used on rating scales: (1) intensity, (2) evaluation, (3) frequency, (4) quantity, and (5) comparison.

Intensity Anchors

Intensity anchors measure the degree or intensity of a respondent's *feelings toward a behavior* in a statement. The most widely used anchors of this type are the *agree–disagree scales.* These are the anchors originally employed on Likert scales. They are *bipolar,* meaning there are both positive anchors and negative anchors. The number on each side should be equal so they are balanced, not biased toward one direction. Even-numbered scales, such as 2-point, 4-point, and 6-point scales have equal numbers of positive and negative anchors. Examples of these (with alternative adverbs) are shown on page 87. Odd-numbered scales contain the addition of a middle anchor, usually labeled "Neutral," "Undecided," or "Uncertain."

2-POINT	4-POINT	6-POINT
Agree	Strongly Agree	Strongly Agree (Completely)
Disagree	Agree	Moderately Agree (Mostly)
	Disagree	Slightly Agree (Somewhat, Mildly)
	Strongly Disagree	Slightly Disagree (Somewhat, Mildly)
		Moderately Disagree (Mostly)
		Strongly Disagree (Completely)

Evaluation Anchors

Evaluation anchors ask the respondent to evaluate the *quality of a behavior* according to a particular dimension with descriptors such as *excellent–poor, excellent–unacceptable, effective–ineffective, satisfactory–unsatisfactory, important–unimportant, exceeded expectations–unacceptable,* and *major concern–no concern.* Most of these scales are *unipolar,* starting with the highest level of quality rating and moving toward the lowest level. The direction for the anchors is either high to low or low to high.

These anchors provide a graduated scale of levels of quality. The most popular scales have five points or levels. There is no neutral position. The middle position on an odd-numbered scale usually indicates "Good," "Average," "Moderate," or "Mediocre" quality. Examples of anchors (with alternative adverbs) used to rate teaching behaviors or course characteristics are listed below:

EXCELLENT–POOR (5-POINT)
Excellent
Very Good (Above Average)
Good (Average)
Fair (Below Average, Needs Improvement, Barely Acceptable)
Poor (Very, Extremely Poor)

EXCELLENT–UNACCEPTABLE (5-POINT)
Excellent
Good
Acceptable
Borderline
Unacceptable

EFFECTIVE–INEFFECTIVE (5-POINT)
Extremely Effective
Very Effective

Moderately Effective
Somewhat Effective (Slightly)
Ineffective

SATISFACTORY–UNSATISFACTORY (3-POINT)

Satisfactory
Mediocre
Unsatisfactory

VERY SATISFACTORY–UNSATISFACTORY (4-POINT)

Very Satisfactory
Satisfactory
Not Quite Satisfactory
Unsatisfactory

IMPORTANT–UNIMPORTANT (5-POINT)

Extremely Important   Very Important
Very Important   Important
Moderately Important   Moderately Important
Slightly Important   Of Little Importance
Unimportant   Unimportant

EXCEEDED EXPECTATIONS–UNACCEPTABLE (4-POINT)

Exceeded Expectations
Met Expectations
Below Expectations
Unacceptable

MAJOR CONCERN–NO CONCERN (3-POINT)

You Have a Major Concern
You Have Some Concern
No Concern

Another type of evaluation anchor is the *satisfied–dissatisfied* scale, not to be confused with the preceding *satisfactory–unsatisfactory* scale. This satisfaction scale is frequently used to evaluate the quality of academic services or programs in exit and alumni surveys.

The *satisfied–dissatisfied* scale differs in structure from the preceding unipolar evaluation anchors. It is a bipolar scale that is balanced as an even-numbered scale similar to the intensity scales. It is also possible to insert a "Neutral" anchor in the middle of the scale to create an odd-numbered scale. A typical 6-point scale is shown below.

SATISFIED–DISSATISFIED (6-POINT)
Completely Satisfied
Mostly Satisfied
Somewhat Satisfied
Somewhat Dissatisfied
Mostly Dissatisfied
Completely Dissatisfied

Frequency Anchors

Frequency anchors measure *how often a behavior occurs*. These anchors tend to be the most problematic of the types mentioned so far. Unless actual quantitative times or ranges of the day (once or twice), week, or month are designated in the anchors (Newstead & Collis, 1987), measuring the frequency of behaviors is indefinite and ambiguous (Bryant & Norman, 1980). They range from *nonoccurrence* ("Never") to *constant occurrence* at different levels. The ambiguity is an intractable problem. It even has produced a specific body of research on "vague quantifiers" (Bass, Cascio, & O'Connor, 1974; Chase, 1969; Cliff, 1959; Goocher, 1965; Hakel, 1968; Lichtenstein & Newman, 1967; Parducci, 1968; Pepper & Prytulak, 1974; Simpson, 1994).

Unfortunately, the most popular anchors are generic and nonquantitative, with adverbs such as *frequently, occasionally, usually, rarely,* and *seldom.* What do these words mean? Only the respondent knows for sure. Each respondent assigns his or her own wacky definition to these anchors. This built-in ambiguity renders the interpretation of summary results very difficult. If most students rate "Occasionally" for a particular behavior, we have no clue about the concrete frequency of that anchor. It has relative meaning only compared to the other anchors. Despite this lack of precision in frequency anchors, they are still widely used.

When frequency scales are used to rate behaviors, the anchors chosen are based on opinion. For example, if a student or peer rates the frequency with which an instructor uses profanity in class "Sometimes" or "Seldom," it is an opinion. However, if an employer rates the frequency with which she bops an employee over the head with an issue of *Cosmo,* that rating is regarded as factual. Of course, she can lie or fake her response. In other words, when a person *rates someone else,* it's usually his or her *opinion* or estimate of frequency. Most frequency rating scales of teaching or clinical performance fit this mold. When a person or rodent rates the frequency of his or her *own behavior* or practice, it's supposed to be interpreted as *factual*; however, that rating can be biased.

Examples of some unipolar frequency scales (with alternative adverbs) are as follows:

OFTEN–NEVER (4-POINT)
Often
Sometimes
Seldom
Never

ALMOST ALWAYS–SELDOM (4-POINT)
Almost Always
To a Considerable Degree
Occasionally
Seldom

ALWAYS–NEVER (5-POINT)
Always
Very Often (Usually)
Sometimes (About Half the Time)
Rarely (Seldom)
Never

ALWAYS–NEVER (6-POINT)
Always (Very Frequently)
Very Frequently (Frequently)
Occasionally
Rarely
Very Rarely
Never

Quantity Anchors

Quantity anchors measure *how much* of a behavior or *to what extent* a behavior occurs. These anchors may be found on exit and alumni surveys of instructor, course, or program characteristics. If there were a contest for "Most Ambiguous Anchors," the quantity anchors would be neck and neck with the verbal frequency anchors. Whichever one won, the other would be first runner-up, with an ambiguous tiara and sash. Word combos such as "A Great Deal," "Quite a Bit," "Very Much," and "Fairly Much," scream out for meaning. MEEEANIIING!!! They're as difficult to define and discriminate as the frequency anchors. However, if a quantity scale is required to assess *How much did you like the program?* or *To what extent did the program ruin your life?* then it must be used. The scales include *all–none, a good deal–not at all,* and *a great extent–not at all.* Examples of these unipolar scales are given below:

4-POINT	5-POINT	6-POINT
All	All	All
A Great Amount	A Great Amount	Almost Completely (Entirely)
A Moderate Amount	Quite a Bit	Very Much
None	Some	Fairly Much
	None	To Some Degree
		None

A GREAT DEAL–NOT AT ALL (6-POINT)
>A Great Deal
>Very Much
>Somewhat
>Little
>Very Little
>Not at All

A GREAT EXTENT–NOT AT ALL (4-POINT)
>A Great Extent
>Somewhat
>Very Little
>Not at All

Comparison Anchors

Comparison anchors are used when you want students to *compare characteristics of the course* they are rating *to other courses* they have completed. The comparison courses may be those in the same content area or discipline, department, school, university, or planet. The comparison anchors may be verbal, quantitative, or a combination of both. They compose a unipolar scale because the respondents are evaluating the current course against previous courses from *high–low, more–less, heavier–lighter, faster–slower,* or *difficult–easy.* Although these comparison anchors are used less often on rating scales than the previous types of anchors, they can provide useful information in a separate subscale of topics or phrases describing teaching and course characteristics.

The major weakness of this type of scale is the *unknown reference point,* or *norm group,* of previous courses in the cranium of each student. Those courses are different for all students and unknown to those interpreting the scores. Yet the ratings are based directly on the "norm groups of courses." Then what does the overall rating mean? The interpretation is ambiguous. Proceed cautiously if you plan on using any of the following examples:

HIGH–LOW (5-POINT)
High (highest 10% of courses)
High Average (next 20% of courses)
Average (middle 40% of courses)
Low Average (next 20% of courses)
Low (lowest 10% of courses)

MORE–LESS (5-POINT)
Much More than Most Courses
More than Most Courses
About the Same
Less than Most Courses
Much Less than Most Courses

HEAVIER–LIGHTER (5-POINT)
Much Heavier than Other Courses
Heavier than Other Courses
About the Same
Lighter than Other Courses
Much Lighter than Other Courses

FASTER–SLOWER (5-POINT)
Much Faster than Similar Courses
Somewhat Faster than Similar Courses
About the Same
Somewhat Slower than Similar Courses
Much Slower than Similar Courses

DIFFICULT–EASY (5-POINT)
Much More Difficult than Other Courses
More Difficult than Other Courses
About the Same
Easier than Other Courses
Much Easier than Other Courses

The above anchor scales can be used to rate characteristics such as the following:

- Gaining factual knowledge
- Learning fundamental principles
- Applying course material to real-world situations
- Pace at which instructor covered material
- Assigned reading
- Workload
- Subject matter
- Thinking independently
- Interest in the course content
- Preparation for each class
- Effort put into the course

Another type of unipolar comparison scale focuses on the individual being rated, such as the instructor, administrator, physician, or nurse, rather than characteristics of the courses or program. The respondent is asked to *rate the instructor compared to others he or she knows* with anchors ranging from *best–worst* or *among the best–among the worst*. The comparison is being made to a norm group of instructors in the mind of each respondent. Ambiguity-wise, these comparison anchors are as flawed as the ones listed previously. What does the comparison rating mean when the comparison group is unknown and different for each rating? Summarizing the ratings for all respondents doesn't eliminate that ambiguity. A couple of examples are shown below:

BEST–WORST (5-POINT)
    Best
    Very High
    Average
    Fair
    Worst

AMONG THE BEST–AMONG THE WORST (5-POINT)
    Among the Best
    Top Half
    Average
    Bottom Half
    Among the Worst

MEMORY JOGGER 4.1

RULES FOR SELECTING ANCHORS

1. The anchors should be *consistent with the purpose* of the rating scale.
2. The anchors should *match the statements, phrases, or word topics.*
3. The anchors should be *logically appropriate* with each statement.
4. The anchors should be *grammatically consistent* with each statement.
5. The anchors should provide the most *accurate and concrete* responses possible.
6. The anchors should elicit a *range of responses.*
7. The anchors on *bipolar scales* should be *balanced, not biased.*
8. The anchors on *unipolar scales* should be *graduated appropriately.*

Rules for Selecting Anchors

Given the array of anchors one could choose, here are eight specific rules to guide the choice of your anchors. Again, since you may be familiar with some of these rules, a review of Memory Jogger 4.1 will speed up your coverage of this section. Also, take a whirl at Pop Quiz #2 on page 95.

If you have already picked a set of anchors or you need to critique the quality of the anchors on an existing scale, you might want to use Checklist 4.1 to speed up that review.

1. The anchors should be consistent with the purpose of the rating scale.

If you are designing an instrument to measure students' satisfaction with their undergraduate program, then the anchor choices should consist of an appropriate satisfaction scale rather than, for example, an *excellent–poor* scale. If teaching effectiveness is the purpose of the measurement, then an effectiveness scale would be the first choice of anchors to assess teaching behaviors. If teaching behaviors are mixed with course characteristics, the effective or desirable behaviors may be expressed in the statements, and an *agree–disagree* scale can be used for the entire tool.

POP QUIZ #2

Directions: Please identify the flaw(s) in each of the following six "real" student rating scale statements with different anchor choices. The number of boxes to the left indicates the number of flaws. The anchor choices are listed in each section below.

VE = Very Effective
E = Effective
ME = Moderately Effective
SE = Slightly Effective
IE = Ineffective

Flaw(s)   **Statement**

1. My instructor emphasized important points in class.   *VE E ME SE IE*

2. Instructor's enthusiasm.   *VE E ME SE IE*

E = Excellent
VG = Very Good
G = Good
F = Fair
P = Poor

3. This course was quite interesting.   *E VG G F P*

4. Instructor was boring.   *E VG G F P*

A = Always
VO = Very Often
S = Sometimes
R = Rarely
N = Never

5. Instructor's use of class time.   *A VO S R N*

6. Physical environment was conducive to learning.   *A VO S R N*

Answers: Go to p. 103.

CHECKLIST 4.1

EVALUATION OF RATING SCALE ANCHORS

	YES	NO
1. Are the anchors *consistent with the purpose* of the rating scale?	____	____
2. Do the anchors *match the statements, phrases, or word topics*?	____	____
3. Are the anchors *logically appropriate* with each statement?	____	____
4. Are the anchors *grammatically consistent* with each statement?	____	____
5. Do the anchors provide the most *accurate and concrete* responses possible?	____	____
6. Do the anchors elicit a *range of responses*?	____	____
7. Are the anchors on *bipolar scales balanced, not biased*?	____	____
8. Are the anchors on *unipolar scales graduated appropriately*?	____	____

---

2. *The anchors should* match the statements, phrases, or word topics.

Like, duuuh! This rule seems so obvious. You just select the appropriate statements from the pool supplied by a publisher or you write your own and then use an *agree–disagree* scale. Simple enough. Right? Well, not always. Sometimes that strategy might work, but a more deliberate review to match the anchors to the statements is recommended. In fact, some of the behaviors or characteristics may be phrases or word topics for which an *agree–disagree* scale would be inappropriate. Student rating scales may contain a series of statements in one section and phrases in another. Peer rating scales may use a checklist anchor format with phrases and/or word topics. The other scales may use any of these formats.

A systematic review by a committee of at least 5–7 faculty and 2–4 students should be conducted once the body of the rating scale is in draft form. This is part of the mini-field test (see chapter 7). "Why are students on this committee?" you query. Students will be completing the scale, and their input on the readability of the items and the meaningfulness of the anchors would be extremely valuable. They can identify professional jargon or other terminology that faculty might not notice.

The rest of the rules for selecting anchors can serve to guide this review process. For example, the following steps might be useful:

1. Read each statement.
2. Say to yourself (silently), "Bucko (or Buckette), can I agree or disagree with this statement?"
3. If yes, ask, "Are *agree–disagree* anchors the best choices, or do I want to know how frequently this behavior occurred?"
4. Pending your tentative choice, ask, "Are these anchors
    a. logically appropriate?"
    b. grammatically correct?"
    c. the most accurate and concrete responses?"
    d. going to elicit responses along the entire continuum?"
    e. going to improve my chances of getting tenure?"

Certainly some of these questions would be different for a peer, alumni, or employer scale, but the process would be the same. Each statement, phrase, and/or word topic must be scrutinized to determine the most appropriate anchors. Once this review has been completed, those items requiring the same anchor scale could then be grouped together, resulting in different subscales.

3. *The anchors should be* logically appropriate *with each statement.*

The anchors you select should make sense logically with each statement or phrase.

a. Statements.   Declarative sentences that express a positive or negative behavior or characteristic can usually be rated with intensity or frequency anchors. Other anchors may be inappropriate. For example, how would you mark the statement below?

PUTRID: My instructor uses as much technology as a nuclear submarine.

____ Extremely Effective
____ Very Effective

___ Moderately Effective
___ Somewhat Effective
___ Ineffective

This effectiveness scale and other evaluation anchors are illogical for statements such as the above. The logical anchors would be an *agree–disagree* scale or even an *always–never* frequency scale, if one were interested in how often the behavior occurred.

b. Phrases/words.   When short phrases are chosen as the item format instead of statements, the evaluation anchors may be employed. Phrases usually describe a behavior and may be less strongly worded than statements. Sometimes they are just topics consisting of one or two words. What anchors would fit the phrases/words below?

My instructor's use of technology

or

Use of technology

or

Technology

- Overheads
- PowerPoint®
- Slides
- PC
- CD-ROM
- Course Web site
- Internet
- Videos/DVDs
- Audiotapes/CDs

First notice that there is no positive or negative feeling conveyed. Logically, an *agree–disagree* scale is inappropriate because there is nothing with which to agree. You could use a frequency scale or evaluation scale. *Excellent–poor* and *extremely effective–ineffective* anchor scales can evaluate the "use of technology." These anchors can be found on student rating scales, but more often on peer and interview rating scales where the items are listed as above, with a checklist format for the anchors.

4. *The anchors should be* grammatically consistent *with each question.*

If any items are in question format, the answers must be not only logical, but also grammatically correct. How would you answer the following questions?

PUTRID: Would you take another course with this bozo?

____ Strongly Agree
____ Agree
____ Disagree
____ Strongly Disagree

If there were no anchors above, how would you normally answer the question? The wording of the question suggests either *yes* or *no*. In this case, the *agree–disagree* anchor scale is grammatically inconsistent with that question.

Here are some examples with appropriate anchors:

BETTER: What was the *quality* of the course materials?

____ Excellent
____ Very Good
____ Good
____ Fair
____ Poor

BETTER: How *effective* were the props used in class to illustrate concepts?

____ Extremely Effective
____ Very Effective
____ Moderately Effective
____ Slightly Effective
____ Ineffective

In the "better" items, the question qualifies the behaviors with the key words *quality* and *effective*, which can be rated with grammatically appropriate evaluation anchors.

The acid test, or criterion, in selecting response options for question-format items is: *Ask the respondent to answer the question.* That natural answer should indicate whether to use *yes–no* or one of the anchor scales. Your choice should then be logically and grammatically correct.

5. The anchors should provide the most accurate and concrete responses possible.

Among the three types of anchor scales described previously, the most indefinite, imprecise, and ambiguous were the frequency and quantity anchors. Although *frequency* denotes number of times something occurs, the most common anchors on frequency scales are verbal. If you were to ask students how many times a particular teaching behavior occurred in class, they would answer with a number.

The anchors become foggier when we ask: "How much . . . ?" or "To what extent . . . ?" The *quantity* anchors are also verbal, but there are no obvious numerical alternatives.

a. Verbal anchors.   So why use verbal anchors such as "Always," "Very Frequently," "Occasionally," "Seldom," and the like on rating scales? They are easy to answer, although only the respondents really know what they mean. They furnish generic categories for estimating how frequently a behavior occurs, so that behaviors that are rated near the ends of the scale can furnish meaningful diagnostic information on teaching characteristics. Although the scale presents the illusion of precision, perhaps the greatest area of ambiguity rests near the middle of the scale with anchors such as "Occasionally" and "Sometimes."

The quantity anchors, such as "A Great Deal," "Quite a Bit," and "A Little," are typically the answers respondents would give to a "How much" question. Quantity scales do not convey any real or illusory sense of precision. They are just plain ambiguous.

b. Quantitative anchors.   The obvious alternative to overcome this imprecision is to employ quantitative anchors. Ideally, the actual quantity would be the most accurate response. As anchors, the quantitative scale may be composed of single numbers per week, month, or semester, or number ranges for the specific behaviors. For a series of statements about instructor behaviors during a course, number categories such as *0, 1–2 times, 3–4 times, 5 or more times per semester* may be appropriate. These categories have to be tested with each statement to assure they are meaningful and accurate scales to measure frequency of behavior.

6. *The anchors should elicit a* range of responses.

The anchor scale you choose should tap the entire range of feelings toward the statement being rated. If students across different classes don't pick anchors along the continuum, then they need to be smacked. No. Then either the statement needs to be strengthened or another anchor scale should be considered.

If you can predict the students' responses at one end or the other of the anchor scale, why ask the question? If the statement yields low or no variance, it just confirms your prediction; it provides evidence to support what you already knew. However, you might want to select different anchors. What anchors would be best for this statement?

> My instructor was so involved in lecturing from her notes
> that she didn't even know the class left.

What is the most appropriate anchor scale for the above statement?

A. Agree–Disagree
B. Excellent–Poor
C. Effective–Ineffective
D. Satisfied–Dissatisfied
E. Always–Never
F. None of the Above
G. I have no clue what you want from me.

According to the preceding rules, choices "B," "C," and "D" make absolutely no sense as anchor scales. Choice "A" might work because I can certainly agree or disagree with the statement. If all the students observed this behavior at least once, they would respond agree or strongly agree. Did she or didn't she do that in class? It's factual. There would be very limited variance in the answers. By a process of elimination, how about choice "E"? A frequency scale could be used to measure how often this behavior occurred. This scale would provide a more sensitive range of options and could produce greater response variance.

7. *The anchors on* bipolar scales *should be* balanced, not biased.

Intensity scales and *satisfied–dissatisfied* anchors must have an equal number of positive and negative anchors; otherwise, the respondent is restricted from reacting to a statement along the entire continuum. For example, suppose a student was asked the following question:

PUTRID: How satisfied were you with the quality
of teaching in your program?

____ Satisfied
____ Slightly Dissatisfied
____ Markedly Dissatisfied
____ Severely Dissatisfied

The dice are loaded. How much variance does this scale permit? Not a lot. It seems that the item is designed to tap how dissatisfied students felt rather than how satisfied they were. These anchors are biased. They don't allow students to respond fairly along the entire underlying *satisfied–dissatisfied* continuum. A balanced scale with an equal number of "Satisfied" and "Dissatisfied" anchors would be more appropriate. Such a scale was shown previously under evaluation anchors.

8. *The anchors on* unipolar scales *should be* graduated appropriately.

Should these anchors wear a cap and gown? How about an anchor with a mortar board? Seriously, the unipolar scales are used to rate the quality of teaching performance (*excellent–poor* or *satisfactory–unsatisfactory*), effectiveness of teaching behaviors (*extremely effective–ineffective*), and the frequency with which the behaviors occur (*always–never* or *0–5 or more times per course/semester*).

a. Student rating scales.   On student rating scales where phrases describing behaviors are listed rather than statements, the anchors should be sensitive to those behaviors and graduated to reflect distinct differences in performance. If effectiveness anchors are selected, the number of adjectives (or points) should be appropriate for the students' ability to discriminate among those points. The issue is not the extreme anchors; it is the adverbs such as *very*, *moderately*, and *somewhat* (or *slightly*). Can the students clearly distinguish between "Moderately Effective" and "Somewhat Effective"? Four or five anchors are appropriate for most college students. Six- or seven-anchor scales require a higher level of discrimination, which may not be optimal for all classes (see question 2, chapter 5, p. 109).

b. Peer rating scales.   In contrast to students, faculty can rate a peer on almost any of the unipolar scales. Since phrases and/or word topics are the most common formats on peer rating scales, the quality and effectiveness anchors are the best fit. Most of these are 5-point scales.

POP QUIZ #2 ANSWERS

1. mismatch with anchors
2. mismatch with anchors
3. mismatch with anchors
4. a. mismatch with anchors
   b. will not elicit a range of responses
5. mismatch with anchors
6. mismatch with anchors

REFINING THE ITEM STRUCTURE

Caveat Itemus

Bet you thought you were done with the items. WROOONG! Now that you have a bundle of statements and anchors in draft form, other rather sticky icky issues can be considered that relate to the specific scale format, anchor structure and format, and response bias. The research evidence on these issues will be reviewed to guide your decisions on what adjustments need to be made in your draft rating scale. The seven issues covered in this chapter must be addressed now or later. You decide when you want it. Most of the issues are straightforward; only the nine types of response bias present formidable challenges. The decisions you make will affect the validity and reliability of the scale scores and their interpretation.

 BERK'S NOTES

Faculty—Now you think you have a spiffy collection of items. But are you sure? Stop and consider the anchors for a moment. Should you use a "Neutral" midpoint? Should you label every anchor point or use numbers? How many anchors do you need? How can the anchor structure bias responses to the statements? Some people think the answers to these questions began as "urban myths," such as the albino alligator in the New York City sewers or the president of the United States being elected by some electoral college. Au contraire! (*Foreign Word Translation*: This is a French expression meaning "Your Jacques Cousteau wetsuit is on inside out and backwards.") Anyway, it's time to get back to our topic, which was . . . I forget. Oh, spiffy items. These are basic issues for which there is more than 80 years of research. Take Pop Quiz #3 to test your knowledge of these issues. Your items must conform to the state of research. Read the answers to each question, especially the last section on bias. Those answers will streamline your scale so it will be the latest model on the block. You won't regret it.

Administrators—This chapter deals with the structure of the items, particularly the anchors. Since you may be in the process of leaping over this chapter to the next, you probably aren't reading this note anyway. However, if you are flying over this paragraph or you ignored my leaping recommendation, take the Pop Quiz. The questions and answers will acquaint you with the key issues. The material pertains to all rating scales. You should read the last section, on bias (question 7), because certain types of bias can occur as a result of how you rate faculty and administer scales and who does the administration. You are in a position to minimize some of those biases, if you feel like it.

Preparing for Structural Changes

Before you dive into the seven sticky and thorny issues in scale construction, take a crack at Pop Quiz #3 below to measure how much you already know about these issues. I really hope you do better on this one than on the previous two. I'm watching. Go for it.

POP QUIZ #3

Directions: Circle the *BEST* answer to each of the following questions based on the research and practice in scaling over the past 80 years.

1. What rating scale format is best?
   A. graphic
   B. forced-choice
   C. behaviorally anchored
   D. behavior summary
   E. behavioral observation
   F. It doesn't matter

2. How many anchor points should be on the scale?
   A. 3–5
   B. 5–7
   C. 7–9
   D. 5–9
   E. The more points, the better

3. Should there be a midpoint, "Neutral," or "Uncertain" position on the scale?
   A. Yup
   B. Nope

4. How many verbal anchors should be specified on the scale?
   A. 2 (at the extremes only)
   B. 3 (at the extremes and midpoint)
   C. Every point on the scale

5. Should numbers be placed on the anchor scale (e.g., 0–3, 1–5)?
   A. Yup
   B. Nope

6. Should a "Not Applicable" (*NA*) option be provided on the scale?
   A. Yup
   B. Nope

7. Should a "Not Observed" (*NO*) or "Unable to Assess" (*U/A*) option be provided?
   A. Yup
   B. Nope

8. Can students or faculty bias their ratings with less-than-honest and not entirely impartial responses?
   A. Yup
   B. Nope

Answers: 1. F, 2. B, 3. B, 4. C, 5. B, 6. B, 7. A, 8. A.

How did you do? Yeah, I know what you mean. I got some wrong and I wrote the questions. Anyway, a dense slab of words will be used to explain each of these answers in the following sections.

Issues in Scale Construction

1. What rating scale format is best?

Graphic rating scale formats have been illustrated in the examples throughout this book. The *stimuli* (words, phrases, or statements) are listed and numbered down the left side of the page, and the anchor *response choices* appear horizontally on the right side aligned with each statement. This is the most widely used Likert format for student, peer, alumni, and employer rating scales. Examples of this format for both types of scales are displayed in chapter 6 and also in appendices A and B. Appendix B also presents some of the other formats that provide more detailed behavioral descriptions. These are mentioned below.

The graphic format, however, is only one of several formats that could be used. There are checklist formats, such as forced-choice (Jacobs, 1986) and the mixed standard scale (Blanz & Ghiselli, 1972; Saal & Landy, 1977); formats with varying degrees of behavioral descriptions beyond single statements, such as behaviorally anchored scales (Bernardin & Smith, 1981; Cardy & Dobbins, 1994; Smith & Kendall, 1963), behavior summary scales (Borman, Hough, & Dunnette, 1976; Dunnette, 1966), and behavioral observation scales (Bernardin & Kane, 1980; Kane & Bernardin, 1982; Latham, Fay, & Saari, 1979), which are similar to graphic scales; and behavioral assessment formats (Cone, 1980; Komaki, Collins, & Thoene, 1980). (*Sentence Alert:* This is the longest sentence I have written since freshman English, plus there are a megagillion citations. I think that sentence structure is called a *funicular conundrum* or *infricative imprecation.* I forget which.)

Most of these formats have been developed and applied in the context of personnel and industrial/organizational psychology for a lonnng time, not higher education (Berk, 1986b). Numerous comparative studies of these formats seem to converge on one conclusion: *no one rating scale format has emerged as clearly superior to the alternatives* (Bernardin, 1977; Bernardin & Smith, 1981; Borman, 1979, 1986; Jacobs, 1986; Jacobs, Kafry, & Zedeck, 1980; Kingstrom & Bass, 1981; Kinicki, Bannister, Hom, & DeNisi, 1985; Zedeck, Kafry, & Jacobs, 1976). More than 20 years ago, Landy and Farr (1983) suggested:

> After more than 30 years of serious research, it seems that little progress has been made in developing an efficient and psychometrically sound alternative to the traditional graphic rating scale. . . . It appears likely that greater progress in understanding performance judgments will come from research on the rating process than from a continued search for the "Holy Format." (p. 90)

There appears to be consensus in the performance appraisal literature that small variations in rating scale format are not as important as the quality of the scale. Care in the preparation of the items and the competence of the rater (student, peer, external expert, self, or employer) have a greater effect on validity than the particular rating format used (Cronbach, 1990; Guion, 1986).

2. How many anchor points should be on the scale?

There are two factors to consider in answering this question: (1) the research evidence on the relationship between number of scale points and scale score reliability, and (2) the discrimination ability of the respondents. The first factor is based on rather consistent empirical results; the second is a judgment call.

Scale score reliability. More than a dozen studies on graphic rating scales conducted in the 1950s through the 1970s have yielded remarkably consistent results (Bendig, 1952a, 1952b, 1953, 1954a, 1954b; Finn, 1972; Jenkins & Taber, 1977; Komorita, 1963; Komorita & Graham, 1965; Lissitz & Green, 1975; Masters, 1974; Matell & Jacoby, 1971; Nishisato & Torii, 1970; Peabody, 1962; Symonds, 1924). Those results, which were substantiated by Myford (2002) in this century, led to two conclusions: (1) increases in the number of scale points (3→10) are accompanied by increases in scale score reliability, and (2) those increases reach a point of *diminishing returns after five points.* In other words, there are only miniscule gains in reliability with 6- to 10-point scales. The popular 7- and 9-point scales used to measure teaching effectiveness or job performance may be overkill, plus they may exceed the discrimination ability of the respondents to distinguish all of those points on the scale. It's like using an army tank to crack a walnut.

Respondent discrimination. Respondents have limited capacities for differentiating several levels, or categories, on a scale. For example, distinguishing between "Strongly Agree" and "Agree" is fairly easy for most adult respondents; however, the difference between "Agree" and "Slightly Agree" or "Somewhat Agree" may not be as clear. If the number of anchors is less than the respondent's ability to discriminate, there will be a loss of information. Conversely, as the number of anchors and points increases, the interpretation of differences between adjacent anchors becomes more difficult, ambiguous, and/or time-consuming, especially if the respondents are dumber than a doorknob.

Respondents must be able to discriminate among the anchor options. The tendency is to provide too many points rather than too few. *A balance is needed between the number of scale points, number of items on the scale, and completion time.* For college students to complete a 25–40 item rating scale in less than 10 minutes, a 4- or 5-point scale is adequate. A 6- or 7-point scale will take a little longer. Since the number of items also affects reliability, even a 20-item, 4-point scale or subscales with fewer items can yield reliability coefficients in the .80s and .90s (see chapter 8).

The competence of the rater and his or her ability to clearly discriminate among all points on the scale are reeeally important. Miller's (1956) now famous "seven, plus or minus two" dictum seems to generalize to most rating scales. He demonstrated that the *limit of short-term memory is seven chunks of information* (e.g., five-digit zip codes, seven-digit telephone numbers, nine-digit social security numbers).

Based on the reliability studies and students' and faculty's ability to discriminate points on rating scales measuring teaching effectiveness, *5–7 anchors are adequate*. The answer to the next question may knock this range down to 4–6. Hold on to your anchors. We're not done.

3. Should there be a designated midpoint position, such as "Neutral," "Uncertain," or "Undecided," on the scale?

Bipolar scales, such as *strongly agree–strongly disagree* and *satisfied–dissatisfied*, may have a midpoint option, which is usually an escape anchor. When a respondent picks this anchor, he or she is usually thinking:

> a. "I have no opinion, belief, or attitude on this statement."
> b. "I'm too lazy to take a position on this right now."
> c. "I don't care because there's a scorpion stinging my big toe."

The respondent is essentially refusing to commit to a position for whatever reason. From a measurement perspective, the information provided on teaching performance from a "Neutral" response is NOTHING! ZIPPO! By not forcing students to mark their positions, information is lost. Further, when several students pick the midpoint for an item and the ratings are generally favorable (a.k.a. negatively skewed), the overall faculty rating on the item can be lower or more conservative than when respondents are forced to pick a position.

For rating scales used to measure teaching effectiveness, it is recommended that the *midpoint position be omitted* and an even-numbered scale be used, such as 4 or 6 points. If the items are correctly written and all students, peers, and administrators are in a position to render an informed opinion on the instructor's behavior, then all items should be answered.

4. How many anchors should be specified on the scale?

Many graphic scales present anchors only at the ends; some indicate a mid-point anchor; and others label every point with a verbal/quantitative anchor or behavioral description. Consider the examples below:

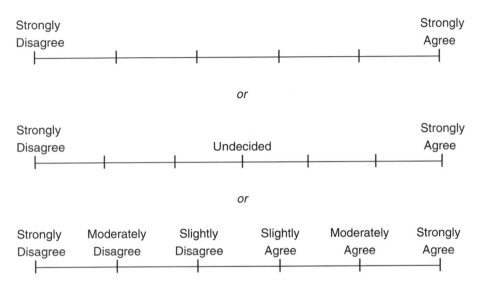

There is very little research on this topic. Those few studies that have compared different response formats with and without anchors indicate there is relatively little difference in responses and reliability (Dixon, Bobo, & Stevick, 1984; Frisbie & Brandenburg, 1979; Newstead & Arnold, 1989; Wildt & Mazis, 1978).

This research suggests that respondents tend to select the same position on the scale whether there is an anchor there or a blank. Adequate and even high reliability coefficients have been found for scales with only end-point anchors. So the issue here is *not* reliability. It's validity. What does the response mean when there is no anchor? Hmmm. Let's probe this issue a bit.

All of the anchor scales used to rate the teaching performance of faculty represent verbal or qualitative feelings. *If anchors are omitted from the scale, there is no way of knowing how a student or peer would describe his or her feeling about the behavior being rated.* The meaning of the response remains in the respondent's cranium. The issue is how to interpret positions on the scale for which no known feeling is rated. It is possible that, even when the same position is selected by a whole class of any size, every student may define that position differently. For example, hypothetically, suppose you take a two-by-four and smack each student in your class upside his or her head, after which each records the level of pain on the following 11-point scale:

(*Note*: This 10 cm scale is called a *visual analog scale*.)

If every student were to pick the position corresponding to 8, how would the students describe their level of pain? Ask them to write down a word or phrase to capture their physical feeling of pain. If you were to actually conduct this experiment in your class, which I don't recommend, there could be 50 different descriptions of that level in a class of 49 students. Ha ha. Just checking to see if you're conscious. If not, I can slug you with my two-by-four. Let me know.

Visual analog scales are, in fact, used to measure pain in adults. There is even a children's version called the Oucher!™ (www.oucher.org), which lists the 11 numbers (0–10) and illustrates six faces, of children expressing different levels of pain, at points along the scale. The instructions for administration tell the clinician to use the anchors "Little," "Middle," and "Big" hurt to describe those areas of the scale. Then children are asked to discriminate among the points on an 11-point scale. YIIIIKES! What were the authors thinking? Are kids capable of that level of discrimination? I can't meaningfully distinguish between that many points. What about you?

These examples serve to illustrate how real this problem is. The meaning of visual analog scales may be adequate for clinical purposes to prescribe pain medication, but not for research if scores are summed and averaged, as when we need to know the meaning of "7" for one sample or class and "4" for another.

From the perspective of score interpretation, it is highly recommended that you *specify as many anchors as necessary* on whatever scale is chosen. This will assure that at least the one- or two-word meaning of the responses will be known when they are picked by the students, peers, or employers. The meaning of the anchors will also be the same, unless they are ambiguous themselves, as in the case of frequency and quantity scales.

5. Should numbers be placed on the anchor scale?

At present, there is no research evidence to know whether students' ratings will be any different when numbers are specified with the anchors compared to when scales contain anchors only. For example, compare the following:

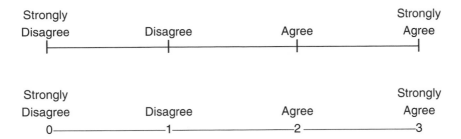

Only one study comparing a positive scale of 0–10 with a negative–positive scale of –5 to +5 found that respondents rated the latter numerical scale higher (Schwarz, Knäuper, Hippler, Noelle-Neumann, & Clark, 1991), indicating that the negative values conveyed a different meaning from the positive values.

For all rating scales, it is advisable to *use anchors only with letter abbreviations*, such as "SA" for "Strongly Agree," if appropriate. The numerical values are for analysis purposes and need not concern the respondents. Omitting the numbers also simplifies the appearance of the whole scale.

6. Should a "Not Applicable" (NA) or "Not Observed" (NO) option be provided?

The issues related to *NA* are different from those associated with *NO*. The reasons underlying these options are also different. "Not Applicable" means the respondent cannot answer because the statement is irrelevant or doesn't apply to the person or object being rated. "Not Observed" indicates the respondent can't rate the statement because he or she hasn't observed the behavior or is not in any position to answer the statement. The choices you have to make regarding use of these options are discussed next.

A few items on a rating scale that might be interpreted as not applicable or inappropriate by some students can be not only irritating and confusing, but also misleading. This problem is usually encountered where a single standard or generic scale is administered in courses that vary widely in content and instructional methods or formats. For example, not all statements may apply to a freshman psychology lecture-format course of 1,500 students as well as to a doctoral political science seminar with five students. Even when one carefully and deliberately generates statements with the intention of creating a "generic" scale, the *NA* problem may still be unavoidable.

One solution rests with attempting to eliminate the source of the problem: the evil *NA* statements. The task is to identify and modify the *NA* statements. Here is a suggested procedure that can be used in the context of the field tests described in chapter 7:

   a. Field-test the total pool of statements in courses that represent the range of content, structure, and method characteristics.
   b. Include the *NA* option with the anchor scale.
   c. Compute the percentage of students picking the *NA* option for every statement.
   d. Identify those statements with an *NA* percentage greater than 10%.
   e. Assemble a panel of reviewers composed of the faculty and a few students from the field-tested courses.
   f. Ask the panel to explain why the identified statements may be *NA* for those courses and to suggest how they may be revised to be promoted to "Applicable."
   g. Either revise or discard the questionable statements.

If the preceding steps were successful in eliminating the *NA* statements, there is no need to include the *NA* option on the final version of the rating scale. However, there is also another reason for not using an *NA* option: It can greatly complicate the analysis of the results. If the rating scale is being used by instructors for formative decisions, and only item-by-item results are presented with the percentage of students picking each anchor, then the *NA* option is not a problem. However, if scale or subscale scores are desired for summative decisions, the *NA* option distribution can distort the scale scores (see chapter 9). Every time the option is chosen by any student, his or her scale score will be different, because one or more items will not be part of the score. In other words, each score will be based on different items and cannot be compared or summed with other scores. This is an analysis nightmare. *Avoid using the NA option on scales intended for group analysis.*

A second solution to the *NA* problem is to develop a "generic" scale applicable to all courses, plus an "optional" subscale to which each instructor can add up to 10 statements related only to his or her course (see "Commercially Published Student Rating Scales" in chapter 2). These course-specific items would allow instructors to customize at least a portion of the total scale to the unique characteristics of their courses. The add-on subscale can also provide valuable diagnostic instructional information to instructors that would otherwise not be reported on the standard scale.

When scales are used for direct observation of performance *and* where the scores to be analyzed involve just a few raters, such as peer observation, colleague ratings, administrator ratings, mentee ratings, and self-ratings, it is permissible to use the *NA* option. Such ratings are summarized differently from student ratings. More judgment is involved. If a statistical summary is computed, the limitations described previously will still apply.

Those rating conditions may also require the addition of a "Not Observed"

(*NO*) or (*NOB*) option, which may also be expressed as "Unable to Assess" (*U/A*) or "Unable to Comment" (*U/C*). This option among the anchors gives respondents an "out" so they do not feel forced to rate behaviors they have not seen or are not in a position to rate (rule 11, chapter 3, p. 76). Such responses would be invalid. In fact, raters should be explicitly instructed in the directions for completing the scale to select *NA* or *NO*, if appropriate, so their ratings of the items they do answer are true and honest appraisals of the behaviors they *can* rate.

7. How can response set biases be minimized?

When students, peers, external experts, self, and administrators rate an instructor's performance, and employers rate employees based on a collection of statements and an anchor scale ranging from "Strongly Disagree" to "Strongly Agree," it is assumed that they will read each statement carefully and make their honest assessment with scrupulous impartiality. (*Editor*: Please insert belly laugh here.) Are we dreaming or is this the real world? The problem is that there are human tendencies or factors that may contaminate their responses, rendering them less than honest and impartial. In fact, these tendencies may be driven by demonic forces, such as those seen on *The X-Files* or appearing in Stephen King's books. Booga booga! Kidding. However, they may be conscious and intentional or unconscious. These tendencies are known as *response sets* or *biases* (Nunnally & Bernstein, 1994).

The five types of bias that can affect most ratings to some degree are halo effect; end-aversion bias; extreme-response bias; acquiescence bias; and gender, racial/ethnic, and sexual orientation bias. There are also four others that particularly afflict peer or administrator ratings: leniency-stringency bias, incompetence bias, buddy bias, and back-scratching bias. All of these biases are described next along with suggestions for minimizing their effects, where possible.

a. Halo effect.   This effect refers to the extent to which a student's, peer's, or administrator's *overall impression of an instructor will affect his or her rating on each statement*. For example, if the global impression is positive and the student really likes the instructor, he or she may simply mark "Strongly Agree" or "Agree" to all statements (d'Apollonia & Abrami, 1997a; Remmers, 1934; Shevlin et al., 2000). However, despite the positive image of a halo on an angel, this effect can also be negative. Where the student hates the instructor, subject matter, or course, the instructor is sure to be demolished on the statements. Thorndike (1920), who coined the name for this effect, defined it as follows: "The judge seems intent on reporting his [or her] final opinion of the strength, weakness, merit, or demerit of the personality as a whole, rather than on giving as discriminating a rating as possible for each separate characteristic" (p. 447).

Possible solutions: Since this is an individual bias, the larger the class, the greater the chance that positive and negative halo effects will cancel out in the instructor's mean, or median, course rating. Small class sizes of 5–10, particularly seminars, can produce significantly inflated or deflated ratings, depending on the direction of the bias. Obviously, there is *no simple solution to control or minimize halo effect.* Even in peer observations, multiple peer ratings by different faculty may reduce the effect, but not eliminate it (see Cooper, 1981). Structurally, expanding the anchors into more detailed, concrete descriptors in the format of a behaviorally anchored rating scale may reduce the bias, but be prohibitive to administer in class or online within 10 minutes or too complex for peer observers and other raters of teaching performance.

b. End-aversion/central tendency bias.   This bias refers to the tendency of students, peers, administrators, or employers to *ignore the extreme anchors on the scale* (Attali & Bar-Hillel, 2003). They may be viewed as too strong. When the extremes are not selected, the ratings may be squished into the middle of the scale, which restricts the range of responses.

Possible solutions: This bias should not be a problem on 4- to 7-point student rating scales, especially in the *agree–disagree* format. However, peer rating scales consisting of 5 or more evaluation anchors, such as *excellent–poor,* or frequency anchors with absolutes, such as *always–never,* can produce this type of bias. Either *soften the extreme anchors* with "Almost Always" and "Almost Never," or *extend the number of anchors from 5 to 7* with the expectation that the extremes will rarely be chosen. This latter adjustment may improve the variance of the responses.

c. Extreme-response bias.   This tendency is the opposite of the one above. In this case, the respondents may tend to *mark the extreme anchors rather than those in between.* This bias is difficult to detect because the reason for the choice of the extremes may also be due to their honest ratings or the halo effect.

Possible solutions: This type of bias may occur less often than the other sources of bias. It can influence the overall instructor's rating in small classes. (See solutions for halo effect.)

d. Acquiescence/affirmation/agreement/yea-saying bias.   This bias is the tendency to *agree or give positive responses to statements irrespective of their content* (Couch & Keniston, 1960). In our culture, we are socialized to be agreeable, to say "yes" instead of "no," and when asked, "How are you?" we answer ~~"yucky"~~ "fine" whether we honestly mean it or not. On student rating scales, the students may pick "Strongly Agree" and "Agree" more frequently than the disagree anchors because of this response set. Faculty peers may also select "Excellent," "Very Good," and "Good" more often than negative anchors or "Needs Improvement" on an observation checklist. This response set tends to inflate the ratings and skew the distribution toward the upper end of the scale so that an instructor's performance appears much better than it really is.

Possible solutions: There have been various attempts to measure acquiescent tendencies (Bentler, Jackson, & Messick, 1972; Couch & Keniston, 1960; Cronbach, 1946; Edwards, 1963; Edwards & Diers, 1963; Fricke, 1957; Martin, 1964; Rorer, 1965; Rorer & Goldberg, 1965). Unfortunately, most have bombed. The recommended strategy to minimize the effect of acquiescence bias is to *word half of the statements on the scale positively and the other half negatively* (rule 9, chapter 3, p. 74). This 50-50 distribution was first suggested by Likert (1932). Of course, the statements would be randomly ordered so the students or other respondents would not know the difference. They would respond to each statement on the *agree–disagree* anchor scale. This method does not eliminate or reduce the bias; it simply cancels out its effect. Since the negative statement responses are scored in the reverse, each point gained by acquiescing to a positively worded statement is lost by acquiescing to a negatively worded statement. Hence, the net effect of the bias should be zero.

This solution is workable in practice with most rating scales designed to measure educational, psychological, business, management, and health care constructs. However, it doesn't seem appropriate for student rating scales and others measuring teaching effectiveness for three reasons: (1) the reversals in the polarity of the statements throughout the scale, such as positive, positive, negative, positive, negative, and so on, can be confusing, which might result in increased response time and response errors; (2) the *face validity*, or meaning, of the scale on teaching performance is rating the extent which the instructor exhibited positive teaching behaviors, not negative ones; and (3) the strong opinions students and other respondents typically communicate about instructors and courses by the end of a semester suggest that they may not necessarily be in a particularly acquiescent mood when they complete the scales—that is, there may be minimal or no acquiescence bias (Berk, 1979a). For these reasons, it is recommended that *no adjustments be made in the scale structure*. Further, there are no known techniques to control acquiescence bias in peer rating scales, because the item format consists of words or phrases, which do not have a negative form.

e. Gender, racial/ethnic, and sexual orientation bias.   In the interest of fairness and nondiscrimination, this type of bias must be addressed. Since such bias exists in the forms of salary inequity, differential hiring and promotion rates, and available benefits/privileges at the different ranks, cross-gender, cross-race, or straight–gay ratings can exhibit conscious or unconscious bias. This may occur with student, peer, administrator, and employer ratings. Although this bias has not been formally assessed in teaching effectiveness programs, industrial research has indicated that same-race peer evaluations were more positive than cross-race evaluations (Schmitt & Lappin, 1980). The most serious implications of this bias are in uses of peer or administrator ratings for summative decisions.

Possible solutions: *Sensitivity or diversity training* is the most common strategy to minimize this type of bias. Such bias, or prejudice, may manifest itself in so many insidious forms that it is frequently difficult to detect unless the ratings are systematically lower for certain faculty than for others. Even then, those ratings may be justified on nonprejudicial grounds. *Requiring multiple ratings* by a diverse band of raters may tend to counterbalance the bias by any single rater.

f. Leniency-stringency bias. This bias can occur when any person is requested to rate another person. Some raters tend to be more lenient or forgiving, while others are more stringent or unforgiving (Nunnally & Bernstein, 1994). The motives or reasons behind the bias may be unknown.

Consider the winter Olympics, which rolls around every 16 years in a country that has to ship snow in from a neighboring country, and how the ratings are conducted. Although my favorite events are the 8-meter snowball fight and 2-man windshield scrape, the most obvious display of leniency-stringency bias is the pattern of judges' ratings of figure skaters. This provides a prime example of an untainted sport, like boxing, where judges carefully evaluate both the technical merit and artistic impression of each skater's performance and then vote for whomever they were going to vote for anyway. Since each judge represents a particular country, as the competition progresses, a visible trend develops in the judges' ratings. For example, when the ratings for each skater are posted, everyone can see that the judge from France consistently rates lower than all of the other judges. We can only venture to guess that she hates every country because they're inferior and they don't drink as much wine, but it won't matter. That is *stringency bias*. At the other end of the rating spectrum, the judge from Jamaica is so excited just to be in the Olympics with his country's ice hockey team, although the team is made up of Canadians who trained in Frostbite Falls, Minnesota (home of Rocky and Bullwinkle), that he seems to be giving the skaters consistently higher ratings than the other judges. This is *leniency bias*.

Possible solutions: These biases have implications for peer ratings. The biggest problems are that lenient and stringent raters and the reasons for their particular biases are nearly impossible to identify. First, *avoid choosing French professors* to evaluate teaching performance. This is probably a good idea, unless you're in France. Second, peers who rate skating instructors should have *adequate training with the scale and the observational procedures*. That might help minimize the bias. And third, since the confidentiality of the peer rating process may not reveal the identity of the lenient or stringent raters, hire Olivia Benson (a.k.a. Mariska Hargitay) from *Law & Order: SVU* to go undercover and find out who they are. If she's busy, *use multiple peer raters* for each instructor to balance the possible biases. Overall, this type of bias is difficult to detect and to reduce, because the reasons may not be apparent, even if Olivia can pick the perps (a.k.a. perpetrators) out of a lineup.

g. Incompetence bias.   This is the tendency to *assign high ratings because of a lack of competence and/or confidence in rating teaching behaviors* (Root, 1987). An administrator or a peer may have limited or no knowledge of teaching methods or simply lack experience. When observers are incompetent on the characteristics being rated, they tend to give more positive ratings, rather than penalize the faculty member for his or her own shortcomings.

   Possible solutions: Proper training in the particular teaching behaviors or performance being rated may minimize incompetence bias. Alternatively, observers shouldn't be asked to rate the items on the scale that they are unqualified to rate. For example, faculty peers or administrators with the appropriate content expertise, but weak in teaching skills, should complete only the subject-matter items, not the teaching methods section. Another approach, in lieu of peers, is to *hire external experts* to conduct the observations. These raters are trained with the necessary competencies to rate teaching performance.

h. Buddy bias.   Friendship and degree of acquaintance can inflate peer, administrator, and employer ratings. Early studies of peer assessment in the military (Wherry & Fryer, 1949) and private industry (Freeberg, 1969; Hollander, 1956; Love, 1981) suggest this type of bias may be just as applicable to academia.

   Possible solutions: This bias can be eliminated if the *peer rater is chosen by someone other than the peer's "buddy,"* such as an administrator, or if another administrator or employer/supervisor conducts the ratings.

i. Back-scratching bias.   This bias occurs when a *faculty member gives high ratings to peers on the exchange assumption that he or she will then receive high ratings*, kind of a "mutual admiration society" mentality. This mutual back scratching is most common on *The Sopranos* ("That's back stabbing, Bucko." Oops.) when faculty select their own peer raters.

   Possible solutions: If these observers are *selected by an administrator*, such as a department chair, associate dean, or dean, and they are *trained in teaching observation*, back-scratching bias can be minimized and even eliminated.

j. Other response set biases.   There are other types of biases reported in the scaling literature that pertain to self-report rating scales, especially personality measures, in which a person's responses are the focus of the interpretation. In those applications, the respondent may have the tendency to give the socially desirable answer or the one that society regards as positive (*social desirability bias*), to intentionally attempt to create a false positive impression (*faking good*), or to respond with deviant answers to present a negative image (*faking bad/deviation bias*). The latter two types of bias, in fact, can occur in combination, known as the *hello-goodbye effect* (Streiner & Norman, 1995).

When the target of the rating results is someone or something other than the respondent, these biases are not a concern. In formative, summative, and program decisions, the ratings by students, peers, self, administrators, and employers are directed at a specific person (instructor or student graduate), course or program characteristic, or service performed in the school. The respondents' ratings assess the overall quality, performance, effectiveness, or efficiency of these targets. Group-level summary statistics provide the information for decision making (see chapter 9).

6

ASSEMBLING THE SCALE FOR ADMINISTRATION

Scale Improvement

Faculty and administrators, what time is it? "Scale Time!" I'm Ron "The Scale Man" Berk. Not Scaly Man, Scale Man. This box brings you a special edition of *Scale Time*. Today you have a collection of statements and anchors. Tomorrow, who knows? What are you going to do next? All of the pieces need to be assembled into a formal instrument that is self-administering, easy to understand, and simple to complete. Once the tool is in the respondent's hands or on his or her computer screen, it's too late for questions. The respondent should be able to respond thoughtfully to the structured and unstructured items in a whiz. This chapter takes you through the process of completing the scale and then considers the options of paper-based versus online administration.

 BERK'S NOTES

Faculty—If you're involved in building a rating scale and administering it, this chapter is a must. This is where the rubber meets the roadkill, the baby meets the bathwater, and Harry Potter meets the goblet of stone. The first section takes you through the assembly process step-by-step, with a Mayflower® moving van full of real examples. You can also see the final versions of the scales in appendix A, if you haven't already peeked. Finally, review the procedures for administration, both paper-based and online, to consider which approach is best for your scale. Don't skip anything. I'llll be waaatching you.

Administrators—I bet you're starving for some content after all of that leaping. Well, have I got a section for YOU. The first part of the chapter deals with how to assemble a scale. You might want to flip through those pages to get to the best part: the references. Kidding. The last section covers the procedures and up-to-date research and practice on paper-based and online administration of scales. A comparison of the two approaches based on 15 factors is presented in table 6.1 for your convenience. You will need to decide how all of the scales you use for summative decisions will be administered. Estimates of costs are also included.

Assembling the Scale

There are five main sections in most rating scales: (1) identification information, (2) purpose, (3) directions with anchors, (4) structured items, and (5) unstructured items. Descriptions with examples of these sections are given next.

Identification Information

"You keep emphasizing how the identity of rating scale respondents should be kept confidential, and responses, anonymous. Why do I need this section?" I know. But you really haven't given me a chance to describe this section yet. Let's begin.

Student ratings.   You need to track the responses by instructor, course, semester, and year for student ratings, or there will be no way to match "anonymous" student responses to the right instructor. In this case, the information identifies the course not the students. Forms that are scannable or presented online usually have this information preprinted, such as the following:

Course Identifier	Faculty	Semester	Year
NR100.505.0201	Bucko Berk	Spring	2006

Peer ratings.   Peer or external expert observation scales require minimal information for the class observed, such as the following:

Instructor: _____

Observer: _____

Course/Room No.: _____

Class Topic: _____

Date: _____ Time: _____

The peer observer also signs the scale at the end. All of the peer ratings are kept confidential between the instructor and the peer.

Alumni and employer ratings.   When scales are sent out by snail mail or online, certain identifiers are essential to interpret the ratings. However, both confidentiality and anonymity are still preserved. The following tracking information is usually requested:

Agency/Institution Employed: _____

Length of Employment: _____

Degree Earned at Buckeye College: _____

Major Area of Study: _____

Date: _____

Purpose

Before someone takes the time to complete a scale, he or she wants to know its purpose, or what decisions will be made based on its results. Otherwise, why bother filling it out? Students will either refuse to complete the scale or do so grudgingly when they perceive no changes in instructors or courses after previous ratings indicated the need for such changes. Sometimes this information is presented to respondents prior to receiving the scale to promote the importance of the ratings and facilitate a high response rate. At minimum, a simple statement of purpose should be provided, such as the following:

- The purpose of this scale is to evaluate the quality of the course and the teaching effectiveness of your instructor.
- This scale is designed as an observation tool to rate an individual instructor's teaching performance. It is intended to provide a diagnostic profile for teaching improvement.
- The purpose of this scale is to assess the quality of the master's program and your educational experiences while you were a student at our school. Your input will help us improve the program.
- The scale is intended to evaluate the knowledge, skills, and abilities of our graduates based on job performance since graduation.
- The purpose of this scale is to evaluate the mentoring characteristics of _____, who has identified you as an individual with whom he/she has had a professional mentor/mentee relationship.

These statements may also be followed by a confirmation of confidentiality and anonymity:

- All responses will remain anonymous and confidential.
- To preserve confidentiality, DO NOT IDENTIFY THE GRADUATE BY NAME. Only aggregate data will be used to evaluate program outcomes.
- All responses are anonymous. Once group-level analysis is completed, all scales will be destroyed. Only summary statistics will be presented to the faculty committee.

Directions

No assumptions can be made about whether the respondents know how to complete any scale, regardless of their previous background. The rules of the game must be clear and standardized for everyone. Specific instructions must be given on what decision the respondent must make in relation to the anchors, how to respond, and where to mark responses. The directions will also vary depending on the type of administration form—scannable, nonscannable, or online. A few examples are given below:

Directions: Indicate the extent to which you agree or disagree with each statement below. There is no right answer. Completely blacken the box corresponding to your response using the four options. You may use pencil or pen. DO NOT write any stray marks on this form.

SD = Strongly Disagree
D = Disagree
A = Agree
SA = Strongly Agree

Directions: Using the anchors below, check (✓) your rating for each teaching behavior that's applicable for the specific class observed. Check "NA" for items that do not apply.

E = Excellent
VG = Very Good
G = Good
NI = Needs Improvement
NA = Not Applicable

Directions: Check (✓) your rating of Agree (**A**) or Disagree (**DA**) for each of the teaching behaviors listed below. For each **DA** response, please explain in the comments section to the right. For any behaviors Not Applicable (**NA**) or Not Observed (**NOB**), check as appropriate.

Directions: Rate the *quality* of his or her knowledge, skills, and abilities based on performance since graduation/employment. *Circle* your ratings using the following scale:

$$
\begin{aligned}
E &= \text{Excellent} \\
VG &= \text{Very Good} \\
G &= \text{Good} \\
F &= \text{Fair} \\
P &= \text{Poor} \\
NA &= \text{Not Applicable (or Not Observed)}
\end{aligned}
$$

Directions: Please rate how satisfied you were with the following aspects of academic life in the school. Select the bubble that corresponds to your level of satisfaction. If the item is not applicable, click on the bubble for Not Applicable (NA).

○ Very Dissatisfied (VD)
○ Somewhat Dissatisfied (SD)
○ Somewhat Satisfied (SS)
○ Very Satisfied (VS)
○ Not Applicable (NA)

Structured Items

The structured items are presented first. All item stimuli (sentences, phrases, or words) are numbered consecutively down the left side of the form. The anchor options are listed on the right side aligned with the items. An optional sample item may precede the items to warm up respondents and illustrate how to answer the items. The beginning of the item section for a *student rating scale* is shown below

	SD	D	A	SA
SAMPLE: My instructor was hilarious.	☐	☐	☐	■

My Instructor/Course Coordinator:

	SD	D	A	SA
1. Encouraged self-directed learning.	☐	☐	☐	☐
2. Utilized useful audiovisuals, where appropriate.	☐	☐	☐	☐
3. Facilitated critical thinking/problem solving.	☐	☐	☐	☐
4. Appeared knowledgeable about course content.	☐	☐	☐	☐
5. Demonstrated clear relationships between theory and practice.	☐	☐	☐	☐
6. Provided relevant examples to illustrate content.	☐	☐	☐	☐

7. Paced instruction to facilitate learning.   □ □ □ □
8. Encouraged questions, comments, and discussion.   □ □ □ □
9. Provided timely feedback on assignments.   □ □ □ □
10. Provided helpful feedback on assignments.   □ □ □ □

The items may also be grouped into categories that define subscales. These are content groupings that may be supported by statistical evidence (see chapters 7 and 8). Here are items students rate to evaluate nursing faculty, grouped into "Instructional Methods" and "Clinical Experiences."

INSTRUCTIONAL METHODS

My Instructor:

	SD	D	A	SA
1. Provided adequate orientation to my clinical requirements.	○	○	○	○
2. Clarified my learning needs.	○	○	○	○
3. Provided timely written and/or verbal feedback, as appropriate.	○	○	○	○
4. Mentored me in my nursing role.	○	○	○	○
5. Evaluated me fairly.	○	○	○	○
6. Communicated regularly with me.	○	○	○	○
7. Was available for individual advising and counseling.	○	○	○	○
8. Provided assistance when I had questions or was having difficulty.	○	○	○	○
9. Demonstrated respect for me.	○	○	○	○
10. Facilitated my critical thinking and problem solving.	○	○	○	○

CLINICAL EXPERIENCES

My Instructor:

	SD	D	A	SA
1. Provided experiences useful in attaining course objectives/outcomes.	○	○	○	○
2. Assisted me in applying theory and research to clinical practice.	○	○	○	○
3. Provided experiences to meet my learning needs.	○	○	○	○
4. Encouraged me to collaborate with my healthcare team.	○	○	○	○
5. Demonstrated current clinical knowledge.	○	○	○	○
6. Demonstrated skill proficiency.	○	○	○	○
7. Was a positive role model.	○	○	○	○

Other groupings may also appear on a *peer observation scale*, where the peer checks (✓) a box for a rating:

	E	VG	G	NI	NA	Comments:
CONTENT AND ORGANIZATION						
Started and ended class on time						
Presented overview of class content/objectives						
Presented rationale for topics covered						
Presented key concepts						
Presented current material						
Presented information in an organized manner						
Demonstrated accurate knowledge of content						
Used relevant examples to explain major ideas						
Used alternative explanations when necessary						
Made efficient use of class time						
Covered class content/objectives						
COMMUNICATION SKILLS						
Varied pace appropriately						
Enunciated clearly						
Varied modulation						
Varied tone						
Spoke with adequate volume						
Demonstrated confidence						
Demonstrated enthusiasm						
Moved easily about room during presentation						
Used speech fillers (*um, ok, ah*) rarely						

An *alumni ratings satisfaction scale* lists areas of academic life:

	VD	SD	SS	VS	NA
1. Academic advising	○	○	○	○	○
2. Course sequencing	○	○	○	○	○
3. Course scheduling	○	○	○	○	○
4. Course content	○	○	○	○	○
5. Clinical experiences	○	○	○	○	○
6. Classroom instruction	○	○	○	○	○
7. Size of classes	○	○	○	○	○
8. Personal contacts with faculty	○	○	○	○	○
9. Manageability of academic demands	○	○	○	○	○
10. Library services and holdings	○	○	○	○	○

An *employer rating scale* of a graduate's performance focuses on areas of knowledge and skill:

1. Prepared for advanced practice	E	VG	G	F	P	NA
2. Clinical competence	E	VG	G	F	P	NA
3. Application of evidence-based findings to practice	E	VG	G	F	P	NA
4. Application of management skills	E	VG	G	F	P	NA
5. Ethical decision making	E	VG	G	F	P	NA
6. Critical thinking	E	VG	G	F	P	NA
7. Written communication	E	VG	G	F	P	NA
8. Oral communication	E	VG	G	F	P	NA
9. Ability to prioritize	E	VG	G	F	P	NA
10. Leadership skills	E	VG	G	F	P	NA

A *mentorship effectiveness scale* can be completed by a mentee (student or junior faculty) to evaluate mentor characteristics:

1. My mentor was accessible.	SD	D	SLD	SLA	A	SA	NA
2. My mentor demonstrated professional integrity.	SD	D	SLD	SLA	A	SA	NA
3. My mentor demonstrated content expertise in my area of need.	SD	D	SLD	SLA	A	SA	NA
4. My mentor was approachable.	SD	D	SLD	SLA	A	SA	NA
5. My mentor was supportive and encouraging.	SD	D	SLD	SLA	A	SA	NA
6. My mentor provided constructive and useful critiques of my work.	SD	D	SLD	SLA	A	SA	NA

7. My mentor motivated me to improve my
   work product.   SD D SLD SLA A SA NA
8. My mentor was helpful in providing
   direction and guidance on professional
   issues (e.g., networking).   SD D SLD SLA A SA NA
9. My mentor answered my questions
   satisfactorily (e.g., timely response,
   clear, comprehensive).   SD D SLD SLA A SA NA
10. My mentor acknowledged my
    contributions appropriately
    (e.g., committee contributions, awards). SD D SLD SLA A SA NA

Unstructured Items

The last section of the scale contains the open-ended items, usually titled "Comments." It permits the respondent the opportunity to write his or her positive and negative reactions to the instructor/course and suggest areas for improvement. A long list of possible stimuli, or prompts, for this section was provided at the end of chapter 2. It is important that adequate space be given to answer each question on scannable and nonscannable forms. There is no space limitation on online forms. A typical unstructured section on a student rating form is shown below:

COMMENTS

What did you like **MOST** about the course?

What did you like **LEAST** about the course?

What suggestions do you have for **IMPROVEMENT**?

Or, it may be as simple as this:

Strengths:

Areas for Improvement:

_____
                Signature

Or, just:

Comments on Performance:

Appendix A contains complete, "homemade" rating scales for student, peer, employer, and mentee evaluations. Every scale is custom designed to address the preceding five elements. Appendix B has sample scales used to measure clinical teaching and other competencies of physicians. These examples may serve as prototypes for you to assemble your own scales.

Scale Administration

Student rating scales can be administered in three ways: (1) paper-based, in class, on a nonscannable form, (2) paper-based, in class, on a scannable form, or (3) online, for face-to-face and online courses. Nationwide surveys of hundreds of institutions indicate that the vast majority of faculties prefer paper-based evaluations (Dommeyer, Baum, Chapman, & Hanna, 2002). They believe that in-class administrations produce higher response rates and ratings. In fact, Hmieleski's (2000) survey of the 200 "most wired" institutions revealed a whopping 98% in favor of paper-based approaches. More recently, a random sample of 500 institutions indicated 90% use paper-based, scannable (78%), or nonscannable (12%) forms (Hoffman, 2003).

Use of the Internet to evaluate online and face-to-face courses has been increasing at the rate of glacial thawing or soybean growth for vegetarians. Only slightly more than a majority of institutions (56%) evaluated online courses online, while 17% used online administration in face-to-face courses, and another 10% were planning it (Hoffman, 2003). The trend, however, is toward online administration. Currently, 16 universities have campus-wide online systems and more than 40 institutions use online ratings for at least an entire department (Sorenson, 2005). Several issues need to be clarified for faculty before significant progress can be expected. The research over the past five years has facilitated this clarification.

This section critically compares paper-based and online administration procedures according to 15 factors based on the current state of research and practice. The key issues and deterrents to adoption of online administration are examined with alternative solutions suggested. It is hoped that sufficient guidance will be provided to decide on which option to execute and how to execute it effectively.

Paper-Based Administration

The predominant mode of administration for student rating scales is paper-based scannable forms. This approach typically requires considerable time and cost for printing, distribution, scanning, and reporting results. However, it affords standardization of administration conditions in class with the following "best practices":

- There is one time period for completion (~10–15 min.).
- One student is appointed to distribute and collect forms in class and return to processing center.
- Instructor hands packet of forms to appointee for distribution and then leaves room during administration and collection.
- All students follow the same directions for completing scale.

This administration is easy to execute and convenient for students because it is part of class time. No additional times or arrangements outside of class are necessary. It is accessible to all students, except those absent that day. These conditions maintain anonymity and confidentiality of the ratings because the instructor doesn't touch the forms—not before, during, or after the administration. The primary threat to the anonymity of the ratings is the handwritten comments, especially in small classes. Response rates can be maximized by (a) administering scales on a "high attendance" class, such as a test review, (b) communicating to students the importance of the ratings, and (c) making sure designated students collect all forms in class. This level of in-class control yields response rates of 80% or higher and high degrees of validity and reliability of the ratings.

In addition to these well-known benefits of paper-based administration is the relative ease with which scannable forms can be revised and customized for each instructor. Although changes to specific items on the scale may require an act of the faculty senate, technically, the modifications can be completed quite easily and quickly. The optional item section on many scales is also an asset because it allows an instructor the opportunity to add items related specifically to his or her course.

After all of the years of experience with paper-based systems, the single greatest problem is the lag time that occurs in reporting the results back to faculty. Many institutions take from three weeks to two months to several years to put the results into the hands of faculty. The slooow turnaround often precludes faculty from using the feedback to make instructional adjustments for the next semester. This problem has not been licked.

A summary of the advantages and disadvantages of paper-based student ratings is given in table 6.1. A total of 15 factors are rated according to current research evidence and best practices.

TABLE 6.1

Ratings of Paper-Based versus Online Administration of Student Rating Scales

Factor	Paper-Based	Online
1. Response Rates	+ + (80%)	− − (~40%)
2. Response Bias	− −	− −
3. Non-response Bias	− −	− −
4. Ease of Administration	+	+ +
5. Administration Time	− (limited in class)	+ + (flextime)
6. Staff Time	− − (printing, distribution, scanning, reporting)	+ (computer staff)
7. Standardization of Administration	+ + (time, place, distribution, collection)	− − (no control)
8. Accessibility	+ +	−
9. Convenience	+ +	− − (process flaws)
10. Anonymity/ Confidentiality	+ (handwritten comments)	− (perception)
11. Unstructured Item Responses (Comments)		
Quantity	− (few, short)	+ + (many, longer)
Quality	− (less thoughtful)	+ + (more thoughtful)
Anonymity	− (small classes)	+ + (typed)
12. Accuracy of Data Collection	+ (cleaning scannable forms, transcribing written comments)	+ +
13. Costs		
Development	+	− −
Operating	− −	+
Overall	−	+ + (half of paper-based)
14. Turnaround Time	− (weeks to months)	+ + (within days)
15. Ease of Scale Revision	+	+ +

++ Marked Advantage
+ Advantage
− Disadvantage
− − Marked Disadvantage

Other rating scales designed for individual or low-incidence administration, such as peer, self, and administrator ratings and student interviews, can benefit from a simple paper-based system. Unless a statistical summary of results is required or ratings need to be aggregated across instructors or students, even a nonscannable form is fine.

Online Administration

Are ya ready to rumble? This is where the action is. Well, not exactly. But interest in online everything is growing like my weeds. Despite higher education's reluctance to embrace online administration with a bear hug and a smooch, Web-based rating systems are crawling into colleges and universities. All of the commercial student rating systems listed in chapter 2 provide online administration services. Faculty resistance seems to be based on preconceived notions that online administration will decrease response rates, increase bias, and produce lower ratings than paper-based administration. Mounting research evidence and practice in several universities indicate response rates as high as 90% (Sorenson, 2005), with strategies being used to maximize response rates. Further, sources of bias tend to be similar to those in paper-based ratings, and online- and paper-based ratings are comparable, with correlations in the .80s (Hardy, 2003; Johnson, 2003). That being said, what about cost? Overall, online is considerably less expensive than paper-based (Bothell & Henderson, 2003).

Over the past few years, much has been learned about online systems that can address the typical student, faculty, and administrator concerns. Available software used at various institutions includes WebCT, TestPilot, and Snap (also see www.onlinecourseevaluations.com). Table 6.1 summarizes the pluses and minuses on 15 factors based on the state of the art (Sorenson & Johnson, 2003). When compared, it is obvious that both approaches are far from perfect. Let's examine a few of the key online issues.

Response rates. The response rate for online administration can be half the rate of paper-based administration. This is a frequent objection to online ratings reported in faculty surveys. Fear of low response rate has deterred some institutions from adopting an online system. The research on this topic indicates the following possible reasons: student apathy, perceived lack of anonymity, inconvenience, inaccessibility, technical problems, time for completion, and perceived lack of importance (Ballantyne, 2000; Dommeyer, Baum, & Hanna, 2002; Sorenson & Reiner, 2003).

Several institutions have tested a variety of strategies to increase response rate. They have been suggested by faculty and students. Here is a list of the most effective strategies (Johnson, 2003; Sorenson & Reiner, 2003):

- Faculty communicate to students the importance of their input and how the results will be used
- Ease of computer access

- Assurance of anonymity
- Convenient, user-friendly system
- Provide instructions on how to use the system
- Faculty strongly encourage students to complete forms
- Faculty "assign" students to complete forms
- ~~Faculty threaten to smash students' iPods with a Gallagher-type sledge-hammer~~
- System withholds students' early access to final grades
- Faculty provide extra credit or points
- Faculty provide positive incentives
- ~~Faculty require students to pick up dry cleaning and take dog to vet~~

To date, the evidence indicates that students' belief that the results will be used for important decisions about faculty and courses is essential to a successful online system. When faculty members assign students to complete the evaluation with or without incentives, response rates are high. Finally, withholding early access to grades is supported by students as effective but not too restrictive. This "withholding" approach has been very successful at raising response rates.

These strategies have boosted response rates into the 70s and 80s. It is a combination of elements, however, as suggested above, that must be executed properly to ensure a high rate of students' return on the online investment. The research base and track record of online student ratings belies "low response rate" as an excuse for not implementing such a system in any institution.

Standardization. Since students typically complete online rating scales during their discretionary time, there is no control over the time, place, or conditions under which the evaluations occur. In fact, there is no way to ensure that the real student filled out the form. It could be a roommate, partner, alien, or student who has never been to class doing a favor in exchange for a pizza or drugs. Although there is no standardization of the actual administration, the directions given to all students are the same. Therefore, the procedures that the students follow should be similar if they read the directions.

So what's the problem with the lack of standardization? The ratings of students are assumed to be collected under identical conditions according to the same rules and directions. Standardization of the administration and environment provides a snapshot of how students feel at one point in time. Although their individual ratings will vary, they have the same meaning. Rigorous procedures for standardization are required by the *Standards for Educational and Psychological Testing* (AERA, APA, & NCME Joint Committee on Standards, 1999). Groups of students must be given identical instructions under identical conditions to ensure the comparability of their ratings (Standards 3.15 and 3.20). Only then would the interpretation of the scores and, in this case, the inferences about teaching effectiveness be valid and reliable (Standard 3.19).

Without standardization, such as when every student fills out the scale willy-nilly at different times of the day and semester, in different places, using different procedures, the ratings from student to student and instructor to instructor will not be comparable. For example, if some students complete the scale before the final review and final exam and others complete it after, their feelings about the instructor/course can be very different. Exposure to the final exam can significantly affect ratings. The ratings of these two groups of students don't have the same meaning. Students who discuss their ratings with students who haven't completed the form bias the ratings by the latter.

Given the limitations of online administration, what can be done to approximate standardized conditions or, at least, minimize the extent to which the bad conditions contaminate the ratings? Here are three suggestions:

1. Specify a narrow window within which the ratings must be completed, such as one or two days after the final class and before the final exam, or two days after the exam before grades are posted.
2. Set certain time slots during which students have easy access to computers in the lab.
3. Proctor the slots with guards with AK-47s in Kevlar® bullet-proof vests and helmets to eliminate distractions and with computer-geek graduate students to provide technical support for any problems that arise.

Accessibility/convenience.   Once students are taught how to use the online system, it must be user-friendly to execute. In some institutions students complain that it takes too much time to complete the ratings, the log-on process is complicated, they have to wait in line to get into the computer lab, and they encounter computer problems in filling out or submitting the form. These experiences discourage students, especially once they have been told of the importance of their ratings. This contributes to low response rates.

Students value a system that is easy to understand, readily accessible, and convenient to use (Layne, DeCristoforo, & McGinty, 1999; Ravelli, 2000). Sorenson and Reiner (2003) recommend the following elements for an effective, online rating system:

- Ease of access and navigation
- Attractive, simple, and straightforward screen
- Help features to assist with possible problems
- Confirmation of successful submission of the rating form (p. 17)

Anonymity/confidentiality.   Students have doubts about the anonymity and confidentiality of online ratings. Can their identity be preserved when they have to log on with their names and passwords? Students, concerned about privacy, perceive this as an issue in their hesitancy to use the online system (Dommeyer et al., 2002; Hardy, 2002; Layne et al., 1999). They need to be told that the system will not identify individual students; faculty members have no access to individual ratings; and only class data will be reported. Students should be assured and constantly reassured of the anonymity of the ratings and the confidentiality with which they are gathered, analyzed, and reported. The one exceptional advantage of the online system is the anonymity of typed comments as opposed to the handwritten, possibly traceable, comments on paper forms.

Costs.   There have been several studies of the costs of implementing and maintaining paper-based and online rating systems (Bothell & Henderson, 2003; Hmieleski & Champagne, 2000; Kronholm, Wisher, Curnow, & Poker, 1999). The estimates vary considerably depending on how the costs are categorized. In one comprehensive cost analysis at Brigham Young University, Bothell and Henderson (2003) lumped most of the expenses into "development," "operating," and "miscellaneous" categories. A description of what elements fell into these categories for each system is shown in table 6.2.

TABLE 6.2
Description of Costs for Paper-Based versus
Online Administration of Student Rating Scales

Costs	*Paper-Based*	*Online*
Development	Salary and wages for personnel time on ■ Research ■ Designing materials ■ Coordinating and managing project ■ Promoting and educating others ■ Meetings Scanning machine and software	Salary and wages for personnel time on ■ Research ■ Designing materials ■ Coordinating and managing project ■ Promoting and educating others ■ Meetings Hardware and software programming
Operating	Paper and printing Envelopes Labels Scanning and report preparation Class time Distribution and collection of forms	System management Network use Classroom time Promoting new system
Miscellaneous		Web software

You've waited long enough. Here are the one-year costs (P-B = paper-based; O = online):

Development: P-B = $6698; O = $81,339
Operating: P-B = $415,503; O = $101,218
Miscellaneous: P-B = 0; O = $4060
The value of student ratings: PRICELESS

There are some things money can't buy. For everything else, there are

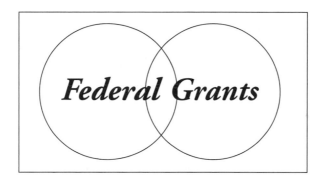

(*Note to Faculty*: Never attempt to present this type of parody of *MasterCard*® in a book or your classroom. This type of joke should be attempted only by a trained humor professional.) (*Note to Trained Humor Professional*: Even then, it appears to be a very bad idea.)

The bottom-line cost difference for the BYU study was $1.06 per student rating form for paper-based and $.47 per form for online. Despite the higher development costs for the online system, the operating costs of the paper-based system were even higher. The areas that accounted for the most savings were decreased time taken away from teaching, reduced printing costs, and reduced personnel time and costs of data collection, processing, and reporting. The online system provided a savings of over 50%, which amounted to about $235,000 in one year. Overall, Bothell and Henderson (2003) found the online system to be considerably less expensive than the paper-based.

Comparability of Paper-Based and Online Ratings

Most of the factors in table 6.1 and the previous sections emphasize the striking differences between the two modes of administration. The only areas of similarity seem to be response and nonresponse biases and the ratings themselves. That news is not very encouraging. But hold on to your mouse. This section examines these topics.

Sources of bias in ratings.   Two of the greatest threats to the accuracy of student ratings are response and nonresponse biases. These biases contaminate the ratings.

Several types of *response bias* were described in chapter 5. Current evidence suggests that these biases can affect student ratings positively and negatively (Berk et al., 2004). However, further research is needed to investigate their differential effects on the overall faculty ratings.

Other response biases relate to the representativeness of the students responding compared to the total class. When response rates are high, such biases may be negligible. Other sources of bias pertain to GPA, year-in-school biases, and department, discipline, or course biases (Goodman & Campbell, 1999; Layne et al., 1999; McGourty, Scoles, & Thorpe, 2002). The findings of studies on these types of bias are inconclusive.

Another threat to the ratings is *nonresponse bias*, which occurs when certain students in a particular demographic category are less likely to complete the rating form than other students. For example, based on a national survey of college students, there is a nonresponse bias against men on student rating scales because they are less likely to complete them than women (Sax, Gilmartin, & Bryant, 2003). This type of gender bias as well as ethnic and sexual orientation nonresponse biases need to be investigated by each institution to assess their effect on ratings. These biases differ from the previous response biases, which relate to prejudices that can deflate ratings.

These various types of response and nonresponse bias can spuriously inflate or deflate the ratings. Since the biases vary in direction and degree, it is difficult to estimate the net effect on any single instructor mean or median rating. Further research is needed to clarify the impact and the previous two sentences.

Paper-based and online ratings.   How do the actual ratings of instructors compare under experimental conditions? The research findings differ according to the structured and unstructured item formats.

Despite all of the differences between paper-based and online administrations and the contaminating biases that afflict the ratings they produce (Surprise! Surprise!), the research reports that *online students and their in-class counterparts rate courses and instructors similarly* (Carini, Hayek, Kuh, & Ouimet, 2003; Hardy, 2003; McGhee & Lowell, 2003; Spooner, Jordan, Algozzine, & Spooner, 1999; Waschull, 2001). The ratings on the *structured items* are not systematically higher or lower for online administrations. The correlations between online and paper-based ratings were .84 (overall instructor) and .86 (overall course) (Johnson, 2003). Although the ratings are not identical, with more than 70% ($.86^2 \times 100$) of the variance in common, any differences in ratings that have been found are small. Further, interrater reliabilities of ratings of individual items and item clusters for both modalities were comparable (McGhee & Lowell, 2003).

The one exception to the above similarities is the *unstructured items,* or open-ended comment, section. The research has consistently indicated that the flexible time permitted to onliners yields *longer, more frequent, and more thoughtful comments than those of in-class respondents* (Hardy, 2002, 2003; Johnson, 2001, 2003; Layne et al., 1999; Ravelli, 2000). Typing the responses is reported by students to be easier and faster than writing them, plus it *preserves their anonymity* (Johnson, 2003; Layne et al., 1999).

Conclusions

Considering all of the pluses and minuses for the 15 factors in table 6.1, the conversion from a paper-based to online administration system seems worthy of serious consideration by every institution using student ratings. The parenthetical notes in the table highlight a few of the major distinctions between the two approaches. When the minuses are addressed, the benefits of online ratings for both face-to-face as well as distance courses far outweigh the traditional paper-based approach. Hopefully, the suggestions proffered to counter typical faculty and administrator concerns will make online administration an attractive option.

Research on the various types of ratings bias and creative efforts to improve standardization of administration procedures are urgently needed. As more and more institutions adopt online administration, imaginative solutions to those issues should be found. Online administration should also be employed for alumni ratings and employer ratings. The costs for these ratings will be a small fraction of the cost of the student rating system.

7

FIELD TESTING AND ITEM ANALYSES

 CAUTION—LIVE PEOPLE AHEAD

After six chapters of fiddling around with your scale, it should be in pretty good shape by now. Ya think? If you meticulously followed all of the scale construction rules, I predict that the item analysis results in this chapter and the validity and reliability evidence described in the next chapter will attest to the quality of your scale, give or take an item or two. "Why do we have to test out the scale?" Because there is only so much *you* can do, and you've done it. Waaaay back in chapter 1, like on page 12, I cited the *Standards* that have guided this whole scale-construction process. Remember? Me neither. This short-term memory loss is driving me crazy. Anyway, those *Standards* require real qualitative and quantitative evidence to support the uses and inferences drawn from the rating scale scores (Standards 1.1, 1.6, 1.11, 14.8, and 14.13). You know what that means: It's time to test-drive your scale on real, live, "flesh and blood" people to determine whether the items are any good. Beeee careful!

 BERK'S NOTES

Faculty—If you are involved in the field testing of a rating scale, either in the planning or as a part of the test sample, you need to read the mini-field test and monster-field test sections. The item analysis section is highly technical, especially

Stage 3 on factor analysis. Unless you are computing the statistics or reviewing the item results to select the best items and structure for the scale, you can hop over that material to chapter 8.

Administrators—If you are coordinating resources, including the budget and computer services, for the field test, you should be familiar with the procedures and sampling requirements for the mini-field test and monster-field test. A basic understanding of the three stages of item analysis might also be helpful. Peruse the introduction only to each analysis. The statistical material is not essential. Jump to chapter 8.

Preparing the Draft Scale for a Test Spin

Now I know many of you consider words like "item-total scale correlation," "interitem correlation matrix," and "eigenvalue" statistical mumbo-jumbo or, even worse, professional profanity. Not to worry, bubby. This chapter is not written in textbook language. It is intended for the mathematically arthritic professor or administrator who needs to ask the right questions to possess a conceptual understanding of the technical landscape, but does not have to plant every tree and fertilize it. In fact, there isn't a formula or Greek letter anywhere. There should be an evaluation center on campus or faculty on board from education, psychology, sociology, or other departments who can assist with the analyses and provide the necessary expertise.

Up to this point, you should have completed the following steps:

1. Decided which rating scale to develop (chapter 1)
2. Specified the purposes or decisions for which the scores will be used (chapters 1 and 2)
3. Defined the domain of teaching job behaviors and course characteristics (chapter 2)
4. Selected and/or generated a pool of statements, phrases, or words to measure those behaviors and characteristics (chapter 3)
5. Picked an appropriate anchor scale (chapter 4)
6. Refined the anchor scale structure (chapter 5)
7. Assembled the statements and anchors into a draft scale (chapter 6)
8. Planned the procedures for administration (chapter 6)

This chapter presents appropriate field test procedures to gather data on the items to furnish evidence of validity and reliability.

Field Test Procedures

The draft rating scale is now ready for testing. We're basically taking the scale out for a test spin to see if it works. However, there are actually two stages of field testing:

1. *Mini-field test* (a.k.a. "pilot test")—A trial run of the scale on a small sample of respondents to critique the quality of the items and directions and to identify errors or flaws in scale construction.
2. *Monster-field test* (a.k.a. "field test")—An administration of the scale to a large sample of respondents to conduct statistical analyses of the items and test structure. This is a mini-field test on steroids. These analyses are intended to refine the item quality and produce evidence of validity and reliability.

Mini-Field Test

This field test is intended to provide information to *revise faulty items, clarify directions, estimate administration time, or correct previously undetected mistakes in the scale* (Berk, 1993). Persons for whom the scale was designed are in the best position to determine, for example, whether the wording is clear and understandable, whether the response choices (anchors) can be selected quickly, whether they are offended by sensitive items or language, whether all of the sections are easy to complete, and whether they can complete it without throwing up. This is also the opportunity to test the "Not Applicable" (*NA*) option. If few or no one picks it, eliminate *NA* from the monster-field test. The feedback from this mini-field test yields valuable insights for improving the scale that would not be disclosed at any other stage of scale development. The respondents' input and the data from the actual administration are essential to evaluate the quality of the scale.

Sample.   Pick a sample of *5–10 students and faculty* similar to those for whom the scale is designed. They should be representative in terms of gender, ethnicity, rank, and any other key sociodemographic characteristics (Standard 3.6).

Scale administration.   There are three administration options: (a) face-to-face individual interview, (b) group administration and interview, and (c) online.

The *group administration is preferable* to the individual. The group format permits discussion that can occur among respondents that can pinpoint important sources of error, such as specific item flaws and confusion about paper-based or online administration that may not be revealed by individual interviews. The group dynamics operating may account for substantively different feedback compared to that produced from individual interviews. If the scale is designed for online administration, it should be administered in face-to-face individual or group format to gather feedback on the scale *and* online to test the technology. Now is the time to eliminate the glitches.

There are two steps:

1. Request the respondents to complete the scale for an imaginary instructor.
2. Request the respondents to answer specific questions about the quality of the scale.

These questions would be asked of the individual or group of respondents in person. In the online administration, the questions would be attached to the end of the scale.

Checklist of probing questions. Once a respondent has completed the scale, questions should be asked to probe for flaws. Sample questions include the following:

1. Did any item seem confusing?
2. Did the response choices fit the (statements, phrases, words)?
3. Were there any words or abbreviations that were unclear?
4. Were there any errors in grammar, punctuation, or spelling?
5. Did any item offend you?
6. Was there any item you did not want to answer?
7. Are there any items that should have been included, but weren't?
8. Did you understand the directions for completing the form?
9. Was the form easy to fill in?
10. Was the form too long?
11. ~~Was the form an absolute scream to complete?~~

The respondents should have the scale available as the questions are asked so they may refer to specific items, words, or parts of the scale. For the individual or group interview, the faculty interviewer should use a checklist format to ask the questions so that the responses can be recorded as they are given (see checklist 7.1). It also helps to tape the interview in case anything was missed. For the online ad-

---

CHECKLIST 7.1

MINI-FIELD TEST QUESTIONS

Question	YES	NO	Corrections
1. Did any item seem confusing?	____	____	
2. Did the response choices fit the (statements, phrases, words)?	____	____	
3. Were there any words or abbreviations that were unclear?	____	____	
4. Were there any errors in grammar, punctuation, or spelling?	____	____	
5. Did any item offend you?	____	____	
6. Was there any item you did not want to answer?	____	____	
7. Are there any items that should have been included, but weren't?	____	____	
8. Did you understand the directions for completing the form?	____	____	
9. Was the form easy to fill in?	____	____	
10. Was the form too long?	____	____	

Comments to improve scale:

Comments to improve administration:

---

ministration, the checklist can be tacked on the scale. An open-ended section to permit comments on the scale and administration procedures should follow.

Summary of results.   The answers to the 10 questions should be summarized according to the sections of the scale: corrections to directions, statements, and anchors. The handwritten or typed comments should also be compiled to address those sections as well as any other aspects of the scale or administration that need attention. The types of errors in the scale and administration dramatically demonstrate that there are limitations to what faculty, measurement experts, and IT specialists can detect prior to field testing. This can be a humbling experience for some; however, it should be viewed more perceptively as respondents making a contribution to scale construction, other than just supplying ratings data.

Committee composition (Murder Board).   Once the summary of possible changes has been prepared, a committee needs to be convened to review the results of the respondents' input. This Murder Board (Berk, 1993) should be composed of the following:

- Faculty involved in selecting and/or writing the items
- A measurement expert, if available
- An IT specialist, if online administration
- Respondents (e.g., students, faculty, alumni, administrators, and/or employers)

The most efficient and effective combination of the above is a gaggle of 5–10 participants. These individuals can furnish unique insights on all aspects of the scale and administration procedures.

Murder Board execution.   The dress code should be Columbo-esque. Rumpled clothing of any kind, especially raincoats, would be appropriate attire. Just sleep in whatever you're wearing to the meeting. The review should systematically consider every error, flaw, suggested change, and comment recorded in the preceding 10-point interview. In other words, the Board potentially murders each item, one by one, from every angle (Berk, 1993). The Board should then decide whether to make each correction, change, or revision. All of the key players on the Board are capable of rewriting directions, rewording statements, and revising online commands or procedures on the spot. This review should be completed in one sitting.

    A new and improved revised scale should emerge from this beating. If major content or administration changes were required, another mini-field test may be conducted to verify that the changes are effective. Otherwise, the draft scale should be scheduled for a formal content review to gather evidence of the content relevance of the items and content representativeness of the item sample. The items must satisfy these criteria. The procedures for assembling an appropriate committee and executing this review are described under "Evidence Based on Job Content Domain" in chapter 8. Once this content review has been completed, the scale can then be prepared for the monster-field test that follows. If this sequence is confusing, that's because it is. Remember: *mini-field test* ⟶ *content review* ⟶ *monster-field test.* Now we're going to skip to the monster.

Monster-Field Test

The scale is now in shape, ready to be administered to a large sample of respondents to assess whether the items and the scale scores behave in accordance with classical measurement theory (Standard 3.8). The item analyses to be performed will help refine the items and scale structure and furnish evidence of the validity and reliability of the scores.

Sample. For student ratings, choose a sample of at least 10 different instructors/courses and 300 students. A diverse sample of 20–30 courses and 500–1,000 students would be even better. The rule of thumb is *5–10 people per item* (Tinsley & Tinsley, 1987). Comrey (1988) and Nunnally and Bernstein (1994) advise a minimum of 200, but prefer 300–400 for scales of 30–40 items, closer to the 10-subjects-per-item rule. If you start with a 50-item pool on your draft scale, you'll need to scrounge up about 500 students. (For a more comprehensive explanation of sample size for factor analysis, see MacCallum, Widaman, Zhang, & Hong, 1999.) Select a wide range of courses, representative of all of the types of courses in your school (Standard 3.8). Stratify your sample to assure a proportionate number of students by department/discipline and level (e.g., undergraduate, master's, and doctoral).

Since the consistency of students' responses to the items and scale are of primary importance, "student" is the unit of analysis. If course or instructor were the unit of analysis, there would be less sensitivity to the students' patterns of responses. The *n* would also be an issue, because 30 courses would be the sample size instead of the large number of students who rated those courses. Another concern is the different class sizes upon which means are estimated. If the sample contains a range of course levels (undergraduate through doctoral), as suggested above, the sizes may vary from 5 students in a doctoral seminar to 500 in an undergraduate survey course. Although weighted means can be computed to adjust for these size differences, those classes with fewer than 20 students will yield unstable means. This needs to be considered in the final reporting of results by instructor. Master's and doctoral courses with small *n*s will likely produce less reliable scores for summative decisions than will super-sized undergraduate courses with typically larger *n*s.

Among the other types of rating scales, only exit and alumni scales usually permit large and diverse sampling, mainly because they are based on graduating or graduated students.

Peer, self, and employer scales rarely afford sample sizes above mini-world. When they are formally administered to the target respondents, the resultant item and scale scores can be analyzed. At that point, it's inconvenient to catch faulty items, though some adjustments can be made.

Scale administration. This field test should simulate a full throttle school-wide scannable, nonscannable, or online administration. The options to consider in these different modes of administration were examined previously. The data from this administration will be used for the comprehensive item analyses described next.

Item Analyses

The entire scale construction process has been driven by the *type of scale* you choose (student, peer, alumni, fish) and the *use of the scale scores* for decision making (formative, summative, program). Do you remember your type of scale and decision use? Me neither. I got lost on "rule of thumb." Go fetch your type and decision use. I'll wait. Okay, get ready. Here we go. The *Standards* require focus on type and use when designing studies to gather evidence of validity and reliability. This is the first time we get to see how the items and scale actually behave "statistically" with live respondents. Are the rules used to write the items (chapters 3–5) confirmed by the ratings?

 FACULTY AND ADMINISTRATOR WARNING

If you are directly involved in conducting the statistical analysis or need to understand how to interpret the results to select the best items, you will have to endure this scintillating section; otherwise, PASS this section, COLLECT 200 smackers, and GO to chapter 8.

Let's begin with the item analyses. There are three stages: (1) item descriptive statistics, (2) interitem and item-scale correlations, and (3) factor analysis.

Stage 1: Item Descriptive Statistics

There are several basic descriptive statistics that can tell you whether the items on the scale are behaving consistently with their purpose in life—which is to measure job performance—or are misbehaving and need to be whooped. The first three are item means, item standard deviations, and item anchor responses.

Item means. An average score *near the center of the score range* is highly desirable for the test sample (for example, this is a score of 1.5 on a 4-point scale of 0–3). Typically, for individual instructors, the mean rating can be very high or very low.

The sample of a range of different instructors, however, should yield a mean in the middle or slightly above to indicate that the item is tapping all possible responses, from one extreme to the other. If, on the other hand, the mean for a diverse sample is at the upper or lower end of the point scale, the item may not be worded strongly enough to create a reaction just short of rioting and looting the campus bookstore (rule 7, chapter 3). Most respondents are either strongly agreeing or disagreeing. Here are some possible outcomes for a four-anchor scale, scored 0–3:

Mean	Rating
1.5	*Excellent*—Bull's-eye.
1 or 2	*Good*—Close enough.
0 or 3	*Lousy*—Send mean to bed with no TV (including *American Idol*) *or* you picked an unrepresentative sample of awful or dynamite instructors.

Item standard deviations.   Consistent with the above, there should be a *wide spread of responses* around the mean across all anchors: that is, relatively high variance, expressed in standard deviation units. The item should be capable of eliciting a range of responses, from *SA* to *SD,* for a heterogeneous sample of instructors. This expectation is consistent with how you wrote the item (rules 7, 19, & 20, chapter 3; rules 6–8, chapter 4). Here are possible values for a 4-anchor scale:

Standard Deviation	Rating
1–1.5	*Excellent*—High variance.
.5–.9	*Good*—Adequate to pass muster.
0	*Lousy*—No variance; evil item.

For any single instructor, the responses may be clumped at one end or the other, depending on his or her lovability.

A sample set of means and standard deviations is displayed in table 7.1 for a 36-item student rating scale administered in 25 courses at the undergraduate, master's, and doctoral levels to 1,586 students. Class sizes ranged from 5 to 126. Based on the previous guidelines, the means are around 2 or slightly above (with a 0–3 scale), which is expected on ratings of faculty; students tend to rate faculty more positively than negatively. Hence, the mean is usually above the midpoint (1.5). Standard deviations are in the .60s and .70s, which indicate an adequate spread of responses. The "Mean" (standard deviation) column should make it possible for you to tell at a glance whether the items are functioning

TABLE 7.1
Student Rating Scale Item Means, Standard Deviations,
and Item-Subscale *rs* (*n* = 1586)

Item	Mean (Std. Dev.)	Item-Subscale r
1	2.39 (.61)	.68
2	2.35 (.63)	.71
3	2.19 (.70)	.71
4	2.12 (.71)	.75
5	2.19 (.66)	.76
6	2.07 (.71)	.74
7	2.11 (.75)	.73
8	1.96 (.87)	.44
9	2.12 (.68)	.82
10	2.13 (.68)	.81
11	2.16 (.64)	.81
12	2.05 (.76)	.79
13	2.15 (.74)	.67
14	2.09 (.83)	.74
15	2.06 (.78)	.77
16	2.40 (.64)	.79
17	2.35 (.71)	.77
18	2.23 (.62)	.63
19	2.11 (.68)	.58
20	2.11 (.71)	.71
21	2.41 (.60)	.74
22	2.23 (.65)	.73
23	2.27 (.63)	.79
24	2.11 (.72)	.72
25	2.28 (.67)	.77
26	2.19 (.72)	.68
27	2.05 (.77)	.71
28	2.23 (.66)	.78
29	2.21 (.68)	.78
30	2.29 (.65)	.74
31	2.22 (.65)	.79
32	2.26 (.70)	.85
33	2.21 (.73)	.86
34	2.23 (.69)	.87
35	2.29 (.60)	.78
36	2.34 (.69)	.78

properly. (*Reader Query*: "What in the world is that last column of decimals under 'Item-subscale *r*'?" Excellent question. I don't have a clue. What do you
think it is? I'm just yanking your chain mail. The topic of item-subscale correlations will be covered shortly. The item results are usually presented together
in the same table for ease of review. Sorry for any mental anguish that may have
caused.)

Item anchor responses.   There should be a distribution of *responses across all anchors*
for all items. After all, this is how you chose the anchors (rules 6–8, chapter 4). If
there are few or no respondents choosing any particular anchor, it serves no useful
purpose. It's a waste of space. This can usually occur on scales with six anchors or
more. For example, peruse the distribution below:

Strongly Disagree	Disagree	Slightly Disagree	Slightly Agree	Agree	Strongly Agree
75	24	3	0	39	148

There are very few responses to "Slightly Disagree" and none to "Slightly
Agree." These are nonfunctioning anchors. If this pattern occurs for several items,
those anchors need to be whacked or the statements scrutinized for possible ambiguity. Usually, that pattern indicates the anchors are duds! If the two anchors are
eliminated, the scale would be smushed down to four anchors. Although four anchors would reduce the potential variance of responses compared to the original
six anchors, do it, because no one is really picking two of the anchors. Only four
are really working. The revised 4-anchor scale should produce a packed distribution of responses.

The visual distribution of responses across anchors should be consistent with
the item mean and standard deviation. There should be a balanced distribution
of responses for the continuum of anchors. If there is a skew, the higher numbers
should usually bunch up at the "Agree" end.

Inspection of the items for the preceding characteristics can flag items that
need to be revised or discarded. Every effort should be made to retain items because they were written to measure certain aspects of teaching effectiveness. Re-
word the statement and/or compress the anchor scale, if possible. This is the
reason for the field test. If an item is not salvageable because of a lopsided mean
and/or low standard deviation, then croak it (Standard 3.7). An item with a high
standard deviation due to skewed responses, similar to the preceding item, would
be acceptable.

ANOTHER FACULTY AND ADMINISTRATOR WARNING

The next section raises the statistical ante a couple of notches. It's based on correlation, which measures the degree of relationship between two things, such as two items or an item and scale score. I'm warning you again because this material is more complex than that in the preceding section. Don't blame me if you blow a gasket over the correlation matrix.

Stage 2: Interitem and Item-Scale Correlations

The next stage of analysis involves the relationships of items to each other and to the scores on the scale (Standards 3.7 and 3.9). These relationships are measured with interitem correlations and item-scale correlations (Berk, 1979a).

Interitem correlations.   If the items on the scale are supposed to measure the same thing—teaching effectiveness—then they should all relate to one another. This thing is the construct, trait, variable, or factor measured by the scale. Initially, the best evidence to inspect whether the items are doing what they are supposed to do is interitem correlations.

All Pearson correlations should be computed between each pair of items and assembled into a matrix. A *matrix* of all items numbered down the left side by all items numbered across the top is the easiest and most compact display of all correlations between every pair of items. Examples are shown in table 7.2 for two subscales. The correlation coefficients should be *positive* and *as high as possible.* The range is –1.00 to +1.00. If items are worded positively, the coefficients should be positive. A negative coefficient is undesirable. It means that respondents who agree with one item disagree with the other, or vice versa. This could be a sign of faulty wording. Examine the pair of items to determine whether one or both items need revision or decapitation.

If the scale is partitioned into sections or subscales, a matrix should be generated for each collection of items in each subscale. Subscale items should cling to each other or cluster (like a peanut cluster, but without the peanuts and chocolate) around the topic of that subscale, such as course organization. *The coefficients of items within a subscale should be higher than those with items from other subscales.* For example, the items in the "Course Organization" subscale should not correlate as highly with those in the Instructional Methods subscale as they correlate with each other. The items within each subscale should have a high degree of clingability, meaning they consistently measure the same thing: the subscale construct.

TABLE 7.2
Interitem Correlation Matrices for Evaluation Methods (Items 9–13)
and Learning Outcomes (Items 14–17) Subscales

Evaluation Methods

Item	10	11	12	13
9	.77	.76	.71	.61
10		.81	.69	.55
11			.68	.57
12				.65

Learning Outcomes

Item	15	16	17
14	.69	.65	.64
15		.69	.66
16			.75

Interitem correlation matrices are shown in table 7.2 for the Evaluation Methods and Learning Outcomes subscales. Each matrix presents the correlations between all possible pairs of items. Coefficients greater than +.50 are desirable. These matrices indicate that the items seem to be consistently measuring the respective subscale constructs.

Item-scale correlations.   Another index to measure consistency in item responses is the correlation between an item and the score on the scale. Respondents who exhibit a high level of agreement on an item should also have a high score, or level of agreement, on the total scale consisting of all remaining items; similarly, those who disagree on an item should have a low score, or level of disagreement, on the total scale. (*Note*: Before the correlation is computed, the item score is removed from the total score to avoid overlap, which would inflate the correlation [Berk, 1978]. This is done automatically for every item-total scale correlation in statistical packages that compute item analysis statistics.) Here again, the coefficients should be positive *and* as high as possible. Values greater than +.30 indicate the direction and magnitude of consistency desired. Negative coefficients suggest inconsistency in responses. Such items mean the respondents disagree with the statement, but agreed with the other statements, or vice versa. Rewriting those items may resolve that inconsistent behavior. Coefficients that are low or zero also signal inconsistencies. Either revise or discard items that do not contribute to the consistent measurement of the construct.

If the scale has subscales, the procedure followed with the interitem correlations should be followed here. First, for each subscale, compute item-subscale correlations. These coefficients indicate the relationship between each item and the respective subscale score, with the item score deleted as previously. It is not uncommon for these to be somewhat higher than the item-scale correlations. They may range from the .50s to .80s. This is perfectly logical if the items defining a subscale are more homogeneous than the collection of items across all subscales.

Table 7.1 lists the item-subscale correlations by subscale (separated by broken lines) for all 36 items. Note the size of the coefficients. Most are in the .70s, several reach the low .80s, and a couple are in the .40s and .50s. Carefully examine the range of coefficients within each subscale. If one or more items has a coefficient relatively lower than the rest, it may be a sign of inconsistent items, which may not belong in the subscale to which they were assigned. For example, in subscale 1, item 8 has an item-subscale correlation (r) = .44, which is much lower than the other seven coefficients. The subscale measures "Course Content and Organization." The item is "The course requirements were appropriate for the number of credits." This doesn't relate as strongly to the topic as the remaining items. Because it is an important item, it will be retained, but may be relocated to a different subscale later.

All of the coefficients were high enough to lead to the decision: Keep 'em all. Although the range varied slightly from one subscale to another, there was still a high degree of consistency within each subscale.

Stages 1 and 2 item analyses are minimum requirements for any field test of a rating scale. Certainly the sample size must be large enough ($n \geq 200$) to compute the statistics previously described. The item means and standard deviations, interitem *r*s, and item-scale/item-subscale *r*s provided a lot of information on the technical quality of the items (Standard 3.9). Frequently, *those statistics are adequate to flag dysfunctional or inappropriate items* and to revise or discard them as necessary. Tables 7.1 and 7.2 also reveal how consistently the items measure the constructs they were written to measure.

 FINAL FACULTY AND ADMINISTRATOR WARNING

I really mean it this time. You think I'm just kidding around. Well, I am, but that's beside the point. This section can induce a stroke or MI. If you're actually planning to read about factor analysis just for fun, please schedule a stress test with your favorite cardiologist first. You should at least be taking Lipitor®, Crestor®, Vytorin™, or some other statin drug for several months before even looking at the frightening statistical terms in this section. Proceed at your own risk.

Stage 3: Factor Analysis

That being said, an additional analysis can be conducted on the items to determine the internal scale structure. Does the scale consist of items that measure only one construct (unidimensional)? Or, do the items tend to group or cluster into several sets (multidimensional), each of which measures a different category of teaching behaviors or course characteristics? (*Refresher:* Remember when you wrote or picked the statements to fit into specific categories, such as Evaluation Methods, Learning Outcomes, and Instructional Methods? Sure you do. That occurred early in the process.) Those item groupings based on the content of the statements were established *a priori* (pronounced "feng shui"), before any analysis. Those groupings seemed to make sense then. Do the relationships among the items, using real responses, support those content categories, or is there only one construct: teaching effectiveness?

The most appropriate technique to answer these questions about scale structure is *factor analysis*, which is actually a family of statistical methods. (Yes, believe it or not, statistics have families, too.) It is a "data reduction" strategy that allows you to *squish all of the items in a scale down to a smaller, more manageable number of subscales for ease of interpretation.* Only a brief conceptual explanation with an example will be presented here. This will be scary enough for some of you. For more detailed descriptions, see Nunnally and Bernstein (1994), Tabachnick and Fidell (2001), or DeVellis (2003).

Instead of the tiny interitem correlation matrices for each subscale described previously (see table 7.2), suppose we compute a ginormous matrix for the total set of items in the scale. Following the previous example, imagine a 36-item matrix for the student rating scale. Wow, what an image. I'll spare you the reality of that image, but you must promise to retain the image. Initially, factor analysis ferrets out an order or pattern in the correlations that can be explained by one factor. (*Clarification Time Out:* The term *factor* is synonymous with *construct, dimension, latent variable, trait, component, hypothetical thing,* and lots of other confusing words.) If one factor doesn't do the job, a search party is then formed to find clots or clumps among the intercorrelations from which to extract additional factors. These clumps emerge as groups of items, called subscales. The overall goal is to determine the *fewest number of factors that can explain the most information* in the matrix, thereby representing all of the item interrelationships.

This approach fits the method known as exploratory factor analysis (EFA), the intent of which is to *explore* the interrelationships among scale items to provide insight into the scale structure. There are three major steps involved in conducting an EFA: (1) statistical assumptions, (2) factor extraction, and (3) factor rotation. EFA contrasts with confirmatory factor analysis (CFA), which involves more complex procedures to *confirm* specific hypotheses or theories about the underlying scale structure.

Statistical assumptions.   Before we can factor-analyze (EFA) the guts out of the scale, there are two statistical requirements: *adequate sample size* and *strong interitem correlations.* Consistent with the preceding guidelines for sample size of the monster-field test, large samples are recommended to ensure the stability of the correlations from sample to sample and the generalizability of the results. At least 300 students are essential for student rating scales, including exit and alumni scales, in the 30–40 item range. Certainly larger samples would be even better. With regard to the interitem correlations, most of the coefficients should be above .30 (Tabachnick & Fidell, 2001). Bartlett's test of sphericity and the Kaiser-Meyer-Olkin measure of sampling adequacy can be used to test these assumptions.

Factor extraction.   Despite the image of its dental counterpart, this step isn't painful in the same way; it's painful in other ways. The question is: How many factors underlie the scale structure? The goal is to find the simplest solution (a.k.a. fewest factors) possible, but explain as much of the job content in the items as possible. *The factors should define substantive content categories that will ultimately condense the items into several subscales.* There are three criteria typically used to decide how many factors will be generated: (1) Kaiser's eigenvalue-1.0 criterion, (2) Cattell's scree plot, and (3) Horn's parallel analysis. Kaiser's technique is the most common, but Horn's is the most accurate. An *eigenvalue* is the amount of information (variance) captured by a factor. Only factors with an eigenvalue of 1.0 or more are retained in the first method; whereas only those eigenvalues that exceed the values from a randomly generated data set are retained in the third method.

Factor rotation.   Rotating the tires on your car extends their life; rotating the factors from Step 2 extends my life in this chapter, plus the items' correlations with each factor and our ability to interpret the clumps. *Items that clump together should have a higher correlation with one factor than any other.* This correlation, or weight, is called the *factor loading.* (*Déjà vu*: This is by the same logic as the interitem *r*s for the subscales described previously, in which each item should correlate higher with the items in its respective subscale than with the items in any other subscale.)

Different types of rotation affect these loadings and the meaning of the factors. The two methods are *orthogonal*, which assumes the factors are uncorrelated, and *oblique*, which permits correlations among the factors. The two approaches can produce similar solutions, especially when there is a distinct pattern in the item correlations. Within these approaches are specific rotational techniques, such as *varimax* (orthogonal) and *direct oblimin* (oblique). The former widely used technique is designed to minimize the number of items that have high loadings on a given factor, which is an extremely desirable outcome. (*Note*: The term "varimax" is actually the abbreviation for "variable interest rate loan.")

Student rating scale application.   An illustration of these procedures with the 36-item student rating scale is shown in table 7.3. The visual image of the actual items and factors will hopefully clarify the concepts just described. Since there were five original subscale content groupings, the purpose of the factor analysis was to determine how closely the faculty content judgments matched the real response patterns of the data to furnish evidence for the internal structure. Five analyses were run, one for each possible factor solution—one through five. Since the items and these five groups were constructed from scratch and did not resemble any existing scale, it was not assumed that the factors would be correlated. We simply did not know. Consequently, a varimax rotation was chosen to maximize the differences between the factors and their loadings. In retrospect, an oblique rotation would have been more appropriate because the factors turned out to be correlated with each other. The column numbers under each factor are the loadings. The bold numbers identify the items with the **highest loadings** that most strongly correlate with one of the factors. The eigenvalue-1.0 criterion produced a 5-factor solution. Note the eigenvalues at the bottom of the columns, ranging from 18.342 down to 1.030. Those factors explained 68.1% of the information (variance) in the 36 items (sum of percentages in last row).

So what happened? Consistent with previous factor analytic studies of student rating scales, the internal structure is multidimensional. With some item juggling, the original content item groupings under the subscale titles on the left came very close to the factor loadings. The strongest item loadings were Learning Atmosphere (Factor 1), Learning Outcomes (Factor 4), and Evaluation Methods (Factor 3). A few items loaded moderately on several factors (4, 7, 26). The cross-loadings of items in Course Content and Organization and Instructional Methods were somewhat perplexing from a content perspective. The first four items related to the content of the syllabus and course materials (Factor 5), and the remaining four addressed difficulty of materials, content of assignments, and course requirements (Factor 3). The latter group loaded strongly with the five evaluation items. Item 7 on course organization cross-loaded on Factors 2–5. It needed a home. Finally, it landed on Factor 4 with Learning Outcomes.

The Instructional Methods items loaded well on Factor 2 with three exceptions: items 20, 26, and 27. Item 20 on critical thinking ended up in Learning Outcomes, and 26 and 27 on feedback to students fell into Learning Atmosphere.

After the items were redistributed according to their highest loadings, the first subscale was renamed "Course Content," and the third, "Course Value." With this

TABLE 7.3
Varimax Rotated Factor Loadings for 36-Item Student Rating Scale (*n* = 1586)

Item	5-Factor Solution				
	Factor 1	Factor 2	Factor 3	Factor 4	Factor 5
Course Content/Organization					
1	.234	.163	.193	.167	**.799**
2	.261	.186	.222	.186	**.784**
3	.207	.191	.315	.263	**.664**
4	.137	.318	.408	.339	**.492**
5	.138	.339	**.511**	.287	.404
6	.169	.302	**.506**	.381	.355
7	.193	.361	.392	**.423**	.389
8	.059	.299	**.604**	.039	.031
Evaluation Methods					
9	.291	.212	**.667**	.252	.369
10	.333	.180	**.676**	.164	.338
11	.289	.225	**.722**	.189	.291
12	.277	.213	**.651**	.344	.207
13	.315	.128	**.547**	.404	.123
Learning Outcomes					
14	.186	.296	.263	**.692**	.173
15	.198	.272	.289	**.698**	.162
16	.186	.178	.122	**.794**	.248
17	.179	.156	.130	**.813**	.193
Instructional Methods					
18	.280	**.449**	.259	.362	.021
19	.172	**.605**	.294	.125	.038
20	.308	.450	.278	**.501**	.047
21	.342	**.639**	.117	.259	.209
22	.233	**.624**	.150	.381	.240
23	.297	**.664**	.205	.296	.239
24	.305	**.635**	.318	.113	.180
25	.529	**.557**	.190	.154	.159
26	**.442**	.420	.218	.179	.242
27	**.551**	.419	.295	.114	.161
28	.534	**.561**	.242	.148	.132
29	.358	**.623**	.244	.244	.246
30	.353	**.606**	.181	.238	.250
Learning Atmosphere					
31	**.764**	.224	.135	.235	.172
32	**.822**	.240	.185	.146	.122
33	**.800**	.227	.235	.178	.158
34	**.833**	.210	.162	.155	.171
35	**.736**	.252	.164	.163	.169
36	**.698**	.319	.173	.206	.180
Eigenvalue	18.342	2.384	1.517	1.247	1.030
Explained Variance	50.95%	6.62%	4.21%	3.46%2	.86%

TABLE 7.4
Original Student Rating Scale and Revised Factor-Loaded Scale Subscale Correlation Matrix

Subscale	Original Scale					Revised Scale				
	2	*3*	*4*	*5*	*Scale*	*2*	*3*	*4*	*5*	*Scale*
1. Course Content	.79	.69	.75	.61	.89	.75	.68	.66	.60	.80
2. Evaluation Methods		.64	.73	.62	.86		.75	.75	.67	.89
3. Course Value			.67	.53	.78			.75	.63	.86
4. Instructional Methods				.77	.94				.80	.92
5. Learning Atmosphere					.82					.87

empirically determined subscale structure, how do the revised subscales based on the five factors compare to the original? Correlations were computed between subscales and total scale. The matrix is shown in table 7.4. How muddy is this water? All of the subscales are moderately correlated with each other and highly correlated with their respective total scale scores. Overall, the differences between the original and revised scales are trivial. This factor analysis and the previous correlations in Stage 2 provide support for the original structure and also help to fine-tune the subscale item clumps.

8

COLLECTING EVIDENCE OF VALIDITY AND RELIABILITY

A Twisted Mind

Does the title of this chapter scare you? "Terrified, mortified, petrified, stupe-fied of the title."* Me too. Well, I've postponed the inevitable for four sentences. Time to hunker down. We have to tackle the two most important topics in scale construction: hokey and pokey. Oops! I mean *validity* and *reliability*. The title of this chapter is really misleading. You have actually been gathering barrels of evidence throughout all of the preceding chapters. That's kind of sneaky, I know, but you should know me pretty well by chapter 8. This chapter is the convergence of all of your work, including qualitative and quantitative results up to this point. The Holy Grail of rating scale construction (a.k.a. the *Standards*) will guide the criteria in this chapter as it has in every other one. This wacky, fun-filled romp through five types of validity evidence and three types of reliability evidence will be unforgettable. It concludes with an epilogue on the care and feeding of a rating scale.

---

*From *A Beautiful Mind*, John Nash's response to classmates at Princeton challenging him to play chess.

 BERK'S NOTES

Faculty—If you are conducting validity and reliability studies for a rating scale or need to interpret the results from other studies, particularly commercially produced scales, for a variety of scales, this chapter is required reading. Otherwise, you might want to just check out the basic concepts for gathering evidence, skim the technical material and reliability theory, and move on to the finale.

Administrators—If you want to be familiar with the technical criteria for judging the quality of any rating scale, an understanding of the evidence essential for validity and reliability is a must. In the reliability section, the interpretation of the standard error of measurement (*SEM*) is especially important. It will be used in the interpretation of scale scores for summative decisions described in the next chapter.

Validity Evidence

Validity refers to the *degree to which evidence and theory support the interpretations of scale scores entailed by proposed uses of the scale* (AERA, APA, & NCME Joint Committee on Standards, 1999). What? *Translation*: It involves accumulating evidence to provide a sound scientific basis for interpreting the scale scores. This is the academic equivalent of *CSI* (*Crime Scene Investigation*). Instead of gathering evidence to solve a crime on a forensic fantasy TV drama, you are assembling a *body of evidence* in order to justify the uses of the scores for specific purposes. This means that the rating scale should not be administered and decisions should not be made from its scores until the validity evidence has been evaluated as adequate. We serve as *ASIs* (Academic Scene Investigators) in determining what evidence needs to be collected and when it satisfies the *Standards* to permit the use of the rating scale scores. As Gil Grissom emphasizes ad nauseum, "It's all about the evidence."

Before we continue with this presentation on validity, I must digress. Some of you may not be familiar with this definition of validity. There are legitimate reasons for that. Come over here and let me explain.

There are two types of validity evidence: logical and empirical. *Logical* evidence consists of the opinions or judgments of qualified experts about key characteristics of the scale and what it measures. The judgments are gathered through systematic reviews that yield qualitative information, although they can be summarized quantitatively. In contrast, *empirical* evidence is obtained from the actual responses of students, faculty, or employers during the field tests and the subsequent statistical analyses of particular item and scale properties. This evidence is quantitative. Both forms of evidence are required for all of the rating scales identified in chapter 1.

Digression Alert

Over the past 2006 years, give or take a month, there has been a lot of confusion and inconsistency in validity terminology. This has been evident especially in the basic, social, and behavioral sciences and the health professions. In an effort to clarify where we've been and where we are now, I have traced the changes in the terms used in the national *Standards for Educational and Psychological Testing* from 1 A.D. to the present (APA, AERA, & NCME Joint Committee on Standards, 1966; AERA, APA, & NCME Joint Committee on Standards, 1974, 1985, 1999):

1 A.D.–1985	*1985 Standards–1999*	*1999 Standards–Present*
Content Validity	Content-Related Validity	Evidence Based on the Scale Content
Criterion Validity Concurrent Predictive	Criterion-Related Validity	Evidence Based on Relations to Other Variables
Construct Validity	Construct-Related Validity	Evidence Based on the Internal Structure

We have moved from the simple "holy trinity representing three different roads to psychometric salvation" (Guion, 1980, p. 386) prior to 1985 to a broadened unified conceptualization of different sources of evidence related to a scale score's specific uses, interpretations, and inferences (Messick, 1989, 1995; Ory & Ryan, 2001; Shepard, 1993). The 1999 *Standards* reflects the most recent wisdom by leading measurement experts on the topic of validity and the qualitative and quantitative methods for collecting evidence for various score uses and interpretations. Those *Standards* will guide the terminology and recommendations in the remainder of this chapter. *End of Digression.*

So where do we begin? First, the purpose of the rating scale and uses of scores must be clear. All of the evidence hinges on those uses (Standard 14.1). Here 'tis:

Purpose—Each scale is supposed to measure specific job content related to teaching effectiveness.

Uses—The scores will be used for formative decisions, such as teaching improvement; summative decisions, such as renewal/dismissal, merit pay, promotion, and tenure; and/or program decisions, such as curriculum revision, mentoring program effectiveness, and course scheduling.

How do you collect the necessary evidence for these score uses? Actually, you can draw on all available evidence relevant to the technical quality of the faculty evaluation system, including proper scale construction procedures (chapters 2–5), appropriate scale assembly and administration (chapter 6), carefully executed field testing and item analyses (chapter 7), and appropriate score interpretation (chapter 9). All of these elements contribute evidence of the validity of the intended score interpretations.

There are also other formal analyses that must be conducted to obtain evidence for a scale used for employment decisions. Consistent with my unified conceptualization or 360° assessment of teaching effectiveness, it is desirable and appropriate for academic administrators to integrate information from multiple sources of evidence (Standard 14.13). However, it is essential that each source has sufficient validity evidence. According to the *Standards*, there are five types of evidence pertinent to the rating scales identified in chapter 1 and the triangulation of results from those scales: (1) job content domain, (2) response processes, (3) internal scale structure, (4) relationships with other measures, and (5) consequences of ratings.

Evidence Based on Job Content Domain

This evidence requires a *thorough and explicit definition of the job content domain* of teaching (Standard 14.8). Since each rating scale has a different purpose with different respondents (e.g., students, peers, alumni, employers, administrators), the domain may also be different (see chapter 2). In every case, teaching effectiveness must be clearly defined in terms of specific teaching tasks, or KSAs (which, you'll recall, stands for Krispy Kreme® Doughnuts) (Standard 14.10). One source of these behaviors is the criteria for promotion to each rank. Teaching outcomes may be specified to differentiate the expectations at assistant, associate, and full professor levels. If these outcomes are available, the behaviors will shoot out of the blocks; if not, you'll have to reload and find another source.

The definition may consist of a list of the representative behaviors that describe effective teaching in your institution. This list should have been compiled in chapter 2. If you skipped this step, you should be ashamed of yourself. It needs to be done. If a colleague asks, "What does the peer rating scale measure?"

you can either run for your life or pull the list of behaviors out of your back pocket, or front pocket if you're wearing cargo pants.

The next step is to establish a *formal link between the job content and the rating scale* (Standard 14.9). Although the scale statements, phrases, or topics were generated from the job content list, a review of the completed scale against the job behaviors must be conducted. Such a review can furnish evidence to satisfy two criteria:

1. *Content relevance*—Each item measures the job behavior/characteristic/outcome it was intended to measure.
2. *Content representativeness*—The scale items collectively provide a representative sample of all possible items that could be used to tap the construct of teaching effectiveness.

These criteria are nonnegotiable. They must be met. The review of the match, or congruence, between item and characteristic and representativeness is based entirely on judgment. This logical analysis produces the qualitative evidence based on the job content domain.

Content committee composition.   The faculty chairperson should be knowledgeable about this entire process, possess outstanding interpersonal skills, and have an IQ greater than a reasonably bright fungus. The committee of faculty ($n = 7–15$) should be selected systematically for this content review. These faculty members should be different from those who served on the committee to develop the scale. They should have at least a familiarity and, preferably, experience with the latest teaching techniques and represent a range of content disciplines and levels (undergraduate, master's, and doctoral) to which the rating scale will be applied. Diversity with regard to rank, gender, and race/ethnicity should also be considered in the composition of the group.

A profile of their characteristics should be created to document the qualifications of these "experts" (Standards 1.7 and 3.5). Without verification of this expertise, the content review probably would be meaningless and misdirected. It would be not unlike turning the controls of a 747 over to a chimpanzee. The burden of proof for validity evidence from the review rests on the judgments by these faculty members (Berk, 1990a). Ultimately, they receive the credit or blame for the content of the scale when it goes before the entire faculty for approval. Everyone will have a vested interest in the quality of the final product. A tabular summary of their characteristics can meet these standards. Here is an example:

Judge	Rank	Primary Discipline	Gender	Race / Ethnicity	Course Level	No. of Years Teaching
1	Assoc.	Econ.	M	C	U	11
2	Full	Psych.	F	A	D	22
3	Full	History	M	A-A	U	31
4	Assist.	Bio.	M	C	M	4
5	Assoc.	Chem.	F	C	U	8

The review process requires a form on which the faculty judges can easily and quickly rate all of the statements against the job characteristics. A checklist format with a few unstructured items can elicit all of the information needed. A sample format is provided (see checklist 8.1).

Review: Round 1.   How should this review process be executed? Dress is usually casual, so instructors can kick off their Birkenstocks® and jump into a hammock. For this first round, the form should be *administered independently to all faculty members on the committee* rather than in a formal group meeting. This ensures individual input without the influence of the other faculty judges. It should be sent online, with a 2- to 3-week window for completion.

Once all forms are returned, the results should be summarized on one master form. For each statement, calculate the percentage of faculty who checked "yes" and the percentage who checked "no," plus the suggested revision or explanation. At the bottom of the form, compute the percentages for "yes" and "no" and list the recommended additions for characteristics and statements.

Review: Round 2.   The chairperson of the committee involved in developing the scale should convene the original committee members to consider the results of the content review. The purpose of this meeting is to *address all of the "no's" on the statements and suggested changes* as well as the additions to the characteristics and statements. For this second round, a revised form incorporating all changes should be sent to the reviewers, or, if feasible, have them *meet to discuss the changes*. All changes should be highlighted to facilitate the speed of this second review. The "gold standard" is to obtain 100% "yes" on every statement–characteristic match and 100% "yes" to the representativeness of the item sample. Although there may be a few disgruntled or dissatisfied faculty members, support must be at least 80%, or the scale is not going to fly with the rest of the faculty.

Review: Round 3.   The final version of the scale with the blessing of the content review committee should then be *sent to the entire faculty* who will be evaluated with that scale. (*Suggestion*: A full description of the scale development process should also accompany the tool.) They need to be given the opportunity to re-

---

CHECKLIST 8.1

CONTENT REVIEW COMMITTEE RATING FORM

Rating Scale Statement	*Teaching Characteristic*	*Does the statement measure the teaching characteristic?*
My instructor is a knucklehead.	Sensitivity to students' needs	YES _____ NO _____ If NO, please revise item or explain: _____ _____
My instructor uses theatrical techniques effectively.	Innovative/creative teaching methods	YES _____ NO _____ If NO, please revise item or explain: _____ _____

Were any important teaching characteristics omitted?
YES _____ NO _____   If YES, please add: _____

_____

Should any statements be added to measure specific characteristics?
YES _____ NO _____   If YES, please add: _____

_____

Collectively, do all of the statements provide a representative sample of all possible statements to measure teaching effectiveness?
YES _____ NO _____   If NO, please explain: _____

_____

---

view the scale and to be informed of how the scores will be used. A special meeting should be scheduled for faculty to raise questions about the tool, its administration, and score interpretation and use. The faculty involved in the construction phase and content review should be present to address any questions or issues that arise. This review may require one or more meetings. During our approval process, my colleagues and I went into the faculty meetings to receive our monthly beatings until all of the faculty members were satisfied with the content and all issues were addressed. All comments and suggestions should be recorded at the meetings, and faculty should be encouraged to e-mail other comments during the week following each meeting.

The point person or chair for the project should set a time for the development committee to review all faculty comments. The scale should be revised accordingly. All suggested changes need to be addressed, either in the scale or with an explanation. The product of this review should be sent back to the faculty for a vote of approval at the next faculty meeting. This cements the accountability of the stakeholders in the assessment of teaching effectiveness process.

This vote of confidence allows the committee to proceed with the monster-field testing and subsequent technical analyses. In other words, the evidence of validity based on the job content review and faculty approval should occur after the mini-field test and before the performance-enhanced, super-sized monster-field test.

Evidence Based on Response Processes

How do students, peers, self, and administrators actually respond to the items on a rating scale? What psychological and cognitive processes are operating? Evidence is required to determine the *fit between how we expect respondents to answer the items and how they actually respond* (Standard 1.8). The most direct method to gather such evidence is (Are you ready for this?): Ask them. Formally interviewing students about the rating process might reveal that their ratings of one instructor are based on the performance of their other instructors that semester or that their motivation to complete the form is to just do it, without careful deliberation over every item.

An interview questionnaire containing structured and unstructured questions (What else would you expect? This is a book on rating scales!) should be developed for each type of respondent. The questions should address the following:

- meaning of the statements or phrases
- meaning of the response anchors
- motivation to answer
- standard for ratings
- time period of observation on which ratings are based
- other factors that affect ratings

There have been studies of a variety of variables that can influence the rating process and why and how someone responds. In this research, student ratings have been correlated with a wide range of student, instructor, and course characteristics (Aleamoni, 1999; Braskamp & Ory, 1994; Centra, 1993; Feldman, 1989b; Theall & Franklin, 2001). Overall, there are few, if any, potentially biasing influences on the rating process. McKeachie (1997) concluded that what influences have been found have relatively small effects.

In addition to the above, the specific sources of response bias described in chapter 5 need to be investigated. When the ratings measure something other than what they were intended to measure, the interpretations can be misleading. Validity studies should be conducted to obtain evidence of suspected bias. Student, exit, and alumni scales should be examined for end-aversion, extreme-response, and gender, racial/ethnic, and sexual orientation biases (Standards 7.12 and 12.2). Differences in the meaning and interpretation of the items across relevant subgroups of students should be studied to determine, for example, whether "international students" rate differently than other students (Standard 3.6). Systematic strategies to minimize leniency-stringency, incompetence, buddy, and back-scratching biases in peer, administrator, and employer ratings should also be considered.

Unless evidence is obtained of the degree of rating bias or intentional steps are taken to control, minimize, or eliminate it, the bias will contaminate the ratings, infect the ratees, possibly cause a full-scale epidemic in your institution, and, ultimately, may affect the decisions rendered based on those ratings. Until Merck or Pfizer pharmaceuticals create a vaccine, which will take 50 years of clinical trials for the FDA (stands for "Internal Revenue Service") to approve and then withdraw a year later, you need to consider the sources of bias in interpreting the ratings. When summative decisions are made about our future in academia, the consequences can be significant.

Once validity evidence of the response processes and specific sources of bias have been documented, there will still be uncontrollable response bias in the ratings that must be considered as random error. This error can be estimated as a type of reliability evidence, which will be presented later in the chapter.

Evidence Based on Internal Scale Structure

Where the previous evidence based on the job content domain was derived from the logical analysis of faculty judges, the evidence on the scale structure is gathered from the *technical "empirical" analyses from the monster-field test administration* (Standards 1.1 and 1.11). Here the focus is on the responses to the items and their relationships to one another. Does the pattern of responses conform to the hypothesized *a priori* (Latin expression meaning "seize the day") structure of the scale?

All of the field test data presented in tables 7.2–7.4 contribute empirical validity evidence about the internal structure of the scale (a.k.a. the "guts"). The *item means and standard deviations* indicate the extent to which the intended purpose of the items to spread out responses across the continuum of anchors actually occurred. The *item-subscale correlations* provide evidence on whether the items written on a specific topic tend to cluster around that topic. The *interitem correlations* by subscale are really measures of the items' clingability (a.k.a. homogeneity) for each subscale. All of the item-subscale and interitem correlations are actually "validity coefficients." The magnitude and consistency of those coefficients furnish support for the degree to which the items belong in each subscale. Each item has the need to belong. If it doesn't find a home in a subscale, it may end up in another scale or, worse, join a gang and get into all kinds of trouble.

Your worst nightmare of results from the first two stages of item analysis might be:

- noncentral mean
- limited spread of responses
- low and/or negative item-subscale correlations
- weak interitem correlations

This evidence negates our purpose-driven scale construction. The item scores are not consistent with the proposed internal structure of the scale.

A final Stage 3 analysis can also boost the evidence level a few notches. As long as the sample size is large enough, the factor analysis can provide a rigorous test of the dimensionality of the scale and of the construct of teaching effectiveness. Is teaching effectiveness unidimensional or multidimensional? The literature is packed with factor analytic studies that support the multidimensionality of the construct (Marsh, 1984; Marsh & Dunkin, 1992). Although specific factors vary, Centra (1993) compiled a list of the six most commonly identified factors:

1. Organization, planning, and/or structure
2. Teacher–student interaction or rapport
3. Clarity, communication skill
4. Workload, course difficulty
5. Grading and examinations, assignments
6. Student learning, student self-ratings of accomplishments or progress (pp. 57)

Despite the number of factors, there still tend to be moderate correlations (.50s–.70s) between them. Global, or overall, ratings also correlate with several of the factors. These relationships add to the complexity of interpreting teaching effectiveness. The evidence displayed in table 7.4 falls into this interpretation.

There are four levels of score interpretation: anchor, item, subscale, and total scale (see chapter 9 for details). When the results are used for diagnostic purposes or teaching improvement, the first three levels are most appropriate. Administrators concentrate on subscale and total scale scores for summative decisions. Program, especially curriculum, decisions are based on item and subscale scores.

The validity evidence described above must support all of these uses. The most significant issue from all of the analyses is the evidence for subscales (Standards 1.12). Since subscales pinpoint areas of teaching effectiveness or ineffectiveness, subscale scores can be extremely informative. *If the item-subscale correlations, interitem correlations by subscale, and factor loadings furnish sufficient evidence for a multidimensional structure, subscale scores can be interpreted.* If the evidence is weak or inconsistent, the internal structure should be regarded as unidimensional, and subscale scores should not be computed.

For which rating scales is the validity evidence most appropriate? The best answer is ALL. However, there is a feasibility problem. Validity studies require certain sample sizes to ensure the stability and meaningfulness of the statistical results. No one wants wobbly correlations. The available field test sample size should be at least 200 to conduct analyses at Stages 1 and 2. But, the sample size guidelines given in chapter 7 for the Stage 3 factor analysis require 300–500, depending on the number of items. These sizes will restrict the analyses of several rating scales. Adequate *n*s are usually accessible for student, exit, and alumni ratings, but self-ratings are limited by the number of courses. Employer ratings are more difficult to collect, and peer ratings are the most restrictive of all.

Evidence Related to Other Measures of Teaching Effectiveness

The quantitative analyses required to obtain evidence of the internal scale structure were based on correlations between items, subscale scores, and total scores. This section examines the evidence that *relates the different rating scales selected to measure teaching effectiveness.* Yup, that's what I said. If you picked student, self, and peer ratings as your path to teaching effectiveness, you now need to consider the relationships among those three sources (Standard 1.14).

If you chose multiple measures of teaching effectiveness, it is possible to perform a *logical* and *empirical* analysis of their interrelationships. For example, a content review of the items on student and peer rating scales might reveal only a small percentage of overlap. These scales are designed to tap different dimensions of teaching effectiveness. Student and peer scales often measure complementary behaviors and dissimilar constructs (Centra, 1993; Doyle & Crichton, 1978; Feldman, 1989b). A low correlation between the scores of the two scales furnishes evidence of their *discriminant validity.*

In contrast, two rating scales known to measure the same construct can be correlated to determine the degree of *convergent validity.* One example would be student and self-(faculty) ratings. The same scale may be used for both. The cor-

TABLE 8.1
Convergent and Discriminant Validity Evidence on
Multiple Measures of Teaching Effectiveness

Scale	2	3	4	5
1. Student	.46*	.76*	.86	.81
2. Peer		.88	–	–
3. Self			–	–
4. Exit				.73
5. Alumni				–

*Based on course mean ratings

relation between the instructor's ratings of all items and the average student ratings for all items should be high (Feldman, 1989b; Marsh, Overall, & Kessler, 1979). This type of convergence might also be expected between peer and external expert ratings and peer and self-ratings, which would be based on the same peer scale.

This validity evidence can best be displayed in the form of a correlation matrix. A hypothetical example is shown in table 8.1. To control for the method by which each construct is measured (Campbell & Fiske, 1959), the same type of rating scale was used for each measurement: a Likert scale. Students' online responses have to be coded to preserve anonymity but permit matching scores on in-class ratings, exit ratings one to two months before the students graduate, and alumni ratings a year later. The student sample size shrinks longitudinally at each measurement point. Peer ratings are based on the average of two or three faculty observers per faculty member. They are correlated against class mean ratings only. Self-ratings were obtained on two forms: the student and peer scales. Self–student and self–peer correlations were computed from the respective forms.

Convergent evidence appears strongest across the three sets of student ratings: student, exit, and alumni (see Feldman, 1989b; Overall & Marsh, 1980). There is also a high degree of convergence between self- and peer ratings. Discriminant evidence is most pronounced between peer and student ratings.

Evidence Based on the Consequences of Ratings

There are both intended and unintended consequences of the use of the various ratings of teaching effectiveness. It is expected that some *benefits will accrue from the intended uses* of student, peer, self, alumni, and other rating scale scores. On an individual faculty level, these might include improved quality of teaching, increased student success, receiving a teaching award, promotion to the next rank, and being given 50-yard-line football tickets for the homecoming game. However, there are also *negative consequences*, such as being denied tenure, no merit pay, no renewal of contract, and being served a subpoena to the president's trial for embezzlement. At an institutional level, the ratings may influence faculty search and hiring decisions, merit increases, promotion and tenure decisions, and course assignments (Kulik, 2001).

Validity evidence needs to be collected on *whether these consequences of the rating scale score interpretations and the decisions based on these interpretations are actually occurring.* Are the anticipated benefits, for example, in improving the overall quality of teaching, being realized? Evidence of both the positive and negative consequences of the formative, summative, and program decisions for which the rating scale scores are used can be very helpful for decision makers.

The evidence may be logical and/or empirical. It should address the intended consequences (Standards 1.22 and 1.23) as well as the unintended consequences (Standard 1.24). Ory and Ryan (2001) have compiled a grocery list of nonedible consequences related to student rating scales. That list is a useful starting point. Many of the consequences are also applicable to other rating scales. Consider how the following consequences relate to your institution and what evidence could be collected for each:

Intended Consequences

- Instructors collect ratings, value the input, and make improvements in their teaching and courses.
- Instructors are rewarded for having excellent rating results (salary, promotions, awards, recognition).
- Instructors with very low ratings are encouraged by their department to seek help, possibly from colleagues or a campus faculty development office.
- Students perceive and use ratings as a means for indicating suggestions for improvement.
- Students have more information on which to base their course selections.
- Instructors use ratings as motivation to improve their teaching.
- Students perceive ratings as a vehicle for change.

Unintended Consequences
- Instructors alter their teaching in order to receive high ratings (lower content difficulty, provide less content, give only high grades).
- Due to their convenience, the campus looks to student ratings as the *only* measure of teaching quality.
- The content of the student rating form may determine what is addressed in the classroom.

- Students reward poor teaching by believing they can give high ratings in return for high grades.
- Ratings are used to make discriminations between instructors that cannot be supported by the data.
- Due to the high stakes involved, instructors fail to follow proper administration procedures.
- The rating process becomes a meaningless activity that is performed by students and instructors only because it is mandated. (adapted from pp. 39–40)

Reliability Evidence

Reliability is the *degree to which scale scores are consistent over repeated administrations*; the degree to which scores are *free of errors of measurement* (AERA, APA, & NCME Joint Committee on Standards, 1999). This characteristic is all about error—*random error*—which can lead to score inconsistencies. How can we generalize over time, items, and raters? My dream is that one day our students, peers, and administrators will be able to give their true ratings of our teaching performance, unaffected by error. Unfortunately, like other evil forces, error is random and unpredictable. The error stems from unsystematic and uncontrollable elements in the respondents' environment that can affect their ratings. It may be rooted in *internal factors*, such as the respondent's state of mind (e.g., motivation, interest, attention, hallucinations) or body (e.g., nausea, low blood sugar, fatigue, pain, bleeding from gunshot wounds) at the time the scale is completed, or *external factors*, such as distractions, room temperature, time pressure, and online administration glitches. Poorly worded or unclear directions, faulty items, inappropriate anchors, and inadequate item sample are also sources of error.

Classical Reliability Theory

Measurement *error* (*E*) contaminates the *true rating* (*T*) of teaching performance. According to classical reliability theory, we are stuck with the realization that a respondent's *observed rating* (*X*), or raw score, consists of two additive components, *true rating* and *error*, or

$$X = T + E$$

Our task is to estimate the amount of *E* (or *T*) with two indices: $r_{xx'}$, the reliability coefficient, and *SEM*, the standard error of measurement.

Theoretically, these indices are derived from certain assumptions:

1. If a student were tied to his chair (*Note*: The male pronoun is used because only a guy would be considered for this experiment) and requested to complete a rating scale at least 100 times, this would resemble a torture not unlike that used on the TV program *24*. Theoretically, all of his 100+ total score ratings (*X*s) would take on the shape of a normal distribution. In reality, hypothetically, before this distribution took shape, usually at around 62 or 63 scales, the student's brain would explode all over the classroom. EWWW! The spread of his gray matter and *X*s in this hypothetical distribution represents the degree to which the estimate of that student's true score (*T*) is likely to fluctuate on repeated measurements due to error (*E*). That fluctuation from measurement to measurement may be narrow and compressed around the middle, or it may be wide. The width of that band is a function of the amount of *E*, or inconsistency in the scores.
2. The hypothetical average of all of the student's *X*s would equal his *T*, and the standard deviation of the errors would be *SEM* (pronounced "brăk ō lee"). *SEM* can circumscribe the width, or band, of error.
3. This single student model can be extended to all students completing the rating scale so that there are group distributions of *X*, *T*, and *E* and variance for each.
4. A *reliability coefficient* is the *proportion of observed score* (X) *variance explained by true score* (T) *variance for a sample of respondents.*

Summated Rating Scale Theory

The preceding model was originally conceived for tests, not rating scales. In fact, there are several currently popular alternative theories that may be considered as well, such as generalizability theory and item response theory (see Brennan, 2001; DeVellis, 2003; Streiner & Norman, 1995). Unfortunately, those theories will not be examined here for three reasons:

1. They are beyond the scope of coverage in this chapter;
2. I'm already stretching the limits of my meager abilities with this material; and
3. I don't know anything about them.

The point is that the two components (*T* + *E*) work for tests in which items are answerable as right or wrong. When they are applied to scales, in which items have no right answer—they're simply expressed feelings or opinions about what is being rated—the two components are inadequate. Spector (1992) proposed a third component to address another source of contamination: *Bias* (*B*). He added *B* to the model:

$$X = T + E + B$$

Bias consists of systematic influences on the respondent's raw score (*X*) that do not reflect the *true rating* (*T*). *B* is the Darth Vader (a.k.a. Anakin Skywalker, *Sith* fans) of rating scale scores. These influences are not random and cannot be averaged with multiple items. They are separate from *Error*. The nine sources of response-set bias described in chapter 5 and the other types of bias identified in the "Response Processes" section on validity fall into *B*. In this case, if we know who the enemy is, we can take steps to control and, perhaps, minimize its impact on *X*. Rarely could the bias be completely eliminated. Validity studies need to be conducted of all known sources of bias in order to reduce its effect on *X* and the reliability of the scores.

Methods for Estimating Reliability

Now let's bring this hypothetical puppy out of George Lucas's galaxy and down to earth. How do we actually estimate reliability and *SEM*? There is no single preferred approach or single index that adequately conveys all of the relevant information on measurement error. The choice of technique and the minimum acceptable level for any index rests on professional judgment.

Like the various types of validity evidence, the empirical evidence of reliability is contingent on the uses and interpretation of the scale scores. Where field testing is possible using the same data from the validity studies, internal consistency reliability should be estimated for total scale scores *and* subscale scores, where appropriate (Standards 2.1 and 2.7). This is possible for student, exit, alumni, and, maybe, employer rating scales. For the peer rating scale, every effort should be made to estimate interobserver agreement or reliability with two or three observers per instructor (Standard 2.10). Finally, the *standard error of measurement* (*SEM*) should be computed from one of the preceding reliability coefficients. A further description of these indices follows.

Internal consistency reliability.   This type of reliability, as the name suggests, estimates *how consistently the scale items measure the construct*. It is also called *item homogeneity*. The error that lowers this reliability relates to the job content domain and sample of items that compose the scale. If the content domain is disorganized or incomplete and the item sample is small, unrepresentative, heterogeneous, and discombobulated, the reliability index can be low.

Let's reminisce a bit. Since chapter 2, I have recommended rating scale construction procedures that emphasize a clear and comprehensive definition of the job content domain and then writing items to collectively provide a representative sample of all possible items to measure that definition of teaching effectiveness. The preceding section on validity evidence documented the products of this work, especially in regard to the criteria of content relevance and content representativeness.

The empirical evidence based on the internal structure of the scale confirmed the logical evidence of the job content, plus it delineated the unidimensionality or multidimensionality of the items. After all, the primary purpose of the item-scale/subscale correlations, interitem correlations, and factor analysis was to determine whether all of the items consistently measure one construct (unidimensional) or several (multidimensional). The student rating scale example of five subscale item groupings illustrated the following:

- High item-subscale *r*s indicated the items consistently measured the subscale job characteristics.
- High interitem *r*s indicated a consistently high degree of relationship among the subscale items.
- Factor loadings on the 36 items produced five homogenous item clusters, or subscales, slightly different from those originally projected based on content alone.

All of the procedures and analyses up to this point have been planned systematically to produce a high degree of internal consistency reliability for the subscale scores. The correlations computed in Stages 2 and 3 of the field test to furnish quantitative validity evidence can now be summarized into a single number for each subscale: *coefficient alpha* (Cronbach, 1951). (*Paragraphus Interruptus*: I know I promised no Greek letters at the beginning of this chapter, but "alpha" is a name. At least I didn't use α.) In other words, if we were searching for an index that could reflect the item homogeneity of the list of item-subscale *r*s and interitem *r* matrix, alpha would do the trick. This coefficient, in essence, is your reward for correctly building a bunch of homogeneous item clusters called subscales. If you did your job well, the coefficients for all subscales should be high.

Coefficient alpha can be computed directly from the same *single administration* rating scale data base used for the validity analyses. Once the subscale groupings are determined, coefficient alpha should be computed for each subscale and the total scale. Its values can range from 0 to +1.00. A 0 means "all *E* (error)" and

TABLE 8.2
Original Student Rating Scale and Revised Factor-Loaded Scale
Subscale Structure and Reliabilities (*n* = 1586)

Subscale	Original Scale				Revised Scale			
	No. of Items	*Coefficient Alpha*	*SEM*	*SD*	*No. of items*	*Coefficient Alpha*	*SEM*	*SD*
Course Content	8	.90	1.39	4.31	4	.87	.81	2.25
Evaluation Methods	5	.91	.89	3.01	8	.91	1.36	4.50
Course Value	4	.89	.85	2.58	6	.90	1.15	3.62
Instructional Methods	13	.94	1.63	6.71	10	.93	1.37	5.13
Learning Atmosphere	6	.94	.87	3.56	8	.93	1.17	4.60
Total	36	.81	7.67	17.69	36	.81	7.67	17.69

a +1.00 means "all *T* (true score) and no *E* (error)." The coefficients for the original student-rating-scale subscales and the revised subscales based on the factor analysis are shown in table 8.2.

If the internal structure of the scale is partitioned into subscales, the alphas for the subscales should be higher than the alpha for the total scale. There is greater response consistency and item homogeneity within each set of subscale items than across all 36 items. In fact, the whole scale is composed of a heterogeneous mix of items measuring five somewhat different subdomains.

Notice the item distribution for the subscales in the original scale and revised scale. *The number of items and variance affect the size of alpha.* Although the numbers are different for every subscale, the alphas are almost identical. The smallest subscale has the lowest coefficient in both versions. Longer subscales with relatively higher variances (or standard deviations) usually yield higher alphas than shorter ones.

So how high is high enough for alpha? It depends on the importance or seriousness of the decisions made with the individual scores. For rating scale scores used for *summative decisions* about faculty, the coefficients should be in the .90s. The gravity of the decisions dictates the requirement for a very high degree of precision and dependability in the scores. If multiple rating scale scores are used from different measures of teaching effectiveness, the bar can be dropped only slightly to the upper .80s and above.

These guidelines for alpha apply similarly to unidimensional scales. The only difference is that the homogeneous item set is the total scale, and there is only one alpha to measure the degree of internal consistency. Only a single scale score is interpreted as an indication of teaching performance.

The coefficients in table 8.2 provide strong evidence of the internal consistency of ratings to each subscale item sample in order to generalize to the entire domain of all possible subscale items. They also attest to the effectiveness of the job content sampling and the item homogeneity of each subscale in the scale structure.

Interobserver reliability.   We also want to generalize to the entire population of potential observers, who your institution couldn't possibly afford to pay. When scales are used in the direct observation of live or videotaped teaching perform-ance, once again random error is introduced into the rating process. It may take the form of personal and professional biases, idiosyncratic or weird interpretations of behavior, uneven knowledge of course content and teaching methods, or unbridled subjectivity. A well-built peer or external expert observation scale with very specific behaviors and appropriate anchors can reduce some of the error. Training and prac-tice with the scale can also help. However, the fact remains: Human observers are fallible and inconsistent, some a lot more than others. You know who you are. Even when they're whipped into shape through formal training, it is impossible to con-trol all random fluctuations in scoring or recording observations of teaching be-haviors. *E*rror inevitably will creep into *X* and decrease the peer's *T*rue ratings.

. The reliability of observations is a function of the *consistency of independent observers' ratings of a sample of faculty.* At least two peer/outside expert observers need to rate instructors with the same scale under identical conditions. Since this is a very time-consuming process, videos of the classes can be substituted in lieu of live observations to provide flextime in conducting the ratings. At least 10 instructors should be rated by both peers/outside experts. The highly desirable sample size of 30–50 faculty that would permit an interclass (Pearson) correla-tion or more sensitive intraclass correlation would be prohibitive.

Instead, the relationship between the two peers'/experts' ratings of 10 instruc-tors can be evaluated with an *agreement index.* This less rigorous estimate can still furnish adequate evidence of interobserver agreement. Either the straightforward *percentage agreement* between the pair of subscale and total scale scores or the *kappa coefficient,* which is percentage agreement corrected for chance, is worthy of consideration (Berk, 1979b). At least 80% agreement between raters should be at-tained to claim a sufficient level of consistency and objectivity of peer ratings, re-gardless of which peer does the rating.

Standard error of measurement (SEM).   The mathematical relationship between *SEM* and reliability is

$$SEM = SD\sqrt{1 - r_{xx'}}$$

where *SD* is the *standard deviation* of the ratings (subscale or total scale). (*Confession*: Okay, you caught me. This is the only formula. It's still relatively benign, though, without any horrific Greek letters. I'm totally ashamed of myself. Sorry.)

The reliability coefficient, $r_{xx'}$, described previously, *is inversely related to SEM.* Where reliability ranges from 0 to +1.00, *SEM* ranges from 0 to *SD*. However, perfect reliability (+1.00) means zero error (0 *SEM*). This is the only condition under which the *actual rating* (*X*) equals the *true rating* (*T*). The higher the reliability, the lower the *SEM*. The worst possible case is 0 reliability, which is a *SEM* equal to the *SD*. Table 8.2 shows the magnitude of alpha coefficients and the corresponding *SEM*s compared to the *SD*s. With coefficients in the .90s, the *SEM*s for the subscales are approximately 1 score point. (*Tech Note*: Since reliability and *SEM* are related to the number of items, a longer scale [or subscale] will likely have a higher $r_{xx'}$ and lower *SEM* than a shorter scale [or subscale]).

How does any of this relate to decision making? I don't have a clue. Kidding. *SEM* provides an index to link error to an individual instructor's rating, which is usually the class mean from student ratings. You can easily compute the *95% confidence interval*, or *band of error*, around any *X* rating. Just multiply the *SEM* by 2 (or 1.96) and add *and* subtract that product from the *X* rating. For example, from the *SEM*s in table 8.2, suppose an instructor received a rating of 22/27 on the Evaluation Methods subscale. The *SEM* is 1.36.

Follow these steps:

1. $1.36 \times 2 = 2.72$
2. $22 + 2.72 = 24.72$
    $22 - 2.72 = 19.28$
3. Set up interval:

(lower limit) 19.28 ——————— 22 ——————— 24.72 (upper limit)

This is a nearly 6-point band of error around 22. It can be interpreted this way: 95 times out of a 100 that instructor's true rating (*T*) will fall within that band. Only 5% of the time will *T* fall outside.

This approach to score interpretation takes into account the random error associated with any *X* score. *The higher the reliability, the smaller the SEM, and the narrower the band* (if *SD* is unchanged). With perfect reliability and no error, there is no band. The *X* rating of 22 would equal the *T* rating. In reality, however, there will always be error. Hypothetically, even if the alpha for the Evaluation Methods subscale had been .99, the *SEM* would be .45, which translates into a less than a 2-point band of error around 22. Compare the following hypothetical band, with nearly perfect reliability, to the previous real band:

(lower limit) 21.12 ——— 22 ——— 22.88 (upper limit)

There is still error. The only way to reach no-band land is with an alpha of 1.0.

When making decisions about contract renewal or merit pay based on teaching performance, the highest level of accuracy of student ratings or any other ratings is critical. Considering the fallibility of the ratings in the context of these bands of error will hopefully provide more informed and fair judgments about teaching effectiveness to decide on merit pay or other consequential issues. (For details on how to use this approach to interpret the scores from multiple sources, see the "Summative Decisions" section at the end of chapter 9.)

Other reliability evidence.   The foregoing description of reliability methods was, admittedly, limited in scope. The coverage assumed you were developing, refining, and/or analyzing scales in your institution. A typical textbook treatment would also include *test-retest reliability.* Researchers (Murray, Rushton, & Paunonen, 1990) and professional publishers of rating scales have conducted retest studies with student rating scales and found coefficients in the .80s. However, the use of rating scales in your institution for employment decisions rarely allows repeated administrations to students, graduates, alumni, peers, employers, and faculty. In fact, the time of administration for most of the scales determines the meaningfulness of the ratings (see chapter 6). They are time sensitive: on a specific class topic or administered midcourse, end of course, end of program, and 1 to 5 years after graduation. The effort to conduct a test-retest study to estimate the consistency, or stability, of ratings over time may not be justified. It will depend on available resources.

Another omission was *parallel forms reliability.* The job content domain tapped by the various rating scales you construct often precludes the development of parallel or alternate forms of each scale. The specificity of teaching characteristics and behaviors measured by the different scales may not permit a large enough pool of "equivalent" characteristics in the domain to generate parallel forms. Further, there is also the question of the need for such forms in the context of your assessment of teaching effectiveness. Rarely are parallel versions of rating scales required. Typically, administrators and faculty leaders are ecstatic if the faculty approve a single student or peer scale. Don't push it. A revolution could be right around the corner. And then we're back in the '60s again with protests and *The Brady Bunch.* I know you don't want that to happen.

Epilogue

This chapter has been all about collecting a body of evidence to be able to convince a jury of our peers (or external experts) that it is okay for a dean or faculty committee to use the scores on student, peer, and self rating scales to promote or to croak several nontenured faculty. At least the quality of the scales can be high.

Before I continue, listen up. This paragraph is reaaally important. It must be if I used three *a*'s. In fact, put your ear right here ⟶ . Terrific. Since most of this chapter was devoted to validity, just how important do you think this topic is? Take a wild guess. Hmmm. Suppose you wrote items that were *not* related to the teaching knowledge, skills, and abilities (KSAs) of a college professor, yet they were intended to be used to measure teaching effectiveness. Why would I use those items? It makes no sense to use a scale that doesn't measure what it was intended to measure. Would a high reliability coefficient (alpha = .93) bail you out? Nope, because this tells me the scale is simply measuring the wrong content with a high degree of consistency.

☞ BOTTOM LINE

Validity evidence of the link between the scale items and job content domain is more important than any other evidence.

By now you know that when you see a finger, I mean business. If that validity evidence isn't gathered, nothing else really matters. Just pack up your computer and go to a flick or Broadway show. Even a .99 alpha coefficient can't save the scale. Now you can remove your ear. EEEW! (*Note:* This sound effect isn't important because it's only uppercase; no finger in sight.) What is that sticky residue on my paragraph? I can't believe that you actually did that.

All of the sources of validity evidence described previously for the intended interpretations of rating scale scores used to measure teaching effectiveness are required according to the *Standards*. In fact, *the reliability coefficients and standard error of measurement are also subsumed under this validity evidence.* Further, previous research on the scale and evidence gathered from new studies are included.

So, how does the student rating scale evidence presented in chapters 7 and 8 satisfy the *Standards*? Is the evidence adequate to support the uses of the scores for formative and summative decisions? Let's consider what evidence was collected from among the six sources:

1. *Job content domain*—Content review completed
2. *Response processes*—No studies conducted
3. *Internal scale structure*—Comprehensive item analyses completed, including

    - item means, standard deviations, anchor distribution
    - interitem correlations (.57–.81)
    - item-subscale correlations (.44–.87)
    - factor analysis with 5-factor solution for subscales

4. *Other measures of teaching effectiveness*—No studies conducted
5. *Consequences of ratings*—No studies conducted
6. *Reliability*—Estimates of internal consistency reliability and *SEM* (alphas = .87–.93)

Obviously, studies need to be designed and executed to obtain evidence of response processes and the consequences of the ratings. If other measures are used, convergent and discriminant validity studies also need to be completed. For the rating scale by itself, the evidence seems very strong to justify the use of its item, subscale, and total scores for the intended decisions.

9

REPORTING AND INTERPRETING SCALE RESULTS

Coup de Grâce

Are you overjoyed to know this is the last chapter, the finale, the coda? Me, too. The preceding eight chapters should have helped you to generate several scales to measure teaching effectiveness or whatever you decided to measure. After all of the field testing and analyses, I heard that you took an Alaskan cruise and almost served yourself as lunch for a grizzly in Denali Park (also known to most tourists as the "Grand Canyon"). I warned you. Instead, you should have actually administered the scales using the paper-based or online procedures described in chapter 6. The final stage is tabulating the results and assembling them into appropriate report formats so that the decision makers can work their magic. Those decision makers are the instructor and the administrator who evaluates that instructor. According to my calculations, rounding to eight decimal places, and by the process of elimination, one of those is YOU. Don't mess with me; I have a cordless mouse, and I know how to use it. There are a variety of scale reports that can be produced with a few examples in appendix C. This chapter will cover the following remaining topics: (1) generic levels of score reporting, (2) criterion-referenced versus norm-referenced score interpretations, and (3) formative, summative, and program decisions.

 BERK'S NOTES

Faculty—If you need to interpret the scores from any rating scale for *teaching improvement*, focus on the generic levels, the subsection on formative decisions, and appendix C. If you are involved in designing report formats, you'll have to knuckle down and suck in all 450 KB of this chapter (which, in computer storage jargon, is the abbreviation for "Metric Tons"). To negotiate the rating scale results used to evaluate your annual teaching performance and portfolio for promotion review, concentrate on the subsection on summative decisions. Don't miss the final conclusions. They will be unforgettable, maybe.

Administrators—If you have to allocate resources for generating rating scale reports, examine all of the formats and examples, including those in appendix C. If you review faculty for contract renewal, merit pay, or recommendations for promotion, or you just like to say, "You're fired!" like The Donald (Trump), read (a) the generic levels, especially related to norms, (b) the norm-referenced versus criterion-referenced interpretations, and (c) the subsection on summative decisions. If you coordinate or are intimately involved in the preparation of accreditation documents, check out the last subsection on program decisions. The conclusions present a final challenge. See you at the end.

Generic Levels of Score Reporting

Although the Likert-type graphic rating scale was designed to produce a "summative score" across all items, there are several levels of score reporting other than the total scale score that can provide useful information. In fact, there are six possible levels of score interpretation: (1) item anchor, (2) item, (3) subscale, (4) total scale, (5) department/program norms, and (6) subject matter/program-level state, regional, and national norms. These are generic levels applicable to most of the rating scales identified in chapter 1 (see also table 1.1). These levels furnish the summary information bites (*Note to Editor:* Or is it "bytes"?) for the decisions that follow. (*Note to Author:* "You're driving me nuts! I don't care. Nobody will read this far into the book, anyway.")

Item Anchor

The first level of score reporting is to calculate the percentage of respondents picking each anchor, item by item. An example is shown below for student rating scale items with *agree–disagree* anchors:

	SD	D	A	SA	N
Statement 1	1.0%	3.1%	37.5%	58.6%	96
Statement 2	1.0	3.1	24.0	71.9	96
Statement 3	1.1	1.1	28.9	68.9	90

These results can be reported for any word, phrase, or statement stimuli and any response anchors. The anchor abbreviations for "Strongly Disagree" (*SD*), "Disagree" (*D*), "Agree" (*A*), and "Strongly Agree" (*SA*) are listed horizontally, left to right, from unfavorable to favorable ratings. This is the same order as the original scale. The *N* is the number of students that responded to the statement.

The percentages for the four anchors indicate the percentage distribution based on the actual *N*. An instructor would expect low percentages for the first two "Disagree" anchors and high percentages for the second two "Agree" anchors, with the highest for *SA*. The percentages taper off drastically from right to left, with tiny percentages for *D* and *SD* for all three items. (*Note*: The percentages are slightly different for statement 3 compared to statements 1 and 2, particularly the 1.1% to *SD* and *D*. This was due, in part, to the six fewer students who responded to that item [*N* = 90].) This overall response pattern indicates a *negatively skewed* distribution of responses, which is the most common outcome. It occurs when the majority of the responses are *A* and *SA*, but there is also a sprinkling of a few *D*s and *SD*s. The extreme *SD* responses, or *outliers*, create the skew. Realistically, a few students might mark *SD* to every statement to express their desire to see the instructor whacked, while the majority of satisfied customers will choose the two "Agree" anchors.

This information provides the instructor with the *most detailed profile of responses to a single item*. The percentages reveal the degrees of agreement and disagreement with each statement. It is diagnostic of how the class felt about each behavior or characteristic. The instructor can then consider specific changes in teaching, evaluation, or course behaviors to shift the distribution farther to the right, in the *A–SA* zone, the next time the class is taught.

Item

The next level is to calculate a summary statistic for each item. As mentioned previously, most anchor distributions are usually negatively skewed. Since the anchors represent a qualitative continuum that has order, such as high to low or favorable to unfavorable, they comprise a ranked, or *ordinal*, scale. Based on the skewness of the distribution and the ordinality of the scale, the *median is the most appropriate measure of central tendency*. It is not sensitive to the extreme scores or anything else in the world and, therefore, is more accurate than the simple mean, which is biased because it is pulled toward those scores. However, given the range of distribution possibilities in practice, it is recommended that both measures of central tendency be reported.

Qualitative to quantitative scale. Now that we've decided *what* to compute (*mean/median*), we need to decide *how* to compute those indices. The anchors as they appear on the scale are verbal, albeit qualitative, not numerical. Numbers have to be assigned to the anchor options. The qualitative scale has to be transformed into a quantitative one for the purpose of analysis. Equally spaced anchors with 1-point increments are supported by research on how raters actually rank different sets of anchors. Spector (1976) calculated psychological scale values for *intensity* (agreement), *evaluation*, and *frequency* anchor scales. Students' ranks of 4- and 5-point scales resulted in approximately equidistant anchors for all three types of scales. So the assignment of 1-point differences between anchor choices is not as arbitrary as it first appears.

Further, for simplicity and interpretability, *a zero-based scale is recommended*, so that the most negative anchor would be coded as "0." This was originally recommended by Likert (1932). Then the other anchors would be coded in 1-point increments above 0. An example of this coding for a 4-point, *agree–disagree* scale is shown here:

SD	D	A	SA
0	1	2	3

Scoring a blank (no response).   Are we ready to compute means/medians for the items using the 0–3 scale? Not just yet. Hold on to your keyboard. What do you do when a student leaves an item blank? Hmmm (these letters stand for "Sport Utility Vehicle"). The blank is different from "Not Applicable" (*NA*) and "Not Observed" (*NO*), defined in chapter 5. When students or other raters leave a blankorino, it's not because the statement is *NA* or *NO*. It's for some other reason, which I hope I can remember by the time I get to the next paragraph. In the previous anchor distributions, six students didn't answer statement 3. Item statistics have to be based on the same *N* in order to compare results from item to item. Otherwise, the mean/median would be calculated on different students for each item, depending on the number of blanks. Usually, there may be only a few blanks on certain items, but it's best to standardize the *N* for all analyses.

If a student skips an item, we don't know why. It could be because she wanted to think about the answer a little longer and forgot to go back and answer it, or he was distracted by the tornado outside and just proceeded to the next item, or she experienced an attack of the heebie-jeebies. There are numerous "imputation" rules for dealing with missing data on scales (Allison, 2000, 2001; Roth, 1994; Roth, Switzer, & Switzer, 1999; Rubin, 2004). There are at least eight statistical methods described in these sources, ranging from simple listwise or casewise deletion of students to rather complex techniques I can't even pronounce.

Since maximizing the student response rate for every course, especially small ones, is super important, a rule has to be chosen. Deletion of missing responses, either listwise or casewise, will reduce the response rate. Bad decision! Try again. The simplest strategy that will unalter the response rate is to *assign the midpoint quantitative value to the missing response.* Yup, that's what I said. "How do you do that?" Before any analysis is conducted or scores computed, make the following adjustments. For an *odd-numbered scale* containing a midpoint anchor, just assign a 2 on a 5-point scale (0–4) or 3 on a 7-point scale (0–6). For an *even-numbered scale* without a midpoint anchor, a blank is assigned a 1.5 on a 4-point scale (0–3) or 2.5 on a 6-point scale (0–5). Once the blanks have been converted to these midpoint values, the item scores can be calculated.

This strategy *assumes the respondent had no opinion on the behavior being rated or couldn't make a choice* on the item and, therefore, left it blank. This is a reasonable assumption for the few cases that may occur. If blanks appear with regularity on specific items, it's possible those items may be *NA* or *NO* (see question 6, chapter 5). Those items should be examined carefully to assure that all respondents can answer the items. If not, then they may need to be revised (the items, not the respondents).

Item statistics.   Following my own advice above for the preceding 4-point (0–3) *agree–disagree* scale, a 1.5 will be substituted for each blank. The statistics can be computed and added to the anchor results already presented:

	SD	D	A	SA	N	Mean	Median
Statement 1	1.0%	3.1%	37.5%	58.6%	96	2.52	3.00
Statement 2	1.0	3.1	24.0	71.9	96	2.65	3.00
Statement 3	1.1	1.1	28.9	68.9	90	2.57	3.00

As mentioned previously, when the anchor distribution is negatively skewed, the mean will always be lower than the median, as it is for all three items here, because it is being drawn toward the few extremely low ratings. (*Statisticians' Concern*: For as long as statisticians can remember, the mean has always had an attraction for extreme scores. Granted, this affinity for outliers is not normal. However, statisticians have tolerated this abnormal relationship for years, but also felt compelled to create another index that is not so easily swayed: the median. You may now resume this paragraph already in progress.) Depending on the degree of skew, the bias in interpreting the mean can be significant or insignificant.

The problem is that the *mean misrepresents the actual ratings* in a negatively skewed distribution by portraying lower class ratings than actually occurred. This bias *makes the instructor appear worse* in teaching effectiveness, on all of the items, than the ratings indicate. Although means are reported on most commercially published scales, it is strongly recommended that medians be reported as well. Although the median is less discriminating as an index, it is more accurate, more representative, and less biased than the mean under this distribution condition. The lower the degree of skew, the more similar both measures will be. In a perfectly normal distribution, the mean and median are identical. However, ratings of faculty, administrators, courses, and programs are typically skewed.

Since all of the item means/medians are based on the total *N* for the class, they can be compared. They display a profile of strengths and weaknesses related to the different teaching behaviors and course characteristics. On a 0–3 scale, *means/medians above 1.5 indicate strengths; those below 1.5 denote weaknesses.* The means/medians in conjunction with the anchor percentages provide meaningful diagnostic information on areas that might need attention. Again, this report is intended for the instructor's use primarily, although the results on course characteristics may have curricular implications.

Subscale

This is the first level at which item scores can be summed. If the items on the total scale are grouped into clusters related to topics such as instructional methods, evaluation methods, and course content, the item scores can be summed to produce subscale scores. *These scores should only be used for decision making if adequate validity and reliability evidence support that internal scale structure* (Standards 1.12 and 2.7). Since each subscale contains a different number of items, the score range will also be different. This range must be reported to interpret the results.

The summary of subscale score results is derived from the item score results. The statistics are the same. We are just aggregating the item-level data (0–3) into subscale item clusters. For example, here are results for three selected subscales.

INSTRUCTIONAL METHODS (IM)
Subscale score range = 0–39; Midpoint = 19.5
Mean/Median = 34.79/37.00, where *N* = 97

EVALUATION METHODS (EM)
Subscale score range = 0–15; Midpoint = 7.5
Mean/Median = 13.40/15.00, where *N* = 97

COURSE CONTENT (CC)
Subscale score range = 0–24; Midpoint = 12
Mean/Median = 21.97/24.00, where *N* = 97

The interpretation of subscale results is analogous to the item results; only the numbers are bigger. For example, instead of a 0–3 range and a midpoint of 1.5 for an item, each subscale has a range and midpoint based on its respective number of items. So, for the Instructional Methods (IM) subscale with 13 items, a "0" (*SD*) response to every item produces a sum of 0 for the subscale, and a "3" (*SA*) response to all 13 items yields a sum of 39.

The *zero-base* for all score interpretations is easy to remember: *the worst, most unfavorable rating on any item, subscale, or total scale is "0."* What changes is the upper score limit for the most favorable rating on each subscale because the number of items change. Again, for the IM subscale, the mean and median can be referenced to the upper limit of 39 and also the midpoint of 19.5 to locate the position on the continuum, as indicated below:

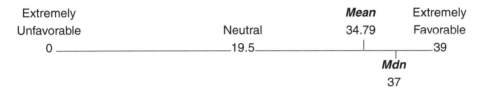

Extremely			**Mean**	Extremely
Unfavorable		Neutral	34.79	Favorable
0 —————————————————————————19.5—————————————— | ————₮————39
			Mdn
			37

The mean/median ratings on the IM subscale are very favorable.

The *subscale results can pinpoint areas of strength and weakness*, but not direct an instructor toward particular aspects of teaching that can be improved or changed. The item and anchor results are intended to provide that detailed level of direction.

Total Scale

The highest level of score summary is the total scale score across all items. If the scale consists of 36 items, each scored 0–3, the following results might be reported:

Total scale score range = 0–108; Midpoint = 54
Mean/Median = 96.43/101, where *N* = 97

The continuum for interpretation would be the following:

Extremely			**Mean**	Extremely
Unfavorable		Neutral	96.43	Favorable
0—————————————————————————— 54 —————————————— | ————₮————108
			Mdn
			101

This score gives a global, or composite, rating that is only as high as the ratings in each of its component parts (anchors, items, and subscales). It represents one *overall index of teaching performance*—in this example, a very high one. However, it is usually a little less reliable and less informative than the subscale scores.

A comparison of the quantitative scales at the previous three levels for a total scale is shown here:

Score Level	Extremely Unfavorable	Neutral	Extremely Favorable
Item	0 _____1_____	1.5 _____2_____	3
Subscale 1 (8 items)	0 _____	12.0 _____	24
Subscale 2 (5 items)	0 _____	7.5 _____	15
Subscale 3 (4 items)	0 _____	6.0 _____	12
Subscale 4 (13 items)	0 _____	19.5 _____	39
Subscale 5 (6 items)	0 _____	9.0 _____	18
Total Scale (36 items)	0 _____	54.0 _____	108

These levels of score reporting and interpretation are based on a single course. This information has the greatest value to the course instructor, the administrator evaluating that instructor, and the curriculum committee evaluating the course. The next two levels aggregate course results at the department/program level and regional and national levels.

Department/Program Norms

The rating scale scores used to evaluate an instructor and course can also be combined with those of other instructors and courses within a single department, such as economics, philosophy, or history, or program level, such as undergraduate, master's, or doctoral. Any combination of courses can be created for program decisions. This combination is referred to as a *norm group*. It represents another aggregate level of performance. The item, subscale, and total scale score ranges, continua, and interpretation remain the same. This time the mean and median for each of those levels are computed for a pre-specified group of courses rather than just one course. Those indices are also computed from course means and medians weighted by the respective class sizes. There are three applications of these norm group ratings: (1) instructor/course evaluation, (2) snapshot program evaluation, and (3) longitudinal program evaluation.

Instructor/course evaluation.   Department or program rating norms can serve as a performance standard against which individual instructor or course ratings can be compared. For example, an instructor's mean and median ratings from an undergraduate economics course can be referenced to the mean and median ratings of all other instructors of undergraduate economics courses. Each norm grouping of courses that is constituted for that type of comparison should provide a meaningful and valid reference group. For a stupid example, suppose a norm group were created based on the ratings from herpetology courses, and your rating as a philosophy instructor were compared to that norm. NOT FAIR!! From everything you've learned in this paragraph, you know that's not a good idea because students like snakes better than Nietzsche, and you might not fare so well. But seriously, whoever would recommend such a comparison probably has a frontal lobe the size and content of a Milk Dud®. Suggest a lobotomy. Frequently, subject-matter discipline and program-level (undergraduate, master's, and doctoral) norms furnish the fairest course normative comparisons.

Snapshot program evaluation.   Department or program-level norm ratings can also be compared annually to provide a snapshot evaluation of one point in time in teaching and course effectiveness. Although somewhat politically volatile, such comparisons may be very revealing. Before releasing those ratings, consider the consequences in your institutional climate. Be careful. You don't want to stimulate bad-natured competition. Despite the legitimacy and value of those ratings, they can create sanguinary feelings among faculty, discourage others, and possibly undo what progress you've achieved in teaching excellence.

Longitudinal program evaluation.   Norm group ratings can also be used to set a baseline teaching performance against which future ratings can be compared longitudinally for semester, annual, and multiyear evaluations. A trend analysis can provide evidence of teaching and course improvements or decrements over time. The caveat above applies here as well. This evidence may be reported in accreditation documents.

Subject Matter/Program-Level State, Regional, and National Norms

It is also possible to create norm groups outside of your institution. For example, a few of the commercially published scales provide national norms by subject matter and program level. The instructor/course ratings at your home institution can be compared to the ratings of similar courses nationwide. This assumes the same scale was administered to all students in those courses at different institutions.

Although a locally developed scale cannot be referenced to national norms, regional norms may be feasible. If the same rating scale is used at several state-sponsored colleges or universities, statewide norms can be generated by subject and program level. Alternatively, private institutions that are members of a consortium of schools in the same region may agree upon a common scale that can be administered to compute regional norms.

Essentially, any norm sample can be composed from any combination of courses, departments, schools, colleges, universities, businesses, conglomerates, cartels, countries, continents, and constellations to provide a norm-referenced interpretation of any single rating. There are international norms for comparing the performance of students on math achievement across different countries. Why not teaching performance? I'm not even going to go there. All comparisons should be fair and appropriate in evaluating one instructor, course, or school against a norm group. In other words, crocodiles should be compared to a norm pond full of Steve "Croc Crazy Guy" Irwin and his staff, not penguins. Course subject matter and/or program level should be matched with the norm characteristics as closely as possible to ensure valid and meaningful interpretations.

Criterion-Referenced versus Norm-Referenced Score Interpretations

The preceding levels of score reporting indicated a variety of *reference points* for interpreting scores. In fact, a single rating at any level has no intrinsic meaning by itself; it's just a number. A number of "2" or "14" has to be referenced to something to have meaning. It can be referenced to the job content domain, possible score range (item, subscale, or scale), a standard (cutoff score) in that range, and/or norm group performance in that range (Berk, 1984). The issue of what this reference point should be to assess teaching effectiveness has been debated in the literature (Abrami, 1993, 2001; Aleamoni, 1996; Cashin, 1992, 1994, 1996; Hativa, 1993; McKeachie, 1996; Theall, 1996). Let's examine each of these reference points.

Score Range

In order to infer high or low performance, a score must be located on its respective score range. A score of "2" on a 0–3 score range is high. Given that the anchors are bipolar, the scores can be assigned positive and negative letter grades as follows:

Anchor	Score	Grade
Strongly Agree	3.0	A
Agree	2.0	B
Midpoint	1.5	C
Disagree	1.0	D
Strongly Disagree	0.0	F

Interpreting a single score against the score or grade range provides perspective for evaluating high or low performance. A similar interpretation can be extended to the subscale and scale levels. Instead of *agree–disagree* anchors, *favorable–unfavorable* anchors are used, such as "Extremely Favorable" (*EF*), "Favorable" (*F*), "Unfavorable" (*U*), and "Extremely Unfavorable" (*EU*). A comparison of item, subscale, and scale score values with anchors and grades is illustrated in the following table.

Score Level	SD	D	Mdpt.	A	SA
Item	0.00	1.00	1.50	2.00	3.00
Subscale	EU	U	Mdpt.	F	EF
1	0.00	6.00	12.00	18.00	24.00
2	0.00	3.75	7.50	11.25	15.00
3	0.00	3.00	6.00	9.00	12.00
4	0.00	9.75	19.50	29.25	39.00
5	0.00	4.50	9.00	13.50	18.00
Total	0.00	27.00	54.00	81.00	108.00
Grade	F	D	C	B	A

Any rating at any score level above can be located on its respective anchor and quantitative score range to interpret performance. The five reference points on all of the scales have the same meaning. For example, an item score of "1" is comparable to a subscale 4 score of "9.75" and total score of "27," as well as a grade of *D*.

The equivalence across score levels is like interpreting currency in different countries. For example, a denomination scale can be created based on U.S. dollars for $100, $150, $200, and $300 and their equivalents in British pounds, Swedish kronas, Russian rubles, Israeli shekels, Czech korunas, and Japanese hondas. Once converted, all currency will have the same meaning at any point on the respective scale. By the way, when you're broke, it doesn't matter what country you're visiting. Zero money is absolute; it means the same thing anywhere in the universe.

Criterion-Referenced Interpretations

Once the score ranges have been determined, one can set a standard, criterion, or benchmark for performance on the scale. For example, all faculty should attain a "Favorable," or *B*, rating or above on all subscales in their courses. This criterion may define teaching effectiveness for the course. It may be linked to merit pay increases or promotion as an incentive to improve the quality of teaching.

Despite its intuitive appeal, standard setting in this rating scale application can be arbitrary. How do you pick the standard? It seems simple enough. Just look at the score range and choose a point. However, this *cardiac approach to standard setting* (I know in my heart that a total scale score of 75/108 indicates effective teaching) is not acceptable. For an administrator to set a standard this way is arbitrary and capricious.

What is a reasonable approach? Assemble a faculty committee to systematically consider cutoff scores on the various subscales. There are more than 50 judgmental procedures this committee could follow to arrive at realistic, defensible standards for teaching performance (see Berk, 1986a, 1996; Cizek, 2001; Jaeger, 1989). Such methods are essential if high-stakes summative decisions by administrators will be made about faculty based on those standards (Standards 4.20 and 4.21). However, student ratings alone should not be used for merit pay and promotion decisions. Other indicators of performance from multiple sources of evidence should be taken into account (Standard 14.13). Strategies for combining those sources for summative decisions are suggested in the next section.

Criterion-referenced interpretation of rating scale scores can be meaningful for administrative decisions about teaching performance and curriculum committee decisions of course effectiveness. However, the validity and fairness of those decisions hinge on the method used to select the criteria and the supplemental evidence beyond those scores that is considered to make the individual or course decisions. Caution should be observed in executing the process to arrive at criterion-referenced interpretations to ensure they are fair and equitable in the context to which they are applied.

Norm-Referenced Interpretations

The norm groups described in the previous sections can be employed in the interpretation of rating scale item, subscale, and total scale scores. Normative comparisons may be of interest to individual faculty, curriculum committees, and administrators at different levels of academia. A norm provides two key pieces of information: (1) a summary of teaching and course ratings at the department level or above or baccalaureate, master's, or doctoral level and (2) the relative position of any instructor, course, or aggregate ratings in relation to a norm.

Summary ratings.   Summary ratings furnish evidence of overall teaching, course, and program effectiveness. These ratings can also be referenced to other norms, such as department performance against a school or college-level norm, or institutional comparisons to a consortium or regional norm. Such interpretations indicate whether the base norm is above or below the reference norm and to what degree.

Instructor/course comparisons. The most basic levels of norm-referenced rating scale interpretation are the item, subscale, and total scale scores. The norms are reported as mean and median ratings. An example for a hypothetical department norm tacked on to the rating results presented previously is displayed here:

	SD	D	A	SA	N	Mean	Median	DEPT. NORM Mean	Median
Statement 1	1.0%	3.1%	37.5%	58.6%	96	2.52	3.00	2.44	3.00
Statement 2	1.0	3.1	24.0	71.9	96	2.65	3.00	2.41	2.00
Statement 3	1.1	1.1	28.9	68.9	90	2.57	3.00	2.39	2.00

Subscale score range = 0–24; Midpoint = 12
Instructor Mean/Median = 21.97/24.00, where N = 97
Department-Norm Mean/Median = 20.01/21.00, where N = 451
Total scale score range = 0–108; Midpoint = 54
Instructor Mean/Median = 96.43/101.00, where N = 97
Department-Norm Mean/Median = 89.51/92.00, where N = 451

The mean and median at every score level can be compared to the norm. These comparisons provide perspective and directions for identifying strengths and weaknesses, particularly at the item and subscale levels. This information can be of value to the individual instructor, administrators, and curriculum committees.

Formative, Summative, and Program Decisions

After considering alternative report formats for scale results and various interpretations, there is only one topic remaining to give closure to this book: Muppets! Everybody loves the Muppets. The issue is this: Do the human hands wear Kermit, Cookie, Elmo, Howdy Doody, and the other Muppets when they rehearse? Or is the rehearsal just a bunch of naked hands talking, singing, and dancing with each other? But seriously, back in rating world, how do we tie all of this together for the decisions about job performance that need to be made? Once you use the scores from rating scales for specific decisions, *timing of feedback* becomes critical. Two rules of thumb should guide the distribution of results to interested parties:

Rule 1. If an instructor doesn't receive rating reports in time to make changes before the following semester, it is unlikely an improvement in teaching will occur; and

Rule 2. If reports from one or more sources of evidence are late or unavailable for summative or program decisions, it is likely those decisions will be made by administrators anyway.

The execution of these decisions based on the 13 sources of evidence described in chapter 1 is presented next.

Formative Decisions

The entire focus of these decisions is on the *diagnosis of specific strengths and weaknesses to improve the quality of teaching.* These decisions may be made by the instructor alone or with the guidance of a trusted colleague or mentor. Most of the information gathered is analyzed confidentially.

Timely, accurate, and relevant *feedback* of the results from the different rating scales can be used for teaching improvement. The value of feedback was central to the success of the 360° multisource assessment in the various applications described in chapter 1. Even better, *consultative feedback* can lead to greater changes in teaching effectiveness (Marincovich, 1999; Penny & Coe, 2004). Consultants may be faculty developers, peers (trained or untrained), or graduate students. The instructor–consultant interaction based on the rating scale scores (student, peer, self, video, etc.) may involve just a brief meeting (Aleamoni, 1978) or extended consultations (Erickson & Erickson, 1979). The multiple sources of evidence provide a more reliable and accurate picture from which the instructor and consultant can identify the teaching problems, design improvement strategies, and determine follow-up steps to improve teaching (Brinko, 1997). In sum, consultative feedback is "a structured, collaborative, problem-solving process that uses information about teaching performance as a basis for discussion about improving teaching practice" (Penny & Coe, 2004, p. 221). In other words, don't do this alone. The full benefits of diagnostic feedback can be realized only with the input of a knowledgeable and wise "consultant."

From among the 13 original colonies—I mean sources of evidence for teaching effectiveness—I have extracted those with the greatest potential for providing diagnostic information. They were previously identified at the end of chapter 1. The sources include (1) student ratings, (2) peer/external expert ratings, (3) self-ratings, (4) videos, (5) student interviews, and (6) exit and alumni ratings. Strategies for using these sources for formative decisions are presented next.

Student ratings.   These ratings are essential. However, although the "student rating scale" is typically administered during the week before finals, shorter versions of that scale can be administered at the midterm or at other key points during the semester. Why wait to get creamed at the end of the term? Get creamed earlier. Further, the diagnostic information given on the final scale will not help you improve during the course. It's only applicable to future courses you teach.

After the first exam or midterm in your course, say to your students:

> Since I have just evaluated your achievement up to this point, and you can now make whatever midterm (or quarter-term) adjustments are necessary to do your best on the next exam, I think I need to do the same. This is similar to trailing by 14 points in a football game at halftime (or end of the first quarter). The coach has to make adjustments if he expects to win the game.
>
>   Well, I need to do what you're doing right now. I have distributed a blank piece of paper or index card (or short rating scale) to everyone. Don't put your name on it. This is anonymous. I would like you to evaluate me. Focus just on my teaching. On the top half of the page, write "Teaching Strengths." Under that heading, write down what I am doing well so far in terms of my specific teaching methods. On the bottom half, write "Areas for Improvement." List those teaching behaviors I need to change or improve to better meet your needs so you can do even better on the next exam. Giving you the answers in advance doesn't count.

I have used this strategy in all of my courses over the past 10 years. The feedback I receive allows me to make adjustments so the students can benefit during the remainder of each course. All of the "Improvement" comments are compiled into a list of the "Top 20 (or whatever number) Areas for Ron's Improvement." This list is presented to the class (following the evaluation), and I address every "area" in one of three ways: (1) I will try really, really, really hard to make that change; (2) I really can't change that until the next semester; or (3) I explain the reason for the problem or indicate I'm not really sure how to fix it. This presentation exposes my weaknesses before the entire class. It builds credibility, trust, and accountability in my teaching. I now have half a semester to improve my teaching in the weak areas. If I don't, they will be reflected in my end-of-course ratings. Without baring my teaching soul to my students, there's no accountability. I have openly committed to my willingness to be a better teacher, and they can hold me accountable. That's why Weight Watchers® is still so successful. Although that weigh-in is a killer. It's about accountability. This strategy is an alternative to the interview procedures described in chapter 1 and again four paragraph heads from here.

INFORMATION NEEDED.   On the rating scale report, there should be at least a 66% response rate, and preferably 80–90%. Anything lower will be unrepresentative of the class and biased ratings. The most valuable information on the structured section is *item means/medians* and *anchor percentages,* although the subscale scores provide an overall profile of strengths and weaknesses.

If the highest median on an item is 3 and you have a 2 or 1, look at the *SD* and *D* anchor percentages to determine what contributed to that median. If only one or two students picked a "Disagree" anchor, don't worry, be happy! Don't obsess over those few. If 10% or more pick either *SD* or *D*, boy, are you in trouble. That may be cause for concern. Remember, the mean will always be less than the median because of the skew toward the *SD* scores.

Analyze the results item by item and anchor by anchor to pinpoint those specific behaviors that need to be changed. Keep in mind that, in general, students give higher ratings to elective courses, higher-level courses, and courses in the humanities; the lowest ratings are reserved for required, lower-level survey courses and quantitative courses in math and statistics. Do your courses fall into any of these categories? I've been in the triple-threat lowest rating categories for the last 20 of my 30 years of teaching. My experiences in that unenviable "slot" can explain the reasons for my uses of humor and the need for the material in this book.

Beyond the quantitative results, a *summary list of all of the comments,* grouped by each unstructured question, can be extremely useful in explaining the low rating to any item and also giving suggestions on what needs to be changed. The voluminous amount of open-ended comments that accompany online administration, compared to paper-based, can point you toward exactly what needs to be done to improve your teaching. Bouncing these suggestions off of a colleague, mentor, or consultant may generate additional insights.

INFORMATION TIMING.   You will benefit from the above ratings feedback only when it is received in a timely manner, *within a week or two after final exams and grades.* Online administration can facilitate this quick turnaround. The week or two after finals is the narrow motivational window within which instructors want the feedback and are charged up enough to make the adjustments in course materials and their teaching before the next semester begins. If feedback is not received for a month or, in some cases, for several years, the motivation is shot for many faculty, and few or no changes will be made.

Peer/external expert ratings.   These ratings may take two forms: direct classroom observation of teaching behaviors and/or review of teaching materials. They may be conducted by a peer or outside expert.

INFORMATION NEEDED.   The ratings report is the actual completed scale with the checked *anchor choices* and *related comments* for all items and summary comments at the end. An additional written report may also be prepared by the observer.

INFORMATION TIMING.   *Immediately following the observation* there should be a 5-minute touch-base session. DeZure (1999) recommends this for three reasons: (1) for clarification of anything that occurred in class, (2) to ask the instructor if that class was "typical," and (3) to thank the instructor and offer some word of support like "milquetoast," "imperious," or "no wonder . . . ," but not formal feedback yet. If this meeting doesn't occur, the instructor may have to wait a week or two before hearing anything and will probably go berserk or ingest several boxes of breath mints (which have been shown in clinical trials to be as effective as Prozac®).The meeting gives temporary closure and reduces anxiety .5–1.0 notch.

Another meeting should be scheduled *a week later.* This post-observation session is intended to furnish the instructor with comprehensive feedback on his or her teaching performance, all in confidence. The instructor should receive the completed rating scale at least a day before. The colleague or expert should be very constructive about all feedback to direct attention to specific classroom behaviors on the scale and how they can be changed. The strengths and weaknesses should be presented in a balanced, tactful manner, being sensitive to the responses of the instructor. If there is more than one observer of the same class or two or three classes observed, the meeting may be organized differently to combine or average ratings and summarize comments to get to the primary behaviors that need to be addressed.

The above meeting is usually the end of the process. However, some institutions require another written report *within a few weeks of the meeting* to incorporate the instructor's reactions to the feedback. This approach fosters a more collaborative, collegial model to classroom observation. Sometimes two reports are prepared—one for formative and a second for summative purposes. The number of institutions using peer observation results for summative decisions is on the rise.

Self-ratings.   This may be a simple, reflective account of one's own teaching using the student or peer rating scale or a complex analysis involving a different scale, video results, or a teaching portfolio. The deliberate activity of just rating your own teaching performance on the student and/or peer scale raises your sensitivity to details of your teaching to which you may not have given much thought. Comparing your responses to those of your students, a peer, or an outside expert can identify teaching behaviors that need attention.

INFORMATION NEEDED.   First, the reports of your students' ratings and peer rating results will provide the benchmark comparisons for your self-ratings. Analyze item by item the *item anchor percentages* of your students against *your anchor choices* and *your perceived anchor choices* of how your students would rate the items. Flag items for which there is a discrepancy between the majority percentage anchor and the anchor you chose. Those behaviors warrant consideration. Second, if peer/external expert ratings are available, you can perform the same discrepancy analysis between the peer's anchor choice and your anchor choice for each item. Flag items with any anchor discrepancy, especially those where your anchor is positive and the peer's is negative.

INFORMATION TIMING.   Self-ratings should be completed *at the same time the student and peer ratings are completed.* This standardizes the administration times and meaning of the ratings being compared.

Videos.   This may be your only opportunity to appear on TV. And you're the star! The video is one of the best sources of evidence to motivate you to change. After you see what you really look like, your reaction might be the same as mine: "Yup, it's time for an Extreme Professor Makeover!"

Document your teaching performance with a video. Use an available checklist, peer rating scale, or your own rating scale to systematically analyze your teaching behaviors. Either alone or with a trusted sidekick, pinpoint your strengths and weaknesses. Then map out a plan to address those weaknesses. That's how you'll improve your teaching.

When the changes have been completed, re-video your classes to witness the evidence of your effort. The pre- to post-video difference should be significant. Go celebrate! Now you know one formula for teaching improvement.

INFORMATION NEEDED.   Once the shock of the video wears off after the first screening, go back and scrutinize your performance with the rating scale. The single rating form with all of *your anchor choices and comments* is all you need to begin your "makeover."

INFORMATION TIMING.   If you are completing the scale, *your results are immediate.* If a peer is doing the rating from the video, the feedback should occur in three steps (see "Peer/External Expert Ratings").

Student interviews.   The instructor-led *quality control circles* (QCC) and colleague- or TA-led class group interviews (SGID, or *small-group instructional diagnosis*) can provide a wealth of information during the course that you can use to adjust your teaching methods. Digesting this feedback can be a humbling experience for some. The students' comments are fresh, candid, and timely. For some instructors, the biggest obstacle to overcome is pride. Suck it in. Listen carefully to what your students are saying. Act on as many suggestions as possible during the course.

Your willingness to subject yourself to open critiques of your teaching conveys to your students, "Leave me alone. You're driving me crazy!" Wait. That's not what it conveys. It says, "I really care about my teaching and YOU, and I'm willing to improve. Just show me the way, bubby." The interview sessions and your responses will test your character and integrity as a teacher. They will also build a strong connection between you and your students. The bonding can only improve what happens in the classroom. The students will frequently tell you that their other instructors will not expose themselves with open critiques or any other formative feedback before the end-of-course ratings. Student interviews can distinguish how you teach from many of your colleagues. They may even improve your teaching.

INFORMATION NEEDED.   Since structured and/or unstructured questions may be employed in these interviews, *item means/medians, anchor percentages,* and a *summary list of student comments* should be reported. This information should be recorded and compiled immediately after the interviews, either by the instructor or TA.

INFORMATION TIMING.   The information from the QCCs should be available *biweekly* or monthly, and the SGID interviews should be completed by *midterm*. Once the feedback is received, you must respond to your students PDQ (Pretty Darned Quick[ly]), or else your intentions may be questioned. This is the accountability issue mentioned previously. You entered into a "good faith" agreement with your students when you requested their input on your teaching. They expect you to use that information to make visible changes. Your credibility and trust are on the line. You must at least address their comments in a timely fashion.

Exit and alumni ratings.   The value of these ratings for teaching improvement depends on their specificity. Surveys of graduating and graduated students are typically much broader in scope than end-of-course ratings. Although one section of the scale may address teaching methods and course characteristics, the overall yield for individual instructors is limited. More feedback may occur in the unstructured comments section.

INFORMATION NEEDED.   A report on these ratings should include *item means/ medians* and *anchor percentages* for appropriate items and a *summary list of comments* pertinent to each instructor and course.

INFORMATION TIMING.   Information from exit ratings should be available at the *end of the term* when most students graduate. This will allow instructors the time to consider the feedback and make changes before the next course begins. Alumni ratings at 1-, 5-, and 10-year intervals should be administered and reported in *as short a time period as feasible*. The delays in processing the results due to slow response or inadequate response rate are normal. Follow-up correspondence to improve the response rate helps, but sometimes you just have to wait longer than you want to get the surveys back. These issues as well as the administration intervals may hinder the usefulness of the results for teaching improvement.

Summative Decisions

We've now come to that part of the book that I know you're as excited to reach as I am: the end. Haha. A little summative humor. No, of course, it's the section that describes how decisions about our future should be made. Based on the unified conceptualization of teaching effectiveness, or 360° assessment, what sources of evidence should be considered? How should they be integrated to reach employment decisions? According to Standard 14.13,

> When decision makers integrate information from multiple [scales] or integrate [scale] and [nonscale] information, the role played by each [scale] in the decision process should be clearly explicated, and the use of each [scale] or [scale] composite should be supported by validity evidence. (p. 161)

Bracket-wise, the translation is this: *The choice of scale scores and sources of evidence should be limited to those for which validity and reliability evidence are available.* Although summative decisions also involve research and publications, service, and practice, this discussion deals with teaching only. Two categories of decisions are examined: (1) renewal/dismissal and merit pay and (2) promotion and tenure.

Renewal/dismissal and merit pay.   The annual review of your teaching performance and productivity is usually based on a formal activity report, or "brag sheet." It doesn't contain most of the sources of evidence recommended throughout this book. Among the 13 sources, there are three that deserve serious consideration—student ratings, self-ratings, and teaching scholarship—and two that are optional—peer/external expert ratings and videos. These two are intended for formative decisions, and their use for summative decisions may be (or may be not) left to your discretion, depending on your institution.

Since administrators like you need to make decisions for all faculty within a short time frame at the end of the academic year (May and June), the information must be displayed in a concise and easily readable form. Here are some suggestions.

NORM-REFERENCED INTERPRETATIONS.   Subscale and total scale scores and/or global item scores can provide a meaningful picture of the students', the department's, and the instructor's ratings of teaching performance. This combo would present a norm-referenced interpretation of the students' and self ratings compared to the department's or school's norm ratings. Those scores are visually comprehensible without oversimplifying the teaching behaviors. Although a few global items are much less reliable than subscale scores, they come highly recommended by experts in the field (Abrami, 2001; Abrami, d'Apollonia, & Rosenfield,1996; Arreola, 2000; Braskamp & Ory, 1994; Cashin, 1999; Centra, 1993). There are two reasons: (1) global items are correlated moderately with student learning, and (2) they provide an easily understandable summary of teaching, like a final course grade. Let's consider how these results can be presented and interpreted.

The *simplest norm-referenced approach* is to rank all faculty members in the department based on their total student rating scale course means at the end of each semester. An individual's performance is contingent on how all other instructors in the department are rated at that point in time. Grouping the instructors into 20% or 33% categories can partition teaching performance into the following scales:

Category	Performance Rating	Score
Top 20%	Excellent	4
High 20%	Very Good	3
Middle 20%	Average	2
Low 20%	Unacceptable	1
Bottom 20% (Morgue)	Disastrous	0
	or	
Top 33%	Superior	2
Middle 33%	Mediocre	1
Bottom 33%	Horrible	0

These ratings can be collected across all courses and averaged using the corresponding scores above for an individual instructor. For example, suppose the ratings for an instructor's six courses over the year on the 0–4 scale are 4, 4, 4, 3,

3, and 2. The mean equals 3.33, which is between "Very Good" and "Outstanding." The instructor's self total rating can then be compared with the mean to arrive at an overall rating based on student data. Alternatively, global item scores can also be used, but with the limitations noted previously. Other sources of evidence can be factored into this annual teaching effectiveness equation as well. A procedure for including multiple sources will be described after the next normative student rating strategy.

 BODILY HARM WARNING

Once faculty members who fell below the top category find out the names of the top instructors, watch out. The games begin. Occasionally, evil thoughts may pass through the minds of the lower performers, people who normally do not harbor such thoughts. Sometimes they will act on those thoughts with ambiguous adverbs such as "occasionally" and "sometimes." Keep close tabs on the rate of physical "accidents" among the toppies, such as broken knee caps, severed fingers, smashed knuckles, gouged out eyeballs, and ruptured spleens. The consequences of competition can rear their ugly heads. Watch your back. You might consider a bodyguard like Kevin Costner.

Another approach to the norm-referenced interpretation of student rating scale results considers the reliability of the scores. It's considerably more complicated than the preceding ranking of faculty. This interpretation focuses on the subscale scores. Given the importance of the decisions to be made, the *standard error of measurement (SEM)* should be reported with each subscale norm mean and the total scale mean. The subscale *SEMs* were approximately 1–1.5 score points for the scale results reported in this chapter and in chapter 8 (see table 8.2, p. 178). The *norm mean* represents the rating of the typical instructor's teaching performance in the department. Is the instructor above or below this rating? The *SEM* can be used to gauge (rather than gouge) an instructor's level of teaching performance against the norm.

The *SEM norm-referenced strategy* mentioned above is another suggested method to assess an instructor's teaching performance in one course. The step-by-step procedure for executing that strategy is as follows:

Step 1. *Present the subscale, total scale, and global item results for the course, department, and self.* A sample report format is shown in table 9.1.

Rationale

Remember in chapter 8 that *SEM* was used to interpret the band of error around an individual rating. However, in the case of student rating scales, an instructor's single rating is actually the *mean rating* for the course. So I set up the band around the course mean. Are you still with me? Just blink. Great.

When comparing an instructor's rating (course mean) to the typical instructor's rating in the department (norm group mean/median), the band of error using the norm's *SEM* is set up around the (guess what?) *norm mean rating*. You nailed it.

In other words, teaching performance in a single course is based on a *norm-referenced comparison of an instructor's rating to the typical instructor's rating in the norm group and the reliability of the scale scores*. (Alternatively, if the standard error of the mean or median were used instead of the *SEM*, performance would be primarily a function of the norm group sample size. Performance would be an artifact of sample size. Small samples would yield wide error bands with few instructors performing well and poorly; large samples would produce narrow bands with loads of instructors performing well and poorly. This approach is not only awkward but unacceptable.)

After reading this rationale, perhaps there are a few skeptics who might question the veracity and soundness of my application of the *SEM* to rating scale mean scores. They may be thinking, "You're an idiot! Where did you learn measurement? This is the dumbest idea yet." In response to these statements, I would like to dig up a trusted American icon to verify the soundness of my proposal before I leave this box:

Abe Lincoln: Ron is telling the truth and nothing but the truth. I'm sorry for rushing, but I have to go to the theater, or else history will be changed forever.

When Abe and I say this rationale is sound, we are not whistling "Dixie."

TABLE 9.1
Sample Norm-Referenced Student Rating Scale Score Report Format

	Course	*Norm*		*Self*
	Mean/Median	*Mean/(SEM)/Median*		*Sum/Total*
Subscale 1	21.97/24	20.01/ (.8) /21		23/24
Subscale 2	13.40/15	12.19/ (1.4) /13		13/5
Subscale 3	9.84/10	9.61/ (1.1) /10		10/12
Subscale 4	34.79/37	32.55/ (1.4) /34		37/39
Subscale 5	16.43/18	15.16/ (1.2) /17		18/18
Total Scale	96.43/101	89.51/ (7.7) /92		101/108
Global Items				
1	2.57/3	2.39	2	3/3
2	2.76/3	2.51	2	3/3
3	2.92/3	2.68	2	3/3

Notice that means/medians are given for the course and department norm, but only individual summed scores can be computed for self.

Step 2. *Visualize the band of error around the department mean in SEM increments of ±1 $\times$ SEM and ± 2 $\times$ SEM*, as shown below for subscale 4 with a *SEM* = 1.4:

−2*SEM*s	−1*SEM*	Dept. Mean	+1*SEM*	+2*SEM*s
29.75————	—31.15 —	———32.55 —	———33.95 —	———35.55

There is ~3-point band of error above and below and mean.

Step 3. *Locate the subscale score of 34.79 on this band.* The self-score would be outside the band to the far right, beyond +2*SEM*s.

−2*SEM*s	−1*SEM*	Dept. Mean	+1*SEM*	+2*SEM*s
29.75————	—31.15 —	———32.55 —	———33.95 ——	—35.55
			34.79	
			Course *Mean*	

Step 4. *Assign an overall rating of teaching performance on the following 5-point scale based on the SEM increments on the band:*

4 = Excellent
3 = Very Good
2 = Good
1 = Fair
0 = Putrid

Consider the following intervals:

			Dept.			
← −2*SEMs*	−1*SEM*		Mean		+1*SEM*	+2*SEMs* →
Deadmeat	*Fair*	*Good*		*Good*	*Very Good*	*Excellent*

Step 5. *What does this all mean?* Basically, if your subscale score falls within 1*SEM* above and below the department mean, your teaching performance is "Good," which is close to the typical faculty rating in the department. Your course rating must fall outside the 2*SEMs* true score (T) band of error (95% confidence interval) of the average rating to be considered "Excellent" or "Deadmeat." Here's a summary of the intervals:

+2*SEMs* or higher = *Excellent* = 4
Above +1*SEM* & below +2*SEMs* = *Very Good* = 3
Between +1*SEM* & −1*SEM* = *Good* = 2
Below −1*SEM* and above −2*SEMs* = *Fair* = 1
−2*SEMs* or below = *Deadmeat* = 0

Step 6. *Determine your course rating and self-rating according to these intervals for each subscale:*

Subscale 1: Course = *Excellent* (4); Self = *Excellent* (4)
Subscale 2: Course = *Good* (2); Self = *Good* (2)
Subscale 3: Course = *Good* (2); Self = *Good* (2)
Subscale 4: Course = *Very Good* (3); Self = *Excellent* (4)
Subscale 5: Course = *Very Good* (3); Self = *Excellent* (4)

Step 7. *Average your class and self-ratings for all five subscales:*

Course mean rating = 2.8
Self mean rating = 3.2

Step 8. *Your overall teaching performance rating for this course is* Deadmeat. Congrats! Oops. Wrong rating. I meant *Very Good.*

Once you've completed a few courses, you can use the interocular perusal technique (eye-balling) to visualize the *SEM* increments above or below the mean. Each course takes only a few minutes. This performance rating should be completed for all courses taught during the preceding year. For example, if an instructor teaches six courses, there should be six ratings. They may vary depending on the size of the class or subject matter. All six ratings can be averaged for an overall performance score. (*Note:* The total scale results are less informative and sometimes less reliable [larger *SEM*] than the subscale scores. The global item results are interesting to review, but are much less reliable and useful for overall performance decisions. The decimal differences between the ratings of the three global items are trivial.)

 CAVEAT MEANUS BIAS

Beware of El Meano (or La Meana) in skewed distributions! This problem was discussed earlier in the chapter. Notice that in table 9.1 all of the course and norm means were lower than the respective medians. An instructor's teaching performance based on means appears lower (worse) than it actually is. Again, remember that the median is the most accurate estimate of typical performance for markedly skewed distributions. The preceding eight-step process for interpreting course-norm-self subscale means can also be applied to the medians. When course subscale distributions are significantly more skewed than the norm's, medians should be used for the course and norm.

If peer/external expert and video ratings are also submitted, only short summaries should be presented. Those summaries should result in an overall rating as well. Finally, teaching scholarship, which is typically part of the activity report, should be evaluated on the same 0–4 scale.

Average the three ratings (course–self, peer–video, and teaching scholarship) for an overall score of teaching effectiveness. This score reflects five different sources of evidence. These sources may vary or be combined differently, but the

TABLE 9.2
Sample Criterion-Referenced Student Rating Scale Score Report Format

	Course	*Self*	*75% Criterion*
	Mean/Median	*Sum/Total*	*Cut/Total*
Subscale 1	21.97/24	23/24	18/24
Subscale 2	13.40/15	13/15	11/15
Subscale 3	9.84/10	10/12	9/12
Subscale 4	34.79/37	37/39	29/39
Subscale 5	16.43/18	18/18	13/18
Total Scale	96.43/101	101/108	81/108

compensatory scoring permits faculty to balance their strengths with their weaknesses. The final "teaching effectiveness" score can then be weighted with research, service, and practice to guide decisions of contract renewal/dismissal and amount of merit pay.

CRITERION-REFERENCED INTERPRETATION.   The preceding norm-referenced approach to interpreting scores from multiple data sources is only one option. A criterion-referenced interpretation should also be considered. For simplicity, suppose course and self medians were used as the scores. Criteria for performance on each subscale and total scale would need to be determined by a faculty committee. A systematic review should indicate a *criterion of expected performance to define teaching effectiveness.* The criteria might be the same for all subscales, such as 75%, the "Favorable" rating point on the "Extremely Unfavorable" to "Extremely Favorable" score continuum displayed on page 195. Separate criteria may also be set for each subscale. The percentage criterion can then be translated into specific cutoff scores for the subscales. The cutoff defines effective performance for a given subscale. The course median *must equal or exceed the cutoff.* An example is shown in table 9.2.

Comparing course and self-medians to the cut scores for the subscales and total indicates that this instructor exceeded all cuts by four or more points, except for subscale 3. An instructor must pass (i.e., reach the cutoff or above) all subscales to satisfy the highest level of teaching effectiveness. *The number of subscales passed by an instructor may be used as an index of performance.* For example, consider the following graduated scale:

No. of Subscales Passed	*Performance Rating*
5	Very Effective
3–4	Moderately Effective
1–2	Slightly Effective
0	Ineffective (Go back to doing research)

These ratings provide an index of the degree of teaching effectiveness for a single course. This analysis would have to be completed for all of an instructor's courses. The overall course ratings may reveal, for example, that the instructor is more effective in large undergraduate courses, but less effective in small master's or doctoral courses. This type of information could be useful not only for retention or merit pay decisions, but also in planning future course assignments and teaching load.

Promotion and tenure.   Administrators and the appointment, promotion, and tenure (APT) committee require a more comprehensive package of source materials over several years to recommend promotion. The teaching component of this review should be based on a well-structured and well-documented teaching portfolio. It can contain as many sources of evidence as the instructor is willing to submit or as you require. He or she can draw on the summaries from the annual activity reports to highlight the growth in teaching effectiveness and scholarly productivity since the previous appointment. The multiyear presentation of all salient results should be easy to review, understandable, and thoroughly documented with appropriate examples.

Program Decisions

Administrators and faculty committees evaluate teaching, courses, curriculum, and other aspects of academic programs from a few of the sources of evidence for teaching effectiveness. This evidence is collected to address program questions and issues, which can be of value when accreditation time rolls around. In each application, the response rate must be at least 60% to render program decisions. Even at that percentage or less, the ratings may be biased and unrepresentative. Uses of the scale scores for these purposes are described for student, exit, alumni, and employer ratings.

Student ratings.   The overall effectiveness and improvement in teaching by level, department, or discipline year after year can be measured by student ratings at the subscale and total scale score levels. *Annual mean/median norms* by semester can furnish the results. This may reveal trends in teaching effectiveness over a five-year period that may be attributable to particular faculty development and innovative teaching programs.

Subscales dealing with course characteristics may be analyzed by curriculum committees to suggest possible content or organizational revisions. *Item and subscale means/medians* can guide such reviews.

Exit and alumni ratings.   Student ratings at graduation and one year or more later can offer valuable perspectives on teaching, specific courses, prerequisites, course sequence, content coverage, and program organization. *Item and subscale means/medians* and the *summary list of comments* to leading unstructured questions can provide useful information for program changes.

Employer ratings.   Employers' feedback on the competence of graduates in terms of program outcomes can be very informative. On-the-job performance ratings are especially useful for professional school programs, such as medicine, nursing, education, cryogenics, hockey, and bull fighting. *Scale item means/medians* and a *summary of employers' comments* can indicate program strengths and weaknesses in teaching and course requirements. Given the difficulty of obtaining an adequate response rate from employers, be cautious with inferences from the results about the program. They may be only suggestive until other evidence can corroborate those findings.

Conclusions

All of the different sources of evidence used for the decisions described in the previous section provide options you may not have considered for assessing teaching effectiveness. The question is, When is this book done? Soon, but that's not the question I had in mind. It was this one: Where do *you* go from here? Here are a few questions to ponder:

- As an instructor or administrator, what can *you* contribute to improve the current state of teaching assessment in your department/school?
- How high of a priority is teaching assessment in your department/school?
- What changes need to be considered to increase the quality of the scales you are now using?
- Who will take ownership for making those changes?
- What additional scales need to be developed?
- Who will assume responsibility for creating these instruments?
- What resources are available or required to build this assessment system?
- How can the scores be interpreted better for formative, summative, and program decisions?

Change is difficult for all organizations; but most of us have experienced changes in our institutions, and we have survived. Spencer Johnson's *Who Moved My Cheese?* conveys the individual dynamics involved in change. The issue here is not whether the changes can take place. It's the level of commitment vested in facilitating those changes.

☞ FINAL BOTTOM LINE

If it's important enough, it'll get done; if it isn't, it won't. How important is this to you? I challenge you to make a difference in your department/school. Take the proverbial bull in the china shop by the nose and lead him to water. "WHAAAT? That makes no sense." I was saving it for the very last paragraph. Let's get back to the topic: proverbs. Both faculty and administrators are the major stakeholders in this process. Both must work together to move the assessment of teaching effectiveness forward. The *Standards,* cited throughout this book to guide the measurement process outlined in Memory Jogger 2.1, should be the gold standard we all strive to attain. Given the gravity of the decisions being rendered, it's a win-win outcome. If you do nothing, the consequence is lose-lose. You decide.

REFERENCES

Abrami, P. C. (1993). Using student rating norm groups for summative evaluation. *Faculty Evaluation and Development, 13*, 5–9.

Abrami, P. C. (2001). Improving judgments about teaching effectiveness using rating forms. In M. Theall, P. C. Abrami, & L. A. Mets (Eds.), *The student ratings debate: Are they valid? How can we best use them?* (New Directions for Institutional Research, No. 109, pp. 59–87). San Francisco: Jossey-Bass.

Abrami, P. C., d'Apollonia, S., & Rosenfield, S. (1996). The dimensionality of student ratings of instruction: What we know and what we do not. In R. P. Perry & J. C. Smart (Eds.), *Effective teaching in higher education: Research and practice.* New York: Agathon.

Aleamoni, L. M. (1978). The usefulness of student evaluations in improving college teaching. *Instructional Science, 7*, 95–105.

Aleamoni, L. M. (1982). Components of the instructional setting. *Instructional Evaluation, 7*, 11–16.

Aleamoni, L. M. (1996). Why we do need norms of student ratings to evaluate faculty: Reaction to McKeachie. *Instructional Evaluation and Faculty Development, 16*(1–2), 18–19.

Aleamoni, L. M. (1999). Student rating myths versus research facts from 1924 to 1998. *Journal of Personnel Evaluation in Education, 13*, 153–166.

Aleamoni, L. M., & Carynnk, D. B. (1977). *Optional item catalog* (Rev. ed.; Information Memorandum No. 6). Tucson, AZ: University of Arizona, Office of Instructional Research and Development.

Allison, P. D. (2000). Multiple imputation for missing data. *Sociological Methods & Research, 28*(3), 301–309.

Allison, P. D. (2001). *Missing data* (Quantitative Applications in the Social Sciences Series, Vol. 136). Thousand Oaks, CA: Sage.

American Association of University Professors. (1974). Committee C. Statement on teaching evaluation. *AAUP Bulletin, 60*(2), 166–170.

American Educational Research Association (AERA), American Psychological Association (APA), & National Council on Measurement in Education (NCME) Joint Committee on Standards. (1974). *Standards on educational and psychological tests.* Washington, DC: APA.

American Educational Research Association (AERA), American Psychological Association (APA), & National Council on Measurement in Education (NCME) Joint Committee on Standards. (1985). *Standards for educational psychological tests.* Washington, DC: APA.

American Educational Research Association (AERA), American Psychological Association (APA), & National Council on Measurement in Education (NCME) Joint Committee on Standards. (1999). *Standards for educational and psychological testing.* Washington, DC: AERA.

American Psychological Association (APA). (1997, November). Learner-centered psychological principles: A framework for school redesign and reform. Retrieved October 15, 2005 from www.apa.org/ed/lcp2/homepage.html

American Psychological Association (APA), American Educational Research Association (AERA), & National Council on Measurement in Education (NCME) Joint Committee on Standards. (1966). *Standards for educational and psychological tests and manuals.* Washington, DC: APA.

Anderson, E. (Ed.). (1993). *Campus use of the teaching portfolio: Twenty-five profiles.* Washington, DC: American Association for Higher Education.

Anderson, L. W., & Krathwohl, D. R. (Eds.). (2001). *A taxonomy for learning, teaching, and assessing: A revision of Bloom's Taxonomy of Educational Objectives.* New York: Longman.

Appling, S. E., Naumann, P. L., & Berk, R. A. (2001). Using a faculty evaluation triad to achieve evidence-based teaching. *Nursing and Health Care Perspectives, 22*, 247–251.

Archer, J. C., Beard, J., Davies, H., Norcini, J. J., & Southgate, L. A. (2005, September). *Mini-PAT (Peer Assessment Tool): Can a multisource feedback tool be a reliable and feasible component of a national assessment programme?* Short communication presented at the annual conference of the Association for Medical Education in Europe, Amsterdam, The Netherlands.

Archer, J. C., Norcini, J., & Davies, H. (2005). Use of SPRAT for peer review of paediatricians in training. *British Medical Journal, 330*, 1251–1253.

Arreola, R. A. (2000). *Developing a comprehensive faculty evaluation system: A handbook for college faculty and administrators on designing and operating a comprehensive faculty evaluation system* (2nd ed.). Bolton, MA: Anker.

Asher, J. J., & Sciarrino, J. A. (1974). Realistic work sample tests: A review. *Personnel Psychology, 27*, 519–533.

Attali, Y., & Bar-Hillel, M. (2003). Guess where: The position of correct answers in multiple-choice test items as a psychometric variable. *Journal of Educational Measurement, 40,* 109–128.

Ballantyne, C. (2000, November). *Why survey online? A practical look at issues in the use of the Internet for surveys in higher education.* Paper presented at the annual conference of the American Evaluation Association, Honolulu.

Barber, L. W. (1990). Self-assessment. In J. Millman & L. Darling-Hammond (Eds.), *The new handbook of teacher evaluation* (pp. 216–228). Newbury Park, CA: Sage.

Bass, B. M., Cascio, W. F., & O'Connor, E. J. (1974). Magnitude estimations of expressions of frequency and amount. *Journal of Applied Psychology, 59,* 313–320.

Baxter, E. P. (1991). The TEVAL experience, 1983–88: The impact of a student evaluation of teaching scheme on university teachers. *Studies in Higher Education, 16,* 151–179.

Bendig, A. W. (1952a). A statistical report on a revision of the Miami instructor rating sheet. *Journal of Educational Psychology, 43,* 423–429.

Bendig, A. W. (1952b). The use of student ratings scales in the evaluation of instructors in introductory psychology. *Journal of Educational Psychology, 43,* 167–175.

Bendig, A. W. (1953). The reliability of self-ratings as a function of the amount of verbal anchoring and of number of categories on the scale. *Journal of Applied Psychology, 37,* 38–41.

Bendig, A. W. (1954a). Reliability and number of rating scale categories. *Journal of Applied Psychology, 38,* 38–40.

Bendig, A. W. (1954b) Reliability of short rating scales and the heterogeneity of the rated stimuli. *Journal of Applied Psychology, 38,* 167–170.

Bennett, W. E. (1987). Small group instructional diagnosis: A dialogic approach of instructional improvement for tenured faculty. *Journal of Staff, Program, and Organizational Development, 5*(3), 100–104.

Bentler, P. M., Jackson, D. N., & Messick, S. J. (1972). A rose by any other name. *Psychological Bulletin, 77,* 109–113.

Berg, I. A. (Ed.). (1967). *Response set in personality assessment.* Chicago: Aldine.

Berk, R. A. (1978). Empirical evaluation of formulae for correction of item-to-tal point-biserial correlations. *Educational and Psychological Measurement, 38,* 647–652.

Berk, R. A. (1979a). The construction of rating instruments for faculty evaluation: A review of methodological issues. *Journal of Higher Education, 50,* 650–669.

Berk, R. A. (1979b). Generalizability of behavioral observations: A clarification of interobserver agreement and interobserver reliability. *American Journal of Mental Deficiency, 83,* 460–472.

Berk, R. A. (Ed.). (1984). *A guide to criterion-referenced test construction.* Baltimore, MD: Johns Hopkins University Press.

Berk, R. A. (1986a). A consumer's guide to setting performance standards on criterion-referenced tests. *Review of Educational Research, 56,* 137–172.

Berk, R. A. (Ed.). (1986b). *Performance assessment: Methods and applications.* Baltimore, MD: Johns Hopkins University Press.

Berk, R. A. (1988). Fifty reasons why student achievement gain does not mean teacher effectiveness. *Journal of Personnel Evaluation in Education, 1,* 345–363.

Berk, R. A. (1990a). Importance of expert judgment in content-related validity evidence. *Western Journal of Nursing Research, 12,* 659–671.

Berk, R. A. (1990b). Limitations of using student achievement data for career ladder promotions and merit pay decisions. In J. V. Mitchell, Jr., S. L. Wise, & B. S. Plake (Eds.), *Assessment of teaching: Purposes, practices, and implications for the profession* (pp. 261–306). Hillsdale, NJ: Erlbaum.

Berk, R. A. (1993). Murder board: Some postmortem thoughts on instrument construction. *Journal of Nursing Measurement, 1,* 107–114.

Berk, R. A. (1996). Standard setting: The next generation (Where few psychometricians have gone before!) *Applied Measurement in Education, 9,* 215–235.

Berk, R. A. (1999). Assessment for measuring professional performance. In D. P. Ely., L. E. Odenthal, & T. J. Plomp (Eds.), *Educational science and technology: Perspectives for the future* (pp. 29–48). Enschede, The Netherlands: Twente University Press.

Berk, R. A. (2002a). *Humor as an instructional defibrillator: Evidence-based techniques in teaching and assessment.* Sterling, VA: Stylus.

Berk, R. A. (2002b). Teaching portfolios used for high-stakes decisions: You have technical issues! In National Evaluation Systems, *How to find and support tomorrow's teachers* (pp. 45–56). Amherst, MA: Author.

Berk, R. A. (2003). *Professors are from Mars®, students are from Snickers®: How to write and deliver humor in the classroom and in professional presentations.* Sterling, VA: Stylus.

Berk, R. A. (2005). Survey of 12 strategies to measure teaching effectiveness. *International Journal of Teaching and Learning in Higher Education, 17*(1), 48–62. (www.isetl.org/ijtlthe)

Berk, R. A., Berg, J., Mortimer, R., Walton-Moss, B., & Yeo, T. P. (2005). Measuring the effectiveness of faculty mentoring relationships. *Academic Medicine, 80,* 66–71.

Berk, R. A., Naumann, P. L., & Appling, S. E. (2004). Beyond student ratings: Peer observation of classroom and clinical teaching. *International Journal of Nursing Education Scholarship, 1*(1), 1–26.

Berliner, D. (2005). The near impossibility of testing for teacher quality. *Journal of Teacher Education, 56*(3), 205–213.

Bernardin, H. J. (1977). Behavioral expectations scales versus summated scales: A fairer comparison. *Journal of Applied Psychology, 62*, 422–428.

Bernardin, H. J., & Kane, J. (1980). A closer look at behavioral observation scales. *Personnel Psychology, 33*, 809–814.

Bernardin, H. J., & Smith, P. (1981). A clarification of some issues regarding the development and use of behaviorally anchored rating scales (BARS). *Journal of Applied Psychology, 66*, 458–463.

Blanz, R., & Ghiselli, E. E. (1972). The mixed standard scale: A new rating system. *Personnel Psychology, 25*, 185–200.

Bloom, B. S., Englehart, M. D., Furst, E. J., Hill, W. H., & Krathwohl, D. R. (1956). *Taxonomy of educational objectives: The classification of educational goals. Handbook I: Cognitive domain.* New York: David McKay.

Bo-Linn, C., Gentry, J., Lowman, J., Pratt, R. W., & Zhu, R. (2004, November). *Learning from exemplary teachers.* Paper presented at the annual Lilly Conference on College Teaching, Miami University, Oxford, OH.

Bonwell, C. C., & Eison, J. A. (1991). *Active learning: Creating excitement in the classroom.* San Francisco: Jossey-Bass.

Border, L. L. B. (2002). The Socratic portfolio: A guide for future faculty. *PS: Political Science & Politics, 25*(4), 739–743. (www.apsanet.org/section_223.cfm)

Border, L. L. B. (2005). Teaching portfolios for graduate students: Process, content, product, and benefits. *Teaching Excellence, 17*(4).

Borman, W. C. (1979). Format and training effects on rating accuracy and rater errors. *Journal of Applied Psychology, 64*, 410–421.

Borman, W. C. (1986). Behavior-based rating scales. In R. A. Berk (Ed.), *Performance assessment: Methods and applications* (pp. 100–120). Baltimore, MD: Johns Hopkins University Press.

Borman, W. C., Hough, L. M., & Dunnette, M. D. (1976). *Development of behaviorally based rating scales for evaluating the performance of U.S. Navy recruiters* (Technical Report TR-76-31). San Diego, CA: U.S. Navy Personnel Research and Development Center.

Bothell, T. W., & Henderson, T. (2003). Do online ratings of instruction make $ense? In D. L. Sorenson & T. D. Johnson (Eds.), *Online student ratings of instruction* (New Directions for Teaching and Learning, No. 96, pp. 69–80). San Francisco: Jossey-Bass.

Boyd, N. M. (2005). 360-degree performance appraisal systems. In J. Rabin (Ed.), *Encyclopedia of public administration and public policy.* Oxford, England: Taylor & Francis.

Boyer, E. (1990). *Scholarship reconsidered: New priorities for the professoriate.* Princeton, NJ: The Carnegie Foundation for the Advancement of Teaching.

Bracken, D. W., Timmreck, C. W., & Church, A. H. (Eds.). (2001). *The handbook of multisource feedback: The comprehensive resource for designing and implementing MSF processes.* San Francisco: Jossey-Bass.

Bradburn, N. M., Sudman, S., & Wansink, B. (2004). *Asking questions: The definitive guide to questionnaire design* (Rev. ed.). Indianapolis: Jossey-Bass.

Braskamp, L. A., Caulley, D. N., & Costin, F. (1979). Student ratings and instructor self-ratings and their relationship to student achievement. *American Educational Research Journal, 16,* 295–306.

Braskamp, L. A., & Ory, J. C. (1994). *Assessing faculty work.* San Francisco: Jossey-Bass.

Braskamp, L. A., Ory, J. C., & Pieper, D. M. (1981). Student written comments: Dimensions of instructional quality. *Journal of Educational Psychology, 73,* 65–70.

Brennan, R. L. (2001). *Generalizability theory.* New York: Springer-Verlag.

Brinko, K. T. (1993). The practice of giving feedback to improve teaching: What is effective? *Journal of Higher Education, 64*(5), 54–68.

Brinko, K. T. (1997). The interactions of teaching improvement. In K. T. Brinko & R. J. Menges (Eds.), *Practically speaking: A sourcebook for instructional consultants in higher education* (pp. 3–8). Stillwater, OK: New Forum.

Bryant, G. D., & Norman, G. R. (1980). Expressions of probability: Words and numbers. *New England Journal of Medicine, 302,* 411.

Campbell, D. T., & Fiske, D. W. (1959). Convergent and discriminant validation by a multitrait-multimethod matrix. *Psychological Bulletin, 56,* 81–105.

Cardy, R. L., & Dobbins, G. H. (1994). *Performance appraisal: Alternative perspectives.* Cincinnati, OH: South-Western.

Carini, R. M., Hayek, J. C., Kuh, G. D., & Ouimet, J. A. (2003). College student responses to web and paper surveys: Does mode matter? *Research in Higher Education, 44*(1), 1–19.

Carnegie Foundation for the Advancement of Teaching. (1994). *National survey on the reexamination of faculty roles and rewards.* Princeton, NJ: Carnegie Foundation for the Advancement of Teaching.

Carusetta, E. (2001). Evaluating teaching though teaching awards. In C. Knapper & P. Cranton (Eds.), *Fresh approaches to the evaluation of teaching* (New Directions for Teaching and Learning, No. 88, pp. 31–46). San Francisco: Jossey-Bass.

Cashin, W. E. (1989). *Defining and evaluating college teaching* (IDEA Paper No. 21). Manhattan, KS: Kansas State University, Center for Faculty Evaluation and Development. (www.idea.ksu.edu)

Cashin, W. E. (1990). *Student ratings of teaching: Recommendations for use* (IDEA Paper No. 22). Manhattan, KS: Kansas State University, Center for Faculty Evaluation and Development. (www.idea.ksu.edu)

Cashin, W. E. (1992). Student ratings: The need for comparative data. *Instructional Evaluation and Faculty Development, 12*(2), 1–6.

Cashin, W. E. (1994). Student ratings: Comparative data, norm groups, and non-comparative interpretations: Reply to Hativa and to Abrami. *Instructional Evaluation and Faculty Development, 14*(1), 21–26.

Cashin, W. E. (1996). Should student ratings be interpreted absolutely or relatively? Reaction to McKeachie. *Institutional Evaluation and Faculty Development, 16*(1–2), 14–19.

Cashin, W. E. (1999). Student ratings of teaching: Uses and Misuses. In P. Seldin & Associates (Eds.), *Changing practices in evaluating teaching: A practical guide to improved faculty performance and promotion/tenure decisions* (pp. 25–44). Bolton, MA: Anker.

Cederblom, D., & Lounsbury, J. W. (1980). An investigation of user acceptance of peer evaluations. *Personnel Psychology, 33*, 567–580.

Center for Teaching Effectiveness. (1996). *Preparing for peer observation: A guidebook.* Austin, TX: University of Texas, The Center for Teaching Effectiveness.

Centra, J. A. (1973a). Effectiveness of student feedback in modifying college instruction. *Journal of Educational Psychology, 65*(3), 395–410.

Centra, J. A. (1973b). Self-ratings of college teachers: A comparison with student ratings. *Journal of Educational Measurement, 10*, 287–295.

Centra, J. A. (1974). The relationship between student and alumni ratings of teachers. *Educational and Psychological Measurement, 32*(2), 321–326.

Centra, J. A. (1975). Colleagues as raters of classroom instruction. *Journal of Higher Education, 46*, 327–337.

Centra, J. A. (1979). *Determining faculty effectiveness.* San Francisco: Jossey-Bass.

Centra, J. A. (1993). *Reflective faculty evaluation: Enhancing teaching and determining faculty effectiveness.* San Francisco: Jossey-Bass.

Centra, J. A., Froh, R. C., Gray, P. J., & Lambert, L. M. (1987). *A guide to evaluating teaching for promotion and tenure.* Acton, MA: Copley.

Cerbin, W., & Hutchings, P. (1993, June). *The teaching portfolio.* Paper presented at the Bush Summer Institute, Minneapolis, MN.

Chase, C. I. (1969). Often is where you find it. *American Psychologist, 24*, 1043.

Chickering, A. W., & Gamson, Z. F. (Eds.). (1991). *Applying the seven principles for good practice in undergraduate education.* (New Directions for Teaching and Learning, No. 47). San Francisco: Jossey-Bass.

Chism, N. V. N. (1999). *Peer review of teaching: A sourcebook.* Bolton, MA: Anker.

Cizek, G. J. (Ed.). (2001). *Setting performance standards: Concepts, methods, and perspectives.* Mahwah, NJ: Erlbaum.

Cliff, N. (1959). Adverbs as multipliers. *Psychological Review, 66*, 27–44.

Cohen, P. A. (1980). Using student rating feedback for improving college instruction: A meta-analysis of findings. *Research in Higher Education, 13*, 321–341.

Cohen, P. A. (1981). Student ratings of instruction and student achievement: A meta-analysis of multisection validity studies. *Review of Educational Research, 51*, 281–309.

Cohen P. A., & McKeachie, W. J. (1980). The role of colleagues in the evaluation of teaching. *Improving College and University Teaching, 28*, 147–154.

Comrey, A. L. (1988). Factor analytic methods of scale development in personality and clinical psychology. *Journal of Consulting and Clinical Psychology, 56*, 754–761.

Cone, J. D. (1980, April). *The overlapping worlds of behavioral assessment and performance appraisal.* Paper presented at the first annual Scientist-Practitioner Conference in Industrial/Organizational Psychology, Old Dominion University, Virginia Beach, VA.

Conway, J. M., & Huffcutt, A. I. (1997). Psychometric properties of multisource performance ratings: A meta-analysis of subordinate, supervisor, peer, and self-ratings. *Human Performance, 10*, 331–360.

Cooper, W. H. (1981). Ubiquitous halo. *Psychological Bulletin, 90*, 218–244.

Couch, A., & Keniston, K. (1960). Yeasayers and naysayers: Agreeing response set as a personality variable. *Journal of Abnormal and Social Psychology, 60*, 151–174.

Cox, M. D. (1995). A department-based approach to developing teaching portfolios: Perspectives for faculty and development chairs. *Journal on Excellence in College Teaching, 6*(1), 117–143.

Cranton, P. (2001). Interpretive and critical evaluation. In C. Knapper & P. Cranton (Eds.), *Fresh approaches to the evaluation of teaching* (New Directions for Teaching and Learning, No. 88, pp. 11–18). San Francisco: Jossey-Bass.

Cronbach, L. J. (1946). Response sets and test validity. *Educational and Psychological Measurement, 6*, 475–494.

Cronbach, L. J. (1951). Coefficient alpha and the internal structure of tests. *Psychometrika, 16*, 297–334.

Cronbach, L. J. (1990). *Essentials of psychological testing* (5th ed.). New York: Harper & Row.

Crouch, C. H., & Mazur, E. (2001). Peer instruction: Ten years of experience and results. *American Journal of Physics, 69*, 970–977.

d'Apollonia, S., & Abrami, P. C. (1996, April). *Variables moderating the validity of student ratings of instruction: A meta-analysis.* Paper presented at the annual meeting of the American Educational Research Association, New York.

d'Apollonia, S., & Abrami, P. C. (1997a). Navigating student ratings of instruction. *American Psychologist, 52*, 1198–1208.

d'Apollonia, S., & Abrami, P. C. (1997b). Scaling the ivory tower, Part 1: Collecting evidence of instructor effectiveness. *Psychology Teaching Review, 6*, 46–59.

d'Apollonia, S., & Abrami, P. C. (1997c). Scaling the ivory tower, Part 2: Student ratings of instruction in North America. *Psychology Teaching Review, 6,* 60–76.

Dale, F., & Chall, J. E. (1948). A formula for predicting readability: Instructions. *Education Research Bulletin, 27,* 37–54.

Davies, H., & Archer, J. (2005). Multi source feedback: Development and practical aspects. *The Clinical Teacher, 2*(2), 77–81.

Davis, B. G. (1993). *Tools for teaching.* Indianapolis: Jossey-Bass.

Davis, J. (2002). Comparison of faculty, peer, self, and nurse assessment of obstetrics and gynecology residents. *Obstetrics and Gynecology, 99,* 647–651.

Dawes, R. M. (1972). *Fundamentals of attitude measurement.* New York: Wiley.

Derry, J., Seibert, W., Starry, A., Van Horn, J., & Wright, G. (1974). *The CAFETERIA system: A new approach to course and instructor evaluation* (Instructional Research Bulletin). West Lafayette, IN: Purdue University.

DeVellis, R. F. (2003). *Scale development: Theory and applications* (2nd ed.). Thousand Oaks, CA: Sage.

DeZure, D. (1999). Evaluating teaching through peer classroom observation. In P. Seldin & Associates (Eds.), *Changing practices in evaluating teaching: A practical guide to improving faculty performance and promotion/tenure decisions* (pp. 70–96). Bolton, MA: Anker.

Diamond, R. M. (2004). *Preparing for promotion, tenure, and annual review: A faculty guide.* (2nd ed.). Bolton, MA: Anker.

Dillman, D. A. (2000). *Mail and internet surveys: The tailored design method* (2nd ed.). New York, NY: Wiley.

Dixon, P. N., Bobo, M., & Stevick, R. A. (1984). Response differences and preferences for all-category-defined and end-defined Likert formats. *Educational and Psychological Measurement, 44,* 61–66.

Dommeyer, C. J., Baum, P., Chapman, K. S., & Hanna, R. W. (2002). Attitudes of business faculty towards two methods of collecting teaching evaluations: Paper vs. online. *Assessment & Evaluation in Higher Education, 27*(4), 455–462.

Dommeyer, C. J., Baum, P., & Hanna, R. W. (2002). College students' attitudes toward methods of collecting teaching evaluation: In-class versus on-line (Electronic version). *Journal of Education for Business, 78*(1), 5–11.

Dori, Y. J., & Belcher, J. (2005). How does technology-enabled active learning affect undergraduate students' understanding of electromagnetism concepts? *Journal of the Learning Sciences, 14*(2), 243–279.

Doyle, K. O., & Crichton, L. A. (1978). Student, peer, and self-evaluations of college instruction. *Journal of Educational Psychology, 70,* 815–826.

Drucker, A. J., & Remmers, H. H. (1951). Do alumni and students differ in their attitudes toward instructors? *Journal of Educational Psychology, 42*(3), 129–143.

Dunnette, M. D. (1966). *Personnel selection and placement.* Belmont, CA: Brooks/Cole.

Dunn-Rankin, P., Knezek, G. A., Wallace, S., & Zhang, S. (2004). *Scaling methods.* Mahwah, NJ: Erlbaum.

Eble, K. E. (1988). *The craft of teaching* (2nd ed.). San Francisco, CA: Jossey-Bass.

Edgerton, R., Hutchings, P., & Quinlan, K. (1991). *The teaching portfolio: Capturing the scholarship in teaching.* Washington, DC: American Association for Higher Education.

Edwards, A. L. (1957). *Techniques of attitude scale construction.* New York: Appleton-Century-Crofts.

Edwards, A. L. (1963). A factor analysis of experimental social desirability and response set scales. *Journal of Applied Psychology, 47,* 308–316.

Edwards, A. L., & Diers, C. J. (1963). Neutral items as a measure of acquiescence. *Educational and Psychological Measurement, 23,* 687–698.

Edwards, A. L., & Kilpatrick, F. P. (1948). Scale analysis and the measurement of social attitudes. *Psychometrika, 13,* 99–114.

Edwards, M. R., & Ewen, A. J. (1996). *360° feedback: The powerful new model for employee assessment and performance improvement.* New York: American Management Association (AMACOM).

Eiszler, C. F. (2002). College students' evaluations of teaching and grade inflation. *Research in Higher Education, 43*(4), 483–502.

Emery, C. R., Kramer, T. R., & Tian, R. G. (2003). Return to academic standards: A critique of students' evaluations of teaching effectiveness. *Quality Assurance in Education: An International Perspective, 11*(1), 37–47.

Erickson, G. R., & Erickson, B. L. (1979). Improving college teaching: An evaluation of a teaching consultation procedure. *Journal of Higher Education, 50*(5), 670–683.

Evans, R., Elwyn, G., & Edwards, A. (2004). Review of instruments for peer assessment of physicians. *British Medical Journal, 328,* 1240–1245.

Feldman, K. A. (1989a). The association between student ratings of specific instructional dimensions and student achievement: Refining and extending the synthesis of data from multisection validity studies. *Research in Higher Education, 30,* 583–645.

Feldman, K. A. (1989b). Instructional effectiveness of college teachers as judged by teachers themselves, current and former students, colleagues, administrators, and external (neutral) observers. *Research in Higher Education, 30,* 137–189.

Fenwick, T. J. (2001). Using student outcomes to evaluate teaching. A cautious exploration. In C. Knapper & P. Cranton (Eds.), *Fresh approaches to the evaluation of teaching* (New Directions for Teaching and Learning, No. 88, pp. 63–74). San Francisco: Jossey-Bass.

Ferguson, L. W. (1941). A study of the Likert technique of attitude scale construction. *Journal of Social Psychology, 13,* 51–57.

Finn, R. H. (1972). Effects of some variations in rating scale characteristics on the means and reliabilities of ratings. *Educational and Psychological Measurement, 32,* 255–265.

Fleenor, J. W., & Prince, J. M. (1997). *Using 360-degree feedback in organizations: An annotated bibliography.* Greensboro, NC: Center for Creative Leadership.

Franklin, J., & Theall, M. (1989, April). *Who reads ratings: Knowledge, attitude and practice of users of students' ratings of instruction.* Paper presented at the annual meeting of the American Educational Research Association, San Francisco, CA.

Freeberg, N. E. (1969). Relevance of rater–ratee acquaintance in the validity and reliability of ratings. *Journal of Applied Psychology, 53,* 518–524.

French-Lazovik, G. (1981). Peer review: Documentary evidence in the evaluation of teaching. In J. Millman (Ed.), *Handbook of teacher evaluation* (pp. 73–89). Newbury Park, CA: Sage.

Fricke, B. G. (1957). A response bias (*B*) scale for the MMPI. *Journal of Counseling Psychology, 4,* 149–153.

Frisbie, D. A., & Brandenburg, D. C. (1979). Equivalence of questionnaire items with varying response formats. *Journal of Educational Measurement, 16,* 43–8.

Fry, E. (1977). Fry's readability graph: Clarification, validity, and extension to level 17. *Journal of Reading, 21,* 249.

Fuller, F. F., & Manning, B. A. (1973). Self-confrontation reviewed: A conceptualization for video playback in teacher education. *Review of Educational Research, 43*(4), 469–528.

Ghorpade, J. (2000). Managing five paradoxes of 360-degree feedback. *Academy of Management Executive, 14*(1), 140–150.

Gibbs, G. (1988). *Creating a teaching profile.* Bristol, England: Teaching and Educational Services.

Goocher, B. E. (1965). Effects of attitude and experience on the selection of frequency adverbs. *Journal of Verbal Learning and Verbal Behavior, 4,* 193–195.

Goodman, A., & Campbell, M. (1999). Developing appropriate administrative support for online teaching with an online unit evaluation system. Retrieved March 28, 2003, from www.deakin.edu.au/~agoodman/isimade99.html

Greenwald, A. G. (1997). Validity concerns and usefulness of student ratings of instruction. *American Psychologist, 52,* 1182–1186.

Greenwald, A. G., & Gillmore, G. M. (1997). Grading leniency is a removable contaminant of student ratings. *American Psychologist, 52,* 1209–1217.

Greimel-Fuhrmann, B., & Geyer, A. (2003). Students' evaluation of teachers and instructional quality: Analysis of relevant factors based on empirical evaluation research. *Assessment & Evaluation in Higher Education, 28*(3), 229–239.

Griffin, B. W. (2001). Instructor reputation and student ratings of instruction. *Contemporary Educational Psychology, 26*, 534–552.

Guion, R. M. (1980). On trinitarian doctrines of validity. *Professional Psychology, 11*, 385–398.

Guion, R. M. (1986). Personnel evaluation. In R. A. Berk (Ed.), *Performance assessment: Methods and applications* (pp. 345–360). Baltimore, MD: Johns Hopkins University Press.

Hakel, M. D. (1968). How often is often? *American Psychologist, 23*, 533–534.

Hall, W., Violato, C., Lewkonia, R., Lockyer, J. M., Fidler, H., Toews, J., Jennett, P., Donoff, M., & Moores, D. (1999). Assessment of physician performance in Alberta: The Physician Achievement Review. *Canadian Medical Association Journal, 161*, 52–57.

Hamilton, J. B., III, Smith, M., Heady, R. B., & Carson, P. P. (1997). Using open-ended questions on senior exit surveys to evaluate and improve faculty performance: Results from a school of business administration. *Journal on Excellence in College Teaching, 8*(1), 23–48.

Hardy, N. (2002, April). *Perceptions of online evaluations: Fact and fiction.* Paper presented at the annual meeting of the American Educational Research Association, New Orleans, LA.

Hardy, N. (2003). Online ratings: Fact and fiction. In D. L. Sorenson & T. D. Johnson (Eds.), *Online student ratings of instruction* (New Directions for Teaching and Learning, No. 96, pp. 31–38). San Francisco: Jossey-Bass.

Hativa, N. (1993). Student ratings: A non-comparative interpretation. *Instructional Evaluation and Faculty Development, 13*(2), 1–4.

Havelka, D., Neal, C. S., & Beasley, F. (2003, November). *Student evaluation of teaching effectiveness: What criteria are most important?* Paper presented at the annual Lilly Conference on College Teaching, Miami University, Oxford, OH.

Helling, B. B. (1988). Looking for good teaching: A guide to peer observation. *Journal of Staff, Program, and Organizational Development, 6*(4), 147–158.

Hesketh, E. A., Anderson, F., Bagnall, G. M., Driver, C. P., Johnston, D. A., Marshall, D., Needham, G., Orr, G., & Walker, K. (2005). Using a 360° diagnostic screening tool to provide an evidence trail of junior doctor performance throughout their first postgraduate year. *Medical Teacher, 27*(3), 219–233.

Hmieleski, K. (2000). *Barriers to online evaluation: Surveying the nation's top 200 most wired colleges.* Troy, NY: Rensselaer Polytechnic Institute, Interactive and Distance Education Assessment (IDEA) Laboratory.

Hmieleski, K., & Champagne, M. V. (2000). Plugging into course evaluation. Retrieved March 28, 2003, from http://ts.mivu.org/default.asp?show=article&id=795

Hoffman, K. M. (2003). Online course evaluation and reporting in higher education. In D. L. Sorenson & T. D. Johnson (Eds.), *Online student ratings of instruction* (New Directions for Teaching and Learning, No. 96, pp. 25–30). San Francisco: Jossey-Bass.

Holden, R. R., Fekken, G. C., & Jackson, D. N. (1985). Structured personality test item characteristics and validity. *Journal of Research in Personality, 19,* 368–394.

Hollander, E. P. (1956). The friendship factor in peer nominations. *Personnel Psychology, 9,* 435–447.

Hutchings, P. (Ed.). (1995). *From idea to prototype: The peer review of teaching,* Washington, DC: American Association for Higher Education.

Hutchings, P. (1996). *Making teaching community property.* Washington, DC: American Association for Higher Education.

Hutchings, P., & Shulman, L. S. (1999). The scholarship of teaching: New elaborations, new developments. *Change, 31*(5), 11–15.

Jacobs, R. R. (1986). Numerical rating scales. In R. A. Berk (Ed.), *Performance assessment: Methods and applications* (pp. 82–99). Baltimore, MD: Johns Hopkins University Press.

Jacobs, R.R., Kafry, D., & Zedeck, S. (1980). Expectations of behaviorally anchored rating scales. *Personnel Psychology, 33,* 595–640.

Jaeger, R. M. (1980). Certification of student competence. In R. L. Linn (Ed.), *Educational measurement* (3rd ed., pp. 485–514). New York: American Council on Education and Macmillian.

Jenkins, G. D., & Taber, T. A. (1977). A Monte Carlo study of factors affecting three indices of composite scale reliability. *Journal of Applied Psychology, 62,* 392–398.

Jenrette, M., & Hayes, K. (1996). Honoring exemplary teaching: The two-year college setting. In M. D. Svinicki & R. J. Menges (Eds.), *Honoring exemplary teaching* (New Directions for Teaching and Learning, No. 65). San Francisco: Jossey-Bass.

Johnson, D., & Cujec, B. (1998). Comparison of self, nurse and physician assessment of residents rotating through an intensive care unit. *Critical Care Medicine, 26,* 1811–1816.

Johnson, T. D. (2001, September). *Online student ratings: Research and possibilities.* Invited plenary at the Online Assessment Conference, Champaign, IL.

Johnson, T. D. (2003). Online student ratings: Will students respond? In D. L. Sorenson & T. D. Johnson (Eds.), *Online student ratings of instruction* (New Directions for Teaching and Learning, No. 96, pp. 49–60). San Francisco: Jossey-Bass.

Kane, J. S., & Bernardin, H. J. (1982). Behavioral observation scales and the evaluation of performance appraisal effectiveness. *Personnel Psychology, 35,* 635–642.

Keig, L. W., & Waggoner, M. D. (1994). *Collaborative peer review: The role of faculty in improving college teaching* (ASHE/ERIC Higher Education Report, No. 2). Washington, DC: Association for the Study of Higher Education.

Keig, L. W., & Waggoner, M. D. (1995). Peer review of teaching: Improving college instruction through formative assessment. *Journal on Excellence in College Teaching, 6*(3), 51–83.

Kingstrom, P., & Bass, A. (1981). A critical analysis of studies comparing behaviorally anchored rating scales (BARS) and other rating formats. *Personnel Psychology, 34*, 263–289.

Kinicki, A. J., Bannister, B. D., Hom, P. W., & DeNisi, A. S. (1985). Behaviorally anchored rating scales vs. summated rating scales: Psychometric properties and susceptibility to rating bias. *Educational and Psychological Measurement, 45*, 535–549.

Knapper, C. (1995). The origins of teaching portfolios. *Journal on Excellence in College Teaching, 6*(1), 45–56.

Knapper, C. (1997). Rewards for teaching. In P. Cranton (Ed.), *University challenges in faculty work: Fresh perspectives from around the world* (New Directions for Teaching and Learning, No. 65). San Francisco: Jossey-Bass.

Knapper, C., & Cranton, P. (Eds.). (2001). *Fresh approaches to the evaluation of teaching* (New Directions for Teaching and Learning, No. 88). San Francisco: Jossey-Bass.

Knapper, C., & Wright, W. A. (2001). Using portfolios to document good teaching: Premises, purposes, practices. In C. Knapper & P. Cranton (Eds.), *Fresh approaches to the evaluation of teaching* (New Directions for Teaching and Learning, No. 88, pp. 19–29). San Francisco: Jossey-Bass.

Komaki, J., Collins, R. L., & Thoene, T. J. F. (1980). Behavioral measurement in business, industry, and government. *Behavioral Assessment, 2*, 151–163.

Komorita, S. S. (1963). Attitude content, intensity, and the neutral point on a Likert scale. *Journal of Social Psychology, 61*, 327–334.

Komorita, S. S., & Graham, W. K. (1965). Number of scale points and the reliability of scales. *Educational and Psychological Measurement, 4*, 987–995.

Kronholm, E. A., Wisher, R. A., Curnow, C. K., & Poker, F. (1999, September). *The transformation of a distance learning training enterprise to an internet base: From advertising to evaluation.* Paper presented at the Northern Arizona University NAU/Web99 Conference, Flagstaff, AZ.

Krueger, R. A., & Casey, M. A. (2000). *Focus groups: A practical guide for applied research* (3rd ed.). Thousand Oaks, CA: Sage.

Kulik, J. A. (2001). Student ratings: Validity, utility, and controversy. In M. Theall, P. C. Abrami, & L. A. Mets (Eds.), *The student ratings debate: Are they valid? How can we best use them?* (New Directions for Institutional Research, No. 109, pp. 9–25). San Francisco: Jossey-Bass.

Kumaravadivelu, B. (1995). A multidimensional model for peer evaluation of teaching effectiveness. *Journal on Excellence in College of Teaching, 6*(3), 95–113.

Landy, F. J., & Farr, J. L. (1983). *The measurement of work performance: Methods, theory, and applications.* San Diego, CA: Academic.

Latham, G. P., Fay, C. H., & Saari, L. M. (1979). The development of behavioral observation scales for appraising the performance of foremen. *Personnel Psychology, 32*, 299–311.

Layne, B. H., DeCristoforo, J. R., & McGinty, D. (1999). Electronic versus traditional student ratings of instruction (Electronic Version). *Research in Higher Education, 40*(2), 221–232.

Lenze, L. F. (1997). Small group instructional diagnosis (SGID). In K. T. Brinko & R. J. Menges (Eds.), *Practically speaking: A sourcebook for instructional consultants in higher education.* Stillwater, OK: New Forum.

Lewis, K. G. (Ed.). (2001). *Techniques and strategies for interpreting student evaluations* (New Directions for Teaching and Learning, No. 87). San Francisco: Jossey-Bass.

Lichtenstein, S., & Newman, J. R. (1967). Empirical scaling of common verbal phrases associated with numerical probabilities. *Psychonomic Science, 9*, 563–564.

Lieberman, D. A. (1999). Evaluating teaching through electronic classroom assessment. In P. Seldin & Associates (Eds.), *Changing practices in evaluating teaching: A practical guide to improved faculty performance and promotion/tenure decisions* (pp. 139–152). Bolton, MA: Anker.

Likert, R. (1932). A technique for the measurement of attitudes. *Archives of Psychology, 140*, 44–53.

Lipner, R. S., Blank, L. L., Leas, B. F., & Fortna, G. S. (2002). The value of patient and peer ratings in recertification. *Academic Medicine, 77*(10S), 64S–66S.

Lissitz, R. W., & Green, S. B. (1975). Effect of the number of scale points on reliability: A Monte Carlo approach. *Journal of Applied Psychology, 60*, 10–13.

Lockyer, J. M. (2002). *Multi source feedback: A critique.* Calgary, Canada: University of Calgary (Work in preparation for PhD candidacy examination).

Lockyer, J. M. (2003). Multi-source feedback in the assessment of physician competencies. *Journal of Continuing Education in the Health Professions, 23*(1), 4–12.

Lockyer, J. M., & Violato, C. (2004). An examination of the appropriateness of using a common peer assessment instrument to assess physician skills across specialties. *Academic Medicine, 79*, 5S–8S.

Love, K. G. (1981). Comparison of peer assessment methods: Reliability, validity, friendship bias, and user reaction. *Journal of Applied Psychology, 66*, 451–457.

Lowman, J. (1990). *Mastering the techniques of teaching* (2nd ed.). Indianapolis: Jossey-Bass.

MacCallum, R. C., Widaman, K. F., Zhang, S., & Hong, S. (1999). Sample size in factor analysis. *Psychological Methods, 4*(1), 84–99.

Marincovich, M. (1999). Using student feedback to improve teaching. In P. Seldin & Associates (Eds.), *Changing practices in evaluating teaching: A practical guide to improved faculty performance and promotion/tenure decisions* (pp. 45–69). Bolton, MA: Anker.

Marsh, H. W. (1984). Student's evaluations of university teaching: Dimensionality, reliability, validity, potential biases, and utility. *Journal of Educational Psychology, 76*, 707–754.

Marsh, H. W. (1987). Student evaluations of university teaching: Research findings, methodological issues, and directions for future research. *International Journal of Educational Research, 11*, 253–388.

Marsh, H. W., & Dunkin, M. J. (1992). Students' evaluations of university teaching: A multi-dimensional perspective. In J. C. Smart (Ed.), *Higher education: Handbook of theory and research* (Vol. 8, pp. 143–234). New York: Agathon.

Marsh, H. W., Fleiner, H., & Thomas, C. S. (1975). Validity and usefulness of student evaluations of instructional quality. *Journal of Educational Psychology, 67*, 833–839.

Marsh, H. W., Overall, J. U., & Kessler, S. P. (1979). The validity of students' evaluations of instructional effectiveness: A comparison of faculty self-evaluations and evaluations by their students. *Journal of Educational Psychology, 71*, 149–160.

Marsh, H. W., & Roche, L. A. (1997). Making students' evaluations of teaching effectiveness effective: The critical issues of validity, bias, and utility. *American Psychologist, 52*, 1187–1197.

Martin, J. (1964). Acquiescence–Measurement and theory. *British Journal of Social and Clinical Psychology, 2*, 216–225.

Masters, J. R. (1974). The relationship between number of response categories and reliability of Likert-type questionnaires. *Journal of Educational Measurement, 11*, 49–53.

Matell, M. S., & Jacoby, J. (1971). Is there an optimal number of alternatives for Likert scale items? Study 1: Reliability and validity. *Educational and Psychological Measurement, 31*, 657–674.

McCarthy, A. M., & Garavan, T. N. (2001). 360 Degree feedback processes: Performance improvement and employee career development. *Journal of European Industrial Training, 25*(1), 3–32.

McGee, D. E., & Lowell, N. (2003). Psychometric properties of student ratings of instruction in online and on-campus courses. In D. L. Sorenson & T. D.

Johnson (Eds.), *Online student ratings of instruction* (New Directions for Teaching and Learning, No. 96, pp. 39–48). San Francisco: Jossey-Bass.

McGourty, J., Scoles, K., & Thorpe, S. (2002, June). *Web-based student evaluation of instruction: Promises and pitfalls.* Paper presented at the 42nd Annual Forum of the Association for Institutional Research, Toronto, Ontario, Canada.

McIver, J. P., & Carmines, E. G. (1981). *Unidimensional scaling.* Newbury Park, CA: Sage.

McKeachie, W. J. (1996). Do we need norms of student ratings to evaluate faculty? *Instructional Evaluation and Faculty Development, 15*(1–2), 14–17.

McKeachie, W. J. (1997). Student ratings: The validity of use. *American Psychologist, 52,* 1218–1225.

McKeachie, W. J., & Kaplan, M. (1996). Persistent problems in evaluating college teaching. *AAHE Bulletin, 48*(6), 5–8.

McNaught, C., & Anwyl, J. (1993). *Awards for teaching excellence at Australian Universities* (Research Working Paper No. 93.1). Melbourne, Australia: University of Melbourne Centre for the Study of Higher Education (ED 368–291).

Me, I. M. (2003). Prehistoric teaching techniques in cave classrooms. *Rock & a Hard Place Educational Review, 3*(4), 10–11.

Me, I. M. (2005). Naming institutions of higher education and buildings after filthy rich donors with spouses who are dead or older. *Pretentious Academic Quarterly, 14*(4), 326–329.

Me, I. M. (2006). Giving a physician a 360° assessment ride for the money. *Journal of Tabpatspratphast Assessment, 12*(7), 69–89.

Me, I. M., & You, W. U. V. (2005). Student clubbing methods to evaluate teaching. *Journal of Punching & Pummeling Evaluation, 18*(6), 170–183.

Me, I. M., & You, W. U. V. (2006a). How to screw up PowerPoint® presentations and alienate students. In U. R. Nuts (Eds.), *Instructional technology for whackos* (Vol. 1, pp. 82,620–82,631). Silicon Crater, CA: Megabyte Me Press.

Me, I. M., & You, W. U. V. (2006b). Tour de ivory tower: Lessons learned from a 360° assessment bicycle ride through academe. *Journal of Rejected Manuscripts, 43,* 4652–4678.

Menges, R. J. (1996). Awards to individuals. In M. D. Svinicki & R. J. Menges (Eds.), *Honoring exemplary teaching* (New Directions for Teaching and Learning, No. 65). San Francisco: Jossey-Bass.

Messick, S. (1989). Validity. In R. L. Linn (Ed.), *Educational measurement* (3rd ed., pp. 13–103). New York: American Council on Education and Macmillan.

Messick, S. (1995). Validity of psychological assessment: Validation of inferences from persons' responses and performances as scientific inquiry into score meaning. *American Psychologist, 50,* 741–749.

Millea, M., & Grimes, P. W. (2002). Grade expectations and student evaluation of teaching. *College Student Journal, 36*(4), 582–591.

Miller, G. A. (1956). The magic number seven plus or minus two: Some limits on our capacity for processing information. *Psychological Bulletin, 63*, 81–97.

Millis, B. J. (1992). Conducting effective peer classroom observations. In D. Wulff & J. Nyquist (Eds.), *To improve the academy* (Vol. 11, pp. 189–201). Stillwater, OK: New Forums Press.

Millis, B. J., & Cottell, P. G., Jr. (1998). *Cooperative learning for higher education faculty.* Phoenix, AZ: American Council on Education Series on Higher Education/Oryx Press.

Millis, B. J., & Kaplan, B. B. (1995). Enhance teaching through peer classroom observations. In P. Seldin & Associates (Eds.), *Improving college teaching* (pp. 137–152). Bolton, MA: Anker.

Morehead, J. W., & Shedd, P. J. (1997). Utilizing summative evaluation through external peer review of teaching. *Innovative Higher Education, 22*(1), 37–44.

Muchinsky, P. M. (1995). Peer review of teaching: Lessons learned from military and industrial research on peer assessment. *Journal on Excellence in College Teaching, 6*(3), 17–30.

Mueller, D. J. (1986). *Measuring social attitudes: A handbook for researchers and practitioners.* New York: Teachers College Press.

Murnane, R. J., & Cohen, D. K. (1986). Merit pay and the evaluation problem: Why most merit pay plans fail and a few survive. *Harvard Educational Review, 56*, 1–17.

Murray, H. G. (1983). Low inference classroom teaching behaviors and student ratings of college teaching effectiveness. *Journal of Educational Psychology, 71*, 856–865.

Murray, H. G. (1991). Effective teaching behaviors in the college classroom. In J. C. Smart (Ed.), *Higher education: Handbook of theory and research* (Vol. 7). New York: Agathon.

Murray, H. G. (1997). Effective teaching behaviors in the college classroom. In R. P. Perry & J. C. Smart (Eds.), *Effective teaching in higher education: Research and practice* (pp. 171–204). New York: Agathon.

Murray, H. G., Rushton, J. P., & Paunonen, S. V. (1990). Teacher personality traits and student instructional ratings in six types of university courses. *Journal of Educational Psychology, 82*(2), 250–261.

Murray, J. P. (1995). The teaching portfolio: A tool for department chairperson to create a climate for teaching excellence. *Innovative Higher Education, 19*(3), 163–175.

Myford, C. M. (2002). Investigating design features of descriptive graphic rating scales. *Applied Measurement in Education, 15*(2), 187–215.

Nasser, F., & Fresko, B. (2002). Faculty views of student evaluation of college teaching. *Assessment & Evaluation in Higher Education, 27*(2), 187–198.

Netemeyer, R. G., Bearden, W. O., Sharma, S. (2003). *Scaling procedures.* Thousand Oaks, CA: Sage.

Newstead, S. E., & Arnold, J. (1989). The effect of response format on ratings of teachers. *Educational and Psychological Measurement, 49*, 33–43.

Newstead, S. E., & Collis, J. M. (1987). Context and the interpretation of quantifiers of frequency. *Ergonomics, 30*, 1447–1462.

Nishisato, N., & Torii, Y. (1970). Effects of categorizing continuous normal distributions on the product-moment correlation. *Japanese Psychological Research, 13*, 45–49.

Noel, L., Levitz, R., Saluri, D., & Associates. (1985). *Increasing student retention: Effective programs and practices for reducing the dropout rate.* San Francisco: Jossey-Bass.

Nordstrom, K. F. (1995). Multiple-purpose use of a peer review of course instruction program in a multidisciplinary university department. *Journal of Excellence in College Teaching, 6*(3), 125–144.

Nunnally, J., & Bernstein, I. H. (1994). *Psychometric theory* (3rd ed.). New York: McGraw-Hill.

O'Neil, C., & Wright, W. A. (1995). *Recording teaching accomplishment: A Dalhousie guide to the teaching dossier* (5th ed.). Halifax, Canada: Dalhousie University Office of Instructional Development and Technology.

Oppenheim, A. N. (1996). *Questionnaire design and attitude measurement.* London: Heinemann.

Ory, J. C., & Braskamp, L. A. (1981). Faculty perceptions of the quality and usefulness of three types of evaluative information. *Research in Higher Education, 15*, 271–282.

Ory, J. C., Braskamp, L. A., & Pieper, D. M. (1980). The congruency of student evaluative information collected by three methods. *Journal of Educational Psychology, 72*, 181–185.

Ory, J. C., & Ryan, K. (2001). How do student ratings measure up to a new validity framework? In M. Theall, P. C. Abrami, & L. A. Mets (Eds.), *The student ratings debate: Are they valid? How can we best use them?* (New Directions for Institutional Research, No. 109, pp. 27–44). San Francisco: Jossey-Bass.

Overall, J. U., & Marsh, H. W. (1979). Midterm feedback from students: Its relationship to instructional improvement and students' cognitive and affective outcomes. *Journal of Educational Psychology, 71*, 856–865.

Overall, J. U., & Marsh, H. W. (1980). Students' evaluations of instruction: A longitudinal study of their stability. *Journal of Educational Psychology, 72*, 321–325.

Parducci, A. (1968). Often is often. *American Psychologist, 23*, 828.

Pascarella, E. T., & Terenzini, P. T. (1991). *How college affects students: Findings and insights from twenty years of research.* San Francisco: Jossey-Bass.

Payne, S. L. (1951). *The art of asking questions.* Princeton, NJ: Princeton University Press.

Peabody, D. (1962). Two components in bipolar scales: Direction and extremeness. *Psychological Review, 69*, 65–73.

Pencavel, J. H. (1977). Work effort, on-the-job screening, and alternative methods of remuneration. In R. Ehrenberg (Ed.), *Research in labor economics* (Vol.1, pp. 225–258). Greenwich, CT: JAI Press.

Penny, A. R., & Coe, R. (2004). Effectiveness of consultation on student ratings feedback: A meta-analysis. *Review of Educational Research, 74*, 215–253.

Pepper, S., & Prytulak, L. S. (1974). Sometimes frequently means seldom: Context effects in the interpretation of quantitative expressions. *Journal of Research in Personality, 8*, 95–101.

Perlberg, A. E. (1983). When professors confront themselves: Towards a theoretical conceptualization of video self-confrontation in higher education. *Higher Education, 12*, 633–663.

Puchta, C., & Potter, J. (2004). *Focus group practice.* Thousand Oaks, CA: Sage.

Ramsey, P., Carline, J. D., Inui, T. S., Larson, E. B., LoGerfo, J. P., & Wenrich, M. D. (1993). Use of peer ratings to evaluate physician performance. *Journal of the American Medical Association, 269*, 1655–1660.

Ravelli, B. (2000). Anonymous online teaching assessments: Preliminary findings. Retrieved March 28, 2003, from www.edrs.com/DocLibrary/0201/ED445069.pdf

Read, W. J., Rama, D. V., & Raghunandan, K. (2001). The relationship between student evaluations of teaching and faculty evaluations. *Journal of Business Education, 76*(4), 189–193.

Remmers, H. H. (1930). To what extent do grades influence student ratings of instruction? *Journal of Educational Research, 21*, 314–316.

Remmers, H. H. (1934). Reliability and the halo effect on high school and college students' judgments of their teachers. *Journal of Applied Psychology, 18*, 619–630.

Remmers, H. H., & Brandenburg, G. C. (1927). Experimental data on the Purdue rating scale for instructors. *Educational Administration and Supervision, 13*, 519–527.

Reynolds, A. (1992). What is a competent beginning teaching? A review of the literature. *Review of Educational Research, 62*(1), 1–35.

Rice, R. E. (1991). The new American scholar: Scholarship and the purposes of the university. *Metropolitan Universities, 1*(4), 7–18.

Richlin, L. & Manning, B. (1995). *Improving a college/university teaching evaluation system: A comprehensive two-year curriculum for faculty and administrators.* Pittsburgh, PA: Alliance.

Roe, E. (1987). *How to compile a teaching portfolio.* Kensington, Australia: Federation of Australian University Staff Associations.

Romberg, E. (1985). Description of peer evaluation within a comprehensive evaluation program in a dental school. *Instructional Evaluation, 8*(1), 10–16.

Root, L. S. (1987). Faculty evaluation: Reliability of peer assessments of research, teaching, and service. *Research in Higher Education, 26,* 71–84.

Rorer, L. G. (1965). The great response-style myth. *Psychological Bulletin, 63,* 129–156.

Rorer, L. G., & Goldberg, L. R. (1965). Acquiescence and the vanishing variance component. *Journal of Applied Psychology, 49,* 422–430.

Roth, P. L. (1994). Missing data: A conceptual review for applied psychologists. *Personnel Psychology, 47,* 537–560.

Roth, P. L., Switzer, F. S., & Switzer, D. (1999). Missing data in multiple item scales: A Monte Carlo analysis of missing data techniques. *Organizational Research Methods, 2*(3), 211–232.

Rubin, D. B. (2004). *Multiple imputation for nonresponse in surveys.* Indianapolis: Wiley.

Ruedrich, S. L., Cavey, C., Katz, K., & Grush, L. (1992). Recognition of teaching excellence through the use of teaching awards: A faculty perspective. *Academic Psychiatry, 16*(1), 10–13.

Saal, F. E., & Landy, F. J. (1977). The mixed standard rating scale: An evaluation. *Organizational Behavior and Human Performance, 18,* 19–35.

Sax, L. J., Gilmartin, S. K., & Bryant, A. N. (2003). Assessing response rates and non-response bias in web and paper surveys. *Research in Higher Education, 44*(4), 409–432.

Schmelkin-Pedhazur, L., Spencer, K. J., & Gellman, E. S. (1997). Faculty perspectives on course and teacher evaluation. *Research in Higher Education, 38*(5), 575–592.

Schmitt, N., & Lappin, M. (1980). Race and sex as determinants of the mean and variance of performance ratings. *Journal of Applied Psychology, 65,* 428–435.

Schön, D. A. (1987). *Educating the reflective practitioner: Toward a new design for teaching and learning in the professions.* San Francisco: Jossey-Bass.

Schriesheim, C. A., & Hill, K. D. (1981). Controlling acquiescence response bias by item reversals: The effect on questionnaire validity. *Educational and Psychological Measurement, 41,* 1101–1114.

Schwarz, N., Knäuper, B., Hippler, H-J., Noelle-Neumann, E., & Clark, L. (1991). Rating scales: Numeric values may change the meaning of scale labels. *Public Opinion Quarterly, 55,* 570–582.

Seifert, C. F., Yukl, G., & McDonald, R. A. (2003). Effects of multisource feedback and a feedback facilitator on the influence behavior of managers toward subordinates. *Journal of Applied Psychology, 88*, 561–469.

Seldin, P. (1980). *Successful faculty evaluation programs.* Crugers, NY: Coventry.

Seldin, P. (1995). *Improving college teaching.* Bolton, MA: Anker.

Seldin, P. (1998, February). *The teaching portfolio.* Paper presented for the American Council on Education, Department Chairs Seminar, San Diego, CA.

Seldin, P. (1999a). Current practices—good and bad—nationally. In P. Seldin & Associates (Eds.), *Changing practices in evaluating teaching: A practical guide to improved faculty performance and promotion/tenure decisions* (pp. 1–24). Bolton, MA: Anker.

Seldin, P. (1999b). Self-evaluation: What works? What doesn't? In P. Seldin & Associates (Eds.), *Changing practices in evaluating teaching: A practical guide to improved faculty performance and promotion/tenure decisions* (pp. 97–115). Bolton, MA: Anker.

Seldin, P. (2004). *The teaching portfolio* (3rd ed.). Bolton, MA: Anker.

Seldin, P., Annis, L., & Zubizarreta, J. (1995). Answers to common questions about the teaching portfolio. *Journal on Excellence in College Teaching, 6*(1), 57–64.

Seldin, P., & Associates. (Eds.). (1999). *Changing practices in evaluating teaching: A practical guide to improve faculty performance and promotion/tenure decisions.* Bolton, MA: Anker.

Seppanen, L. J. (1995). Linkages to the world of employment. In P. T. Ewell (Ed.), *Student tracking: New techniques, new demands.* San Francisco: Jossey-Bass.

Shariff, S. H. (1999). Students' quality control circle: A case study on students' participation in the quality of control circles at the faculty of business and management. *Assessment & Evaluation in Higher Education, 24*, 141–146.

Shepard, L. A. (1993). Evaluating test validity. *Review of Educational Research, 19*, 405–450.

Shevlin, M., Banyard, P., Davies, M., & Griffiths, M. (2000). The validity of student evaluation of teaching in higher education: Love me, love my lectures? *Assessment & Evaluation in Higher Education, 25*(4), 397–405.

Shore, B. M. (1975). Moving beyond the course evaluation questionnaire in evaluating university teaching. *CAUT Bulletin, 23*(4), 7–10.

Shore, B. M., & Associates. (1980). *The teaching dossier: A guide to its preparation and use.* Ottawa, Canada: Canadian Association of University Teachers.

Shore, B. M., & Associates. (1986). *The teaching dossier: A guide to its preparation and use* (Rev. ed.). Ottawa, Canada: Canadian Association of University Teachers.

Shulman, L. S. (1998). Course anatomy: The dissection and analysis of knowledge through teaching. In P. Hutchings (Ed.), *The course portfolio: How faculty can examine their teaching to advance practice and improve student learning*. Washington, DC: American Association for Higher Education.

Siegel, A. I. (1986). Performance tests. In R. A. Berk (Ed.), *Performance assessment: Methods and applications* (pp. 121–142). Baltimore, MD: Johns Hopkins University Press.

Simpson, R. H. (1994). The specific meanings of certain terms indicating differing degrees of frequency. *Quarterly Journal of Speech, 30*, 328–330.

Smith, P., & Kendall, L. M. (1963). Retranslation of expectations: An approach to the construction of unambiguous anchors for rating scales. *Journal of Applied Psychology, 47*, 149–155.

Smither, J. W., London, M., Flautt, R., Vargas, Y., & Kucine, I. (2002, April). *Does discussing multisource feedback with raters enhance performance*. Paper presented at the 17th Annual Conference of the Society for Industrial and Organizational Psychology, Toronto, Canada.

Smither, J. W., London, M., & Reilly, R. R. (2005). Does performance improve following multisource feedback? A theoretical model, meta-analysis, and review of empirical findings. *Personnel Psychology, 58*, 33–66.

Soderberg, L. O. (1986). A credible model: Evaluating classroom teaching in higher education. *Instructional Evaluation, 8*, 13–27.

Sojka, J., Gupta, A. K., & Deeter-Schmelz, D. R. (2002). Student and faculty perceptions of student evaluations of teaching. *College Teaching, 50*(2), 44–49.

Sorenson, D. L. (2005, November). *Online student ratings of instruction*. Paper presented at the annual Lilly Conference on College Teaching, Miami University, Oxford, OH.

Sorenson, D. L., & Johnson, T. D. (Eds.). (2003). *Online student ratings of instruction* (New Directions for Teaching and Learning, No. 96). San Francisco: Jossey-Bass.

Sorenson, D. L., & Reiner, C. (2003). Charting the uncharted seas of online student ratings of instruction. In D. L. Sorenson & T. D. Johnson (Eds.), *Online student ratings of instruction* (New Directions for Teaching and Learning, No. 96, pp. 1–29). San Francisco: Jossey-Bass.

Sorey, K. E. (1968). A study of the distinguishing characteristics of college faculty who are superior in regard to the teaching function. *Dissertation Abstracts, 28*(12-A), 4916.

Spector, P. E. (1976). Choosing response categories for summated rating scales. *Journal of Applied Psychology, 61*, 374–375.

Spector, P. E. (1992). *Summated rating scale construction: An introduction*. Thousand Oaks, CA: Sage.

Spencer, L. M., & Spencer, S. M. (1993). *Competence at work: Models for superior performance*. New York: Wiley.

Spooner, F., Jordan, L., Algozzine, B., & Spooner, M. (1999). Student ratings of instruction in distance learning and on-campus classes. *Journal of Educational Research, 92*, 132–140.

Sproule, R. (2002). The under-determination of instructor performance by data from the student evaluation of teaching. *Economics of Education Review, 21*(3), 287–295.

Streiner, D. L., & Norman, G. R. (1995). *Health measurement scales: A practical guide to their development and use* (2nd ed.) New York: Oxford University Press.

Symonds, P. M. (1924). On the loss of reliability in ratings due to coarseness of the scale. *Journal of Experimental Psychology, 7*, 456-461.

Tabachnick, B. G., & Fidell, L. S. (2001). *Using multivariate statistics* (4th ed.). New York: HarperCollins.

Taylor, W. L. (1957). "Close" readability scores as indices of individual differences in comprehension and aptitude. *Journal of Applied Psychology, 41*, 19–26.

Theall, M. (1996). Who is norm, and what does he have to do with student ratings? A reaction to McKeachie. *Instructional Evaluation and Faculty Development, 16*(1–2), 7–9.

Theall, M., Abrami, P. C., & Mets, L. A. (Eds.). (2001). *The student ratings debate: Are they valid? How can we best use them?* (New Directions for Institutional Research, No. 109). San Francisco: Jossey-Bass.

Theall, M., & Franklin, J. L. (1990). Student ratings in the context of complex evaluation systems. In M. Theall & J. L. Franklin (Eds.), *Student ratings of instruction: Issues for improving practice* (New Directions for Teaching and Learning, No. 43). San Francisco: Jossey-Bass.

Theall, M., & Franklin, J. L. (2001). Looking for bias in all the wrong places: A search for truth or a witch hunt in student ratings of instruction? In M. Theall, P. C. Abrami, & L. A. Mets (Eds.), *The student ratings debate: Are they valid? How can we best use them?* (New Directions for Institutional Research, No. 109, pp. 45–56). San Francisco: Jossey-Bass.

Thorndike, E. L. (1920). A constant error in psychological ratings. *Journal of Applied Psychology, 4*, 25–29.

Thurstone, L. L. (1946). Comment. *American Journal of Sociology, 52*, 39–50.

Thurstone, L. L., & Chave, E. J. (1929). *The measurement of attitude*. Chicago: University of Chicago Press.

Tiberius, R. (1997). Small group methods for collecting information from students. In K. T. Brinko & R. J. Menges (Eds), *Practically speaking: A sourcebook for instructional consultants in higher education*. Stillwater, OK: New Forums Press.

Tinsley, H. E. A., & Tinsley, D. J. (1987). Uses of factor analysis in counseling psychology research. *Journal of Counseling Psychology, 34*, 414–424.

Tinto, V. (1987). *Leaving college: Rethinking the causes and cures of student attrition.* Chicago: University of Chicago Press.

Tornow, W. W., London, M., & CCL Associates. (1998). *Maximizing the value of 360-degree feedback: A process for successful individual and organizational development.* San Francisco: Jossey-Bass.

Trinkaus, J. (2002). Students' course and faculty evaluations: An informal look. *Psychological Reports, 91*, 988.

U.S. Department of Education. (1991, Winter). Assessing teaching performance. *The Department Chair: A Newsletter for Academic Administrators, 2*(3), 2.

Vinson, M. N. (1996). The pros and cons of 360-degree feedback: Making it work. *Training and Development,*° *50*(4), 11–12.

Violato, C., Marini, A., Toews, J., Lockyer, J. M., & Fidler, H. (1997). Feasibility and psychometric properties of using peers, consulting physicians, co-workers, and patients to assess physicians. *Academic Medicine, 72*, 82S–84S.

Wachtel, H. K. (1998). Student evaluation of college teaching effectiveness: A brief review. *Assessment & Evaluation in Higher Education, 23*, 199–212.

Wall, D., Rayner, H., & Palmer, R. (2005, September). *Multi-source feedback: 360° assessment of professional skills of clinical directors.* Short communication presented at the annual conference of the Association for Medical Education in Europe, Amsterdam, The Netherlands.

Wang, K. A. (1932). Suggested criteria for writing attitude statements. *Journal of Social Psychology, 3*, 367–373.

Waschull, S. B. (2001). The online delivery of psychology courses: Attrition, performance, and evaluation. *Computers in Teaching, 28*, 143–147.

Webb, J., & McEnerney, K. (1995). The view from the back of the classroom: A faculty-based peer observation program. *Journal on Excellence in College Teaching, 6*(3), 145–160.

Webb, J., & McEnerney, K. (1997). Implementing peer review programs: A twelve step model. In D. DeZure (Ed.), *To improve the academy* (Vol. 16, pp. 295–316). Stillwater, OK: New Forums Press and the Professional and Organizational Development Network in Higher Education.

Weimer, M. E. (1990). *Improving college teaching: Strategies for developing instructional effectiveness.* San Francisco: Jossey-Bass.

Weimer, M. E. (1993). The disciplinary journals of pedagogy. *Change, 25*, 44–51.

Weimer, M. E. (2002). *Learner-centered teaching.* Indianapolis: Jossey-Bass.

Wenrich, M. D., Carline, J. D., Giles, L. M., & Ramsey, P. G. (1993). Ratings of the performances of practicing internists by hospital-based registered nurses. *Academic Medicine, 68*, 680–687.

Wergin, J. E. (1992, September). *Developing and using performance criteria.* Paper presented at the Virginia Commonwealth University Conference on Faculty Rewards, Richmond, VA.

Wherry, R. J., & Fryer, D. C. (1949). Buddy rating: Popularity contest of leadership criterion? *Personnel Psychology, 2*, 147–159.

Whitehouse, A., Hassell, A., Wood, L. Wall, D., Walzman, M. & Campbell, I. (2005). Development and reliability testing of TAB—A form for 360° assessment of senior house officers' professional behaviour, as specified by the General Medical Council. *Medical Teacher, 27*, 252–258.

Wildt, A. R., & Mazis, A. B. (1978). Determinants of scale response: Label versus position. *Journal of Marketing Research, 15*, 261–267.

Wood, J., Collins, J., Burnside, E. S., Albanese, M. A., Propeck, P. A., Kelcz, F., Spilde, J. M., & Schmaltz, L. M. (2004). Patient, faculty, and self-assessment of radiology resident performance: A 360-degree method of measuring professionalism and interpersonal/communication skills. *Academic Radiology, 11*, 931–939.

Woolliscroft, J. O., Howell, J. D., Patel, B. P., & Swanson, D. B. (1994). Resident–patient interactions: The humanistic qualities of internal medicine residents assessed by patients, attending physicians, program supervisors, and nurses. *Academic Medicine, 69*, 216–224.

Wright, A. W., & Associates (1995). *Teaching improvement practices: Successful strategies for higher education.* Bolton, MA: Anker.

Zahorski, K. J. (1996). Honoring exemplary teaching in the liberal arts institution. In M. D. Svinicki & R. J. Menges (Eds.), *Honoring exemplary teaching* (New Directions for Teaching and Learning, No. 65). San Francisco: Jossey-Bass.

Zedeck, S., Kafry, D., & Jacobs, R. R. (1976). Format and scoring variations in behavioral expectation evaluations. *Organizational Behavior and Human Performance, 17,* 171–184.

APPENDIX A

SAMPLE "HOME GROWN" RATING SCALES

Johns Hopkins University School of Nursing

- Course Evaluation Scale
- Clinical Faculty Evaluation Scale
- Guest Lecturer Evaluation Scale
- Peer Evaluation Scale
- Employer Rating Form—Baccalaureate
- Employer Rating Form—Master's
- Clinical Course Faculty Performance Appraisal Form
- Mentorship Profile Questionnaire
- Mentorship Effectiveness Scale

0820574882   **Johns Hopkins University School of Nursing**
Course Evaluation Scale

Course Identifier	Faculty	Semester	Year
		1=Spring 2=Fall	
. .		3=Winter 4=Summer	

The purpose of this scale is to evaluate the quality of the course and the effectiveness of your instructor/course coordinator. He/she will receive a summary report after grades are submitted to the Registrar. All responses will remain anonymous and confidential. You may use a pencil or pen. Please complete all items. **DO NOT** write any stray marks on this form.

DIRECTIONS: Indicate the extent of your agreement with each statement below. Completely blacken the box ■ corresponding to your response using the scale below:

SD = Strongly Disagree
D = Disagree
A = Agree
SA = Strongly Agree

Course Content and Organization

	SD	D	A	SA
1. Syllabus provided clear statements of how you would be graded.	☐	☐	☐	☐
2. Syllabus provided clear statements of course requirements.	☐	☐	☐	☐
3. Syllabus provided objectives/outcomes that reflected course content.	☐	☐	☐	☐
4. Course materials were useful in attaining course objectives/outcomes.	☐	☐	☐	☐
5. Course materials were at the appropriate level of difficulty for the course level.	☐	☐	☐	☐
6. Assignments were useful in understanding course content.	☐	☐	☐	☐
7. The course was well organized.	☐	☐	☐	☐
8. The course requirements were appropriate for the number of credits.	☐	☐	☐	☐

Evaluation Methods (e.g., exams, projects, presentations)

	SD	D	A	SA
9. Evaluation methods measured course objectives/outcomes.	☐	☐	☐	☐
10. Evaluation methods were fair.	☐	☐	☐	☐
11. Evaluation methods were appropriate for the course level.	☐	☐	☐	☐
12. Evaluation methods covered important content, not trivial information.	☐	☐	☐	☐
13. Evaluation methods required critical thinking/problem solving, not just memorization.	☐	☐	☐	☐

Learning Outcomes

	SD	D	A	SA
14. Attending classes in this course was worthwhile.	☐	☐	☐	☐
15. This course positively changed my thinking about the subject area.	☐	☐	☐	☐
16. I learned new information in this course.	☐	☐	☐	☐
17. What I learned in this course will be useful in my career.	☐	☐	☐	☐

please continue on back

Copyright © 2002 The Johns Hopkins University

Ver. 11/9/2000

Instructional Methods
Instructor/Course Coordinator:

	SD	D	A	SA
18. Encouraged self-directed learning.	☐	☐	☐	☐
19. Utilized useful audiovisuals, where appropriate.	☐	☐	☐	☐
20. Facilitated critical thinking/problem solving.	☐	☐	☐	☐
21. Appeared knowledgeable about course content.	☐	☐	☐	☐
22. Demonstrated clear relationships between theory and practice.	☐	☐	☐	☐
23. Provided relevant examples to illustrate content.	☐	☐	☐	☐
24. Paced instruction to facilitate learning.	☐	☐	☐	☐
25. Encouraged questions, comments, and discussion.	☐	☐	☐	☐
26. Provided timely feedback on assignments and/or tests.	☐	☐	☐	☐
27. Provided helpful feedback on assignments and/or tests.	☐	☐	☐	☐
28. Encouraged students' participation in learning during class.	☐	☐	☐	☐
29. Made clear and understandable presentations.	☐	☐	☐	☐
30. Was thoroughly prepared for each class.	☐	☐	☐	☐

Learning Atmosphere
Instructor/Course Coordinator:

	SD	D	A	SA
31. Was available for individual assistance.	☐	☐	☐	☐
32. Demonstrated respect for each student.	☐	☐	☐	☐
33. Was responsive to students' needs.	☐	☐	☐	☐
34. Was approachable out of class to answer questions.	☐	☐	☐	☐
35. Demonstrated sensitivity to gender and cultural differences.	☐	☐	☐	☐
36. Displayed enthusiasm for teaching.	☐	☐	☐	☐

Comments:

What did you like **MOST** about the course?

What did you like **LEAST** about the course?

What suggestions do you have for **IMPROVEMENT?**

6225149201

Johns Hopkins University School of Nursing
Clinical Faculty Evaluation Scale

ClinicalInstructor

CourseIdentifier	Coordinator	Semester	Year
		1=Spring 2=Fall 3=Winter 4=Summer	

The purpose of this scale is to evaluate the effectiveness of your clinical instructor. The coordinator and instructor will receive a summary report after grades are submitted to the Registrar. All responses will remain anonymous and confidential. You may use a pencil or pen. Please complete all items. **DO NOT** write any stray marks on this form.

DIRECTIONS: Indicate the extent of your agreement with each statement below. Completely blacken the oval ● corresponding to your response using the scale to the right:

SD = Strongly Disagree
D = Disagree
A = Agree
S = Strongly Agree

Instructional Methods

My Instructor:

	SD	D	A	SA
1. Provided adequate orientation to my clinical requirements.	○	○	○	○
2. Clarified my learning needs.	○	○	○	○
3. Provided timely written and/or verbal feedback, as appropriate.	○	○	○	○
4. Mentored me in my nursing role.	○	○	○	○
5. Evaluated me fairly.	○	○	○	○
6. Communicated regularly with me.	○	○	○	○
7. Was available for individual advising and counseling.	○	○	○	○
8. Provided assistance when I had questions or was having difficulty.	○	○	○	○
9. Demonstrated respect for me.	○	○	○	○
10. Facilitated my critical thinking and problem solving.	○	○	○	○

Clinical Experiences

My Instructor:

	SD	D	A	SA
11. Provided experiences useful in attaining course objectives/outcomes.	○	○	○	○
12. Assisted me in applying theory and research to clinical practice.	○	○	○	○
13. Provided experiences to meet my learning needs.	○	○	○	○
14. Encouraged me to collaborate with my healthcare team.	○	○	○	○
15. Demonstrated current clinical knowledge.	○	○	○	○
16. Demonstrated skill proficiency.	○	○	○	○
17. Was a positive role model.	○	○	○	○
18. I would recommend continued use of this clinical site for this course.	○	○	○	○

(For Masters Level Students Only)

	SD	D	A	SA
19. Communicated regularly with my preceptor.	○	○	○	○

Comments:

What aspects of this clinical experience were **EFFECTIVE**?

What aspects need **IMPROVEMENT**?

What suggestions do you have for **IMPROVEMENT**?

Mod 12/12/2002

8733

JOHNS HOPKINS UNIVERSITY
SCHOOL OF NURSING

GUEST LECTURER EVALUATION SCALE

DIRECTIONS: Please fill in the information on this page. Indicate the extent to which you agree or disagree with each statement, and mark the appropriate oval ● on this form. Add any comments regarding the speaker in the space provided.

Coordinator	Course Identifier

Semester   Year   Date
   1=Spring 2=Fall
   3=Winter 4=Summer
☐☐ / ☐☐ / ☐☐

SD = Strongly Disagree
D = Disagree
A = Agree
SA = Strongly Agree

Speaker: _____
Topic _____

	SD	D	A	SA
1. The presentation was useful in attaining course objectives/outcomes.	O	O	O	O
2. The presentation was well organized.	O	O	O	O
3. The presentation was clear and understandable.	O	O	O	O
4. The presenter provided relevant examples to illustrate content.	O	O	O	O
5. The presenter paced instruction to facilitate learning.	O	O	O	O
6. The presenter encouraged questions, comments, and discussion.	O	O	O	O

Comments: ─────────────────

Speaker ID

JOHNS HOPKINS UNIVERSITY SCHOOL OF NURSING
PEER EVALUATION SCALE

Instructor: _____

Observer:_____

Course/Room No.:_____

Class Topic:_____

Date:_____

PURPOSE: This scale is designed as an observation tool to rate an individual instructor's teaching performance. It is intended to provide a diagnostic profile for teaching improvement.

DIRECTIONS: Using the anchors below, check (✓) your rating for each teaching behavior that's applicable for the specific class observed. Check "NA" for items that do not apply.

E	=	Excellent
VG	=	Very Good
G	=	Good
NI	=	Needs Improvement
NA	=	Not Applicable

	E	VG	G	NI	NA	Comments:
Content and Organization						
Started and ended class on time						
Presented overview of class content/objectives						
Presented rationale for topics covered						
Presented key concepts						
Presented current material						
Presented information in an organized manner						
Demonstrated accurate knowledge of content						
Used relevant examples to explain major ideas						
Used alternative explanations when necessary						
Made efficient use of class time						
Covered class content/objectives						
Communication Style						
Varied pace appropriately						
Enunciated clearly						
Varied modulation						
Varied tone						
Spoke with adequate volume						
Demonstrated confidence						
Demonstrated enthusiasm						
Moved easily about room during presentation						
Used speech fillers (um, ok, ah) rarely						
Established and maintained eye contact						
Maintained students' attention						
Questioning Skills						
Encouraged students' questions						
Listened carefully to students' questions						
Answered questions appropriately						
Restated students' questions or comments as necessary						

	E	VG	G	NI	NA	Comments:
Critical Thinking Skills						
Asked probing questions						
Used case studies or scenarios						
Used small-group discussion						
Encouraged students to answer difficult questions by providing cues or rephrasing						
Rapport with Students						
Greeted students at the beginning of class						
Responded appropriately to students' puzzlement or Boredom						
Asked students to clarify questions, when necessary						
Requested very difficult, time-consuming, or irrelevant questions be addressed at a later time						
Used humor and/or anecdotes appropriately						
Demonstrated respect for students and their thoughts/ Concerns						
Learning Environment						
Physical characteristics (temperature, lighting, crowding, seating)						
Class Affect						
Conducive to learning						
Relaxed						
Controlled						
Teaching Methods						
Lecture						
Engagement techniques						
Q&A						
Discussion						
Small-group activities						
Student individual/panel presentations						
Active learning (e.g., think-pair-share)						
One-minute paper						
Other						
Role playing						
Demonstrations/skits						
Simulations						
Games						
Use or integration of technology						
Overheads						
PowerPoint						
Slides						
PC						
CD/ROM						
Course Web site						
Internet						
Videos						
Audiotapes						
Other						
Experimental/Innovative techniques						

	E	VG	G	NI	NA	Comments:
Specify_____						
Other_____						

Strengths:

Areas for Improvement:

_____
Observer Signature

Peereval2.doc

Copyright© 2003 The Johns Hopkins University

*Agency/Institution:*_____

*Department:*_____

*JHU Graduate (1, 2, etc.)#*_____

*Length of employment:*_____

*Date:*_____

EMPLOYER RATING FORM

DIRECTIONS: As an employer of a *new* graduate(s) of the *baccalaureate* program at the Johns Hopkins University School of Nursing for at least 6 months, please complete this form for *each* graduate. To preserve confidentiality, only number the graduate in the blank above. DO NOT IDENTIFY THE GRADUATE BY NAME. Only aggregate data will be used to evaluate program outcomes.

Rate the *quality* of his or her knowledge, skills, and abilities based on performance. *Circle* your ratings using the following scale:

E = Excellent
VG = Very Good
G = Good
F = Fair
P = Poor
NA = Not Applicable (or Not Observed)

1. Readiness for entry-level nursing.	E	VG	G	F	P	NA
2. Application of evidence-based findings to practice.	E	VG	G	F	P	NA
3. Application of principles of science to patient safety.	E	VG	G	F	P	NA
4. Critical thinking.	E	VG	G	F	P	NA
5. Written communication.	E	VG	G	F	P	NA
6. Oral communication.	E	VG	G	F	P	NA
7. Ability to assess the health status of individuals.	E	VG	G	F	P	NA
8. Ability to organize work responsibilities.	E	VG	G	F	P	NA
9. Leadership skills.	E	VG	G	F	P	NA
10. Interpersonal skills with members of the healthcare team.	E	VG	G	F	P	NA

(Continue on Back)

11. Willingness to work on the healthcare team.	*E*	*VG*	*G*	*F*	*P*	*NA*
12. Interpersonal skills with patients.	*E*	*VG*	*G*	*F*	*P*	*NA*
13. Interpersonal skills with families.	*E*	*VG*	*G*	*F*	*P*	*NA*
14. Cultural (diversity) competency skills.	*E*	*VG*	*G*	*F*	*P*	*NA*
15. Ability to delegate responsibilities.	*E*	*VG*	*G*	*F*	*P*	*NA*
16. Fairness and nondiscrimination in nursing activities.	*E*	*VG*	*G*	*F*	*P*	*NA*
17. Professional attitude.	*E*	*VG*	*G*	*F*	*P*	*NA*
18. Professional integrity.	*E*	*VG*	*G*	*F*	*P*	*NA*
19. Utilization of available resources (e.g., equipment, supplies, personnel).	*E*	*VG*	*G*	*F*	*P*	*NA*
20. Overall performance for entry-level nursing practice.	*E*	*VG*	*G*	*F*	*P*	*NA*

21. How satisfied are you with the performance of this employee? (check one)

_____ Extremely Satisfied
_____ Very Satisfied
_____ Somewhat Satisfied
_____ Somewhat Dissatisfied
_____ Very Dissatisfied
_____ Extremely Dissatisfied

COMMENTS ON PERFORMANCE:

*Agency/Institution:*_____   *JHU Graduate (1, 2, etc.) #*_____
                                          Educational Preparation/Specialty Track
                                          (Please check one):
*Department:*_____   _____Primary care NP (family, adult, pediatric)
                                          _____Acute care NP
                                          _____Health Systems Management
*Date:*_____   _____CNS (Clinical Nurse Specialist)
                                          _____Other (Specify:_____)
*Length of employment:*_____

EMPLOYER RATING FORM

DIRECTIONS: If you have employed a graduate(s) of the *master's degree* program at the Johns Hopkins University School of Nursing for at least 6 months, please complete this form for *each* graduate. To preserve confidentiality, only number the graduate in the blank above. DO NOT IDENTIFY THE GRADUATE BY NAME. Only aggregate data will be used to evaluate program outcomes.

Rate the *quality* of his or her knowledge, skills, and abilities based on performance since graduation/employment. *Circle* your ratings using the following scale:

E = Excellent
VG = Very Good
G = Good
F = Fair
P = Poor
NA = Not Applicable (or Not Observed)

1. Preparation for advanced practice.	E	VG	G	F	P	NA
2. Clinical competence.	E	VG	G	F	P	NA
3. Application of evidence-based findings to practice.	E	VG	G	F	P	NA
4. Application of management skills.	E	VG	G	F	P	NA
5. Ethical decision-making.	E	VG	G	F	P	NA
6. Critical thinking.	E	VG	G	F	P	NA
7. Written communication.	E	VG	G	F	P	NA
8. Oral communication.	E	VG	G	F	P	NA
9. Ability to prioritize.	E	VG	G	F	P	NA
10. Leadership skills.	E	VG	G	F	P	NA

(Continue on Back)

11. Management skills (e.g., conflict management & negotiation, change agent).	*E*	*VG*	*G*	*F*	*P*	*NA*
12. Interpersonal skills on the healthcare team.	*E*	*VG*	*G*	*F*	*P*	*NA*
13. Willingness to work on the healthcare team.	*E*	*VG*	*G*	*F*	*P*	*NA*
14. Interpersonal skills with patients/clients.	*E*	*VG*	*G*	*F*	*P*	*NA*
15. Interpersonal skills with families.	*E*	*VG*	*G*	*F*	*P*	*NA*
16. Interpersonal skills with communities.	*E*	*VG*	*G*	*F*	*P*	*NA*
17. Cultural (diversity) competency skills.	*E*	*VG*	*G*	*F*	*P*	*NA*
18. Ability to delegate responsibilities.	*E*	*VG*	*G*	*F*	*P*	*NA*
19. Professional attitudes.	*E*	*VG*	*G*	*F*	*P*	*NA*
20. Professional integrity.	*E*	*VG*	*G*	*F*	*P*	*NA*
21. Utilization of research process in practice.	*E*	*VG*	*G*	*F*	*P*	*NA*
22. Evidence of ongoing professional development.	*E*	*VG*	*G*	*F*	*P*	*NA*
23. Contribution to advancement of the profession.	*E*	*VG*	*G*	*F*	*P*	*NA*
24. Utilization of appropriate resources (e.g., equipment, supplies, personnel).	*E*	*VG*	*G*	*F*	*P*	*NA*
25. Overall performance.	*E*	*VG*	*G*	*F*	*P*	*NA*

26. How satisfied are you with the performance of this employee? (check one)
___Extremely Satisfied
___Very Satisfied
___Somewhat Satisfied
___Somewhat Dissatisfied
___Very Dissatisfied
___Extremely Dissatisfied

COMMENTS ON PERFORMANCE:

JOHNS HOPKINS UNIVERSITY SCHOOL OF NURSING
CLINICAL COURSE FACULTY PERFORMANCE APPRAISAL FORM

Course Coordinator:_____

Clinical Faculty:_____

Course Title (No.):_____

Date:_____

PURPOSE: This scale is designed as an evaluation tool to rate each clinical faculty member. It is intended to provide a diagnostic profile for teaching improvement.

PROCEDURES:

Course coordinator will visit new clinical faculty at least once during the semester to evaluate clinical instruction methods. Additional visits may occur as necessary. Following the initial evaluation, course coordinators will evaluate faculty at least bi-annually.

Clinical faculty member will complete a self-evaluation using this tool, including the two open-ended responses.

A *meeting* will be scheduled between the course coordinator and the faculty member to discuss the results following the clinical site visit. The meeting should occur as soon as possible after the site visit. The self-evaluation form will be used in conjunction with the course coordinator's appraisal to analyze faculty performance and suggest areas for improvement.

DIRECTIONS: Check (✓) your rating of AGREE (**A**) or DISAGREE (**DA**) for each of the teaching behaviors listed below. For each DA response, please explain in the comments section to the right or on the back of this form if more space is needed. For any behaviors NOT APPLICABLE (**NA**) or NOT OBSERVED (**NOB**), check as appropriate.

	A	DA	NA	NOB	Comments:
TEACHING METHODS					
Demonstrates:					
Professionalism					
Enthusiasm					
Respect for students, staff, and patients					
Current clinical knowledge					
Thorough preparation for clinical experience					
Sensitivity to gender and cultural differences					
Effective communication skills (e.g., constructive, nonthreatening feedback, appropriate verbal and nonverbal responses)					
Assures safe application of clinical care					
Assists students to apply theory to practice					
Assures clinical experiences are appropriate for course level					
Facilitates critical thinking skills					
Provides timely verbal feedback					

	A	DA	NA	NOB	Comments:
Provides constructive verbal feedback					
Organizes clinical experiences to maximize learning					
Varies teaching strategies according to student characteristics and abilities					
Provides insightful written feedback to students					
Provides timely written feedback to students (e.g., nursing care plan comments, e-mail, memos)					
Grading clearly discriminates among different levels of performance					
COURSE MANAGEMENT					
Follows clinical course guidelines					
Adheres to established student clinical hours					
Attends clinical course-related meetings					
Develops a written, systematic plan for student improvement, as appropriate					
Provides course coordinator with appropriate feedback on selected students					
Provides course coordinator with timely feedback on selected students					
Seeks assistance from course coordinator as appropriate					
Assists with additional course activities as necessary (e.g., developing care plan guidelines, revising student evaluation tool)					
Submits students' grades promptly					

Strengths:

Areas for Improvement:

_____
Signature

MENTORSHIP PROFILE QUESTIONNAIRE

Your name:_____ Mentor's name: _____

Part I: Description of Relationship

1. What was the *role* of your mentor? _____
    (e.g., teacher, counselor,
    advisor, sponsor, advocate,   _____
    resource)

2. How often did you *communicate*?
    (e.g., e-mail, in person, telephone) _____

3. *How long* have you had this relationship? _____

4. How would you characterize the *strengths* and *weaknesses* of your relationship? _____

    _____

    _____

Part II: Outcome Measures

Directions: Please check all of the following that resulted from your interaction with your mentor and specify or describe below. Supporting documents may be attached, as appropriate.

1. ☐ Publication   _____

2. ☐ Presentation or poster   _____

3. ☐ New teaching method or strategy   _____

4. ☐ Clinical expertise   _____

5. ☐ Conducting research   _____

6. ☐ Service activities
        (e.g. community service, political activity, professional organization)

    _____

    _____

7. ☐ Development of a program:
        (e.g. educational/clinical course or new program of study).

    _____

    _____

8. ☐ Job change/promotion   _____

9. ☐ Grant writing/submission   _____

10. ☐ Other   _____

MENTORSHIP EFFECTIVENESS SCALE

Your name: _____

Directions: The purpose of this scale is to evaluate the mentoring characteristics of _____, who has identified you as an individual with whom he/she has had a professional, mentor/mentee relationship. Indicate the extent to which you agree or disagree with each statement listed below. Circle the letters that correspond to your response. Your responses will be kept confidential.

SD = Strongly Disagree
D = Disagree
SID = Slightly Disagree
SIA = Slightly Agree
A = Agree
SA = Strongly Agree
NA = Not Applicable

SAMPLE: My mentor was hilarious.	SD	D	SID	SIA	A	(SA)	NA

1. My mentor was accessible. — SD D SID SIA A SA NA

2. My mentor demonstrated professional integrity. — SD D SID SIA A SA NA

3. My mentor demonstrated content expertise in my area of need. — SD D SID SIA A SA NA

4. My mentor was approachable. — SD D SID SIA A SA NA

5. My mentor was supportive and encouraging. — SD D SID SIA A SA NA

6. My mentor provided constructive and useful critiques of my work. — SD D SID SIA A SA NA

7. My mentor motivated me to improve my work product. — SD D SID SIA A SA NA

8. My mentor was helpful in providing direction and guidance on professional issues. (e.g., networking). — SD D SID SIA A SA NA

9. My mentor answered my questions satisfactorily (e.g., timely response, clear, comprehensive). — SD D SID SIA A SA NA

10. My mentor acknowledged my contributions appropriately (e.g., committee contributions, awards). — SD D SID SIA A SA NA

11. My mentor suggested appropriate resources (e.g., experts, electronic contacts, source materials). — SD D SID SIA A SA NA

12. My mentor challenged me to extend my abilities (e.g., risk taking, try a new professional activity, draft a section of an article). — SD D SID SIA A SA NA

Please make additional comments on the back of this sheet.

APPENDIX B

SAMPLE 360° ASSESSMENT RATING SCALES

- Multi-Source Feedback: 360° Team Assessment of Behaviour (TAB)
- Team Assessment of Behaviour (TAB): Summary for Appraisal Meeting
- Multi-Source Feedback: 360° Assessment of Professional Skills of Clinical Director
- Sheffield Peer Review Assessment Tool (SPRAT)
- mini-PAT (Peer Assessment Tool—F2 Version
- Self mini-PAT (Peer Assessment Tool)
- PHAST Diagnostic Questionnaire

MULTI-SOURCE FEEDBACK: 360° Team Assessment of Behaviour (TAB)*

Trainee's Name: _____ GMC No: _____ Current post: _____ Date started present post: _____

Please use the comments boxes to commend good behaviour and to describe any behaviour causing you concern. Give specific examples. This form will be sent to the trainee's educational supervisor, who may ask you privately to enlarge on any concern behaviour you report. At least 9 other forms will also be considered. The trainee will receive private feedback, but you will not be identified in person without advance discussion with you.

ATTITUDE AND/OR BEHAVIOUR	No concern	You have some concern	You have a major concern	COMMENTS: *Anything especially good?* If you cannot give an opinion due to lack of knowledge of the trainee say so here. **You must specifically comment on any concern behaviour**, and this should reflect the trainee's behaviour over time – not usually just a single incident.
Maintaining trust / Professional relationship with patients Listens. Is polite and caring. Shows respect for patients' opinions, privacy, dignity and confidentiality. Is unprejudiced.				
Verbal communication skills Gives understandable information. Speaks good English, at the appropriate level for the patient.				
Team-working / Working with colleagues Respects others' roles, and works constructively in the team. Hands over effectively, and communicates well. Is unprejudiced, supportive and fair.				
Accessibility Accessible. Takes proper responsibility. Only delegates appropriately. Does not shirk duty. Responds when called. Arranges cover for absence.				
Name of assessor:	Post/designation:		Signature:	Date:

Please send the completed form, straight away, in a sealed envelope, to the postgraduate centre manager

*Reprinted by permission of Dr. David Wall (9/05). Whitehouse, A., Hassell, A., Wood, L., Wall, D., Walzman, M., & Campbell, I. (2005). Development and reliability testing of TAB—A form for 360° assessment of senior house officers' professional behaviour, as specified by the General Medical Council. *Medical Teacher, 27*, 252–258. (Also see www.wmdeanery.org/.)

Team Assessment of Behaviour (TAB) : SUMMARY FOR APPRAISAL MEETING

Name of Trainee _____   GMC No _____   Present post No: _____   Present speciality /attachment: _____

ATTITUDE AND/OR BEHAVIOUR	How many 'No concern'	How many 'Some concern'	How many 'Major concern'	How many No response	SUMMARY OF COMMENTS
Maintaining trust / Professional relationship with patients Listens. Is polite and caring. Shows respect for patients opinions, privacy, dignity and confidentiality. Is unprejudiced.					
Verbal communication skills Gives understandable information. Speaks good English, at the appropriate level for the patient.					
Team-working / Working with colleagues Respects others' roles, and works constructively in the team. Hands over effectively, and communicates well. Is unprejudiced, supportive and fair.					
Accessibility Accessible. Takes proper responsibility. Only delegates appropriately. Does not shirk duty. Responds when called. Arranges cover for absence.					
Totals					**NB: This summary, and any other evidence of performance, must be made available to the trainee at the appraisal meeting.**

Name of ES:
Date of appraisal meeting: *Signature:*

Multi-Source Feedback: 360° Assessment of Professional Skills of Clinical Director*

Clinical Director's name: _____

Please use this form to commend good skills or to describe issues that cause you concern. Give specific examples. The clinical director has nominated you as one of the 10 individuals who have been sent this form within the directorate. Results will be collated by the medical director and no individual will be identified.

SKILLS	UNACCEPTABLE	BORDERLINE	ACCEPTABLE	GOOD	EXCELLENT	COMMENTS Please state anything exceptionally good. You must make specific comment if there is any area of concern.
1. Operational Management Writing and presenting reports, coping with pressure and deadlines, reasoned thinking						
2. Interpersonal Skills Conflict resolution, sensitivity, communication skills, credibility and adaptability						
3. Creative and Strategic Thinking Developing the learning environment, innovative thinking, leadership, flexibility and challenging traditional practice to introduce new initiatives						

Name of assessor (caps) ....Signature.................Date..........

*Reprinted by permission of Dr. David Wall (9/05). Wall, D., Rayner, H., & Palmer, R. (2005, September). *Multi-source feedback: 360°Assessment of professional skills of clinical directors.* Short communication presented at the annual conference of the Association for Medical Education in Europe, Amsterdam, The Netherlands.

⌐ Sheffield Peer Review Assessment Tool (SPRAT): ⌐

Project No.

The rating system should be viewed as a continuum from 1-6. 1 is the worst practitioner at their level that you have come across and 6 is the best. The descriptors are there to help define the scale's meaning. An average practitioner scores 4 (satisfactory).

Please use a cross to indicate your choice(s) for each question eg. X or write within the spaces provided

1. Practitioner   Surname

   Forename

2. GMC/GDC Number: ⬚   3. Your Gender: ☐ Male   ☐ Female

4. Which clinical environment have you primarily observed the practitioner in? **(Please choose one answer only)**

   ☐ Inpatients   ☐ Outpatients   ☐ Both In and Out-patients   ☐ Admissions
   ☐ A&E   ☐ Intensive Care   ☐ Theatre   ☐ Radiology
   ☐ General Practice   ☐ Community Speciality   ☐ Dentistry
   ☐ Other (Please specify)

5. Your position: ☐ Consultant   ☐ SASG   ☐ SpR   ☐ Foundation/PRHO   ☐ GP
   ☐ Nurse   ☐ SHO   ☐ AHP   ☐ GDS   ☐ CDS
   ☐ Other (Please specify)

6. Length of working relationship (in months): ⬚   7. If you are a Nurse or AHP how long have you been qualified?: ⬚ years

How do you rate this practitioner in their:	Very Poor 1	Poor 2	Needs Development 3	Satisfactory 4	Good 5	Very Good 6	U/C
Good Clinical Care							
1 Ability to diagnose patient problems	☐	☐	☐	☐	☐	☐	☐
2 Ability to formulate appropriate management plans	☐	☐	☐	☐	☐	☐	☐
3 Ability to manage complex patients	☐	☐	☐	☐	☐	☐	☐
4 Awareness of their own limitations	☐	☐	☐	☐	☐	☐	☐
5 Ability to respond to psychosocial aspects of illness	☐	☐	☐	☐	☐	☐	☐
6 Appropriate utilisation of resources e.g. ordering investigations	☐	☐	☐	☐	☐	☐	☐
7 Ability to assess risks and benefits when treating patients	☐	☐	☐	☐	☐	☐	☐
8 Ability to co-ordinate patient care	☐	☐	☐	☐	☐	☐	☐
Maintaining good medical practice							
9 Technical skills (appropriate to current practice)	☐	☐	☐	☐	☐	☐	☐
10 Ability to apply up-to-date / evidence based medicine	☐	☐	☐	☐	☐	☐	☐
11 Ability to manage time effectively / prioritise	☐	☐	☐	☐	☐	☐	☐
12 Ability to deal with stress	☐	☐	☐	☐	☐	☐	☐
Teaching and Training, Appraising and Assessing							
13 Commitment to learning	☐	☐	☐	☐	☐	☐	☐
14 Willingness and effectiveness when teaching/training colleagues	☐	☐	☐	☐	☐	☐	☐
15 Ability to give feedback (private, honest and supportive)	☐	☐	☐	☐	☐	☐	☐

⌐ *U/C Please mark this if you have not observed the behaviour and therefore feel unable to comment.   1387196713 ⌐

	Very Poor	Poor	Needs Development	Satisfactory	Good	Very Good	U/C
	1	2	3	4	5	6	
Relationship with Patients							
16 Communication with patients	☐	☐	☐	☐	☐	☐	☐
17 Communication with carers and/or family	☐	☐	☐	☐	☐	☐	☐
18 Respect for patients' dignity and their right to privacy & confidentiality	☐	☐	☐	☐	☐	☐	☐
Working with colleagues							
19 Verbal communication with colleagues	☐	☐	☐	☐	☐	☐	☐
20 Written communication with colleagues	☐	☐	☐	☐	☐	☐	☐
21 Ability to recognise and value the contribution of others	☐	☐	☐	☐	☐	☐	☐
22 Accessibility/reliability	☐	☐	☐	☐	☐	☐	☐
23 Leadership skills	☐	☐	☐	☐	☐	☐	☐
24 Management skills	☐	☐	☐	☐	☐	☐	☐
Overall							
25 Overall, how do you rate this practitioner compared to other practitioners at the same grade?	☐	☐	☐	☐	☐	☐	☐

U/C Please mark this if you have not observed the behaviour and therefore feel unable to comment.

Do you have any concerns about this practitioner's probity or health?   ☐ Yes   ☐ No

If yes please state your concerns:

What is your ethnic group?:

☐ British   ☐ Chinese   ☐ White and Black Caribbean
☐ Irish   ☐ Other Asian Background   ☐ White and Black African
☐ Indian   ☐ Caribbean   ☐ White and Asian
☐ Pakistani   ☐ African   ☐ Any other mixed background
☐ Bangladeshi   ☐ Any other Black background   ☐ Any other ethnic group

Please use this space to record areas of strength or any suggestions for development.

Strengths   Suggestions for development

Signature: Surname:

--------------------------- |_|_|_|_|_|_|_|_|_|_|_|_|_|_|_| 6404196718

Please refer to curriculum at www.mmc.nhs.uk for details of expected competencies for F1 and F2

mini-PAT (Peer Assessment Tool) - F2 Version

Please complete the questions using a cross: ☒   Please use black ink and CAPITAL LETTERS

Doctor's   Surname

               Forename

GMC Number:

How do you rate this Doctor in their:	Below expectations for F2 completion	Borderline for F2 completion	Meets expectations for F2 completion	Above expectations for F2 completion		U/C*
	1	2	3	4	5	6	

Good Clinical Care

		1	2	3	4	5	6	U/C*
1	Ability to diagnose patient problems	☐	☐	☐	☐	☐	☐	☐
2	Ability to formulate appropriate management plans	☐	☐	☐	☐	☐	☐	☐
3	Awareness of their own limitations	☐	☐	☐	☐	☐	☐	☐
4	Ability to respond to psychosocial aspects of illness	☐	☐	☐	☐	☐	☐	☐
5	Appropriate utilisation of resources e.g. ordering investigations	☐	☐	☐	☐	☐	☐	☐

Maintaining good medical practice

6	Ability to manage time effectively / prioritise	☐	☐	☐	☐	☐	☐	☐
7	Technical skills (appropriate to current practice)	☐	☐	☐	☐	☐	☐	☐

Teaching and Training, Appraising and Assessing

8	Willingness and effectiveness when teaching/training colleagues	☐	☐	☐	☐	☐	☐	☐

Relationship with Patients

9	Communication with patients	☐	☐	☐	☐	☐	☐	☐
10	Communication with carers and/or family	☐	☐	☐	☐	☐	☐	☐
11	Respect for patients and their right to confidentiality	☐	☐	☐	☐	☐	☐	☐

Working with colleagues

12	Verbal communication with colleagues	☐	☐	☐	☐	☐	☐	☐
13	Written communication with colleagues	☐	☐	☐	☐	☐	☐	☐
14	Ability to recognise and value the contribution of others	☐	☐	☐	☐	☐	☐	☐
15	Accessibility/Reliability	☐	☐	☐	☐	☐	☐	☐
16	Overall, how do you rate this doctor compared to a doctor ready to complete F2 training?	☐	☐	☐	☐	☐	☐	☐

Do you have any concerns about this doctor's probity or health?   ☐ Yes   ☐ No
If yes please state your concerns:

*U/C Please mark this if you have not observed the behaviour and therefore feel unable to comment.   2500288218

Anything especially good?

Please describe any behaviour that has raised concerns or should be a particular focus for development:

Please continue your comments on a separate sheet if required

Your Gender: ☐ Male   ☐ Female

Your ethnic group: ☐ British   ☐ Bangladeshi

                         ☐ Irish   ☐ Other Asian Background

                         ☐ Other White Background   ☐ White and Black Caribbean

                         ☐ Caribbean   ☐ White and Black African

                         ☐ African   ☐ White and Asian

                         ☐ Any other Black background ☐ Any other mixed background

                         ☐ Indian   ☐ Chinese

                         ☐ Pakistani   ☐ Any other ethnic group

Which environment have you primarily observed the doctor in?
(Please choose one answer only)
☐ Inpatients   ☐ Intensive Care
☐ Outpatients   ☐ Theatre
☐ Both In and Out-patients ☐ General Practice
☐ A&E/Admissions   ☐ Other (Please specify)
☐ Community Speciality
☐ Laboratory/Research

Your position: ☐ Consultant   ☐ SASG   ☐ SpR   ☐ Foundation/PRHO
                  ☐ Nurse   ☐ SHO   ☐ Allied Health Professional
                  ☐ GP
                  ☐ Other (Please specify)

If you are a Nurse or AHP how long have you been qualified?: ☐☐ years   Length of working relationship: ☐☐ months

What training have you had in the use of this assessment tool?:   ☐ Face-to-Face   ☐ Have Read Guidelines   ☐ Web/CD rom

How long has it taken you to complete this form (in minutes)?:   ☐☐

Your Signature: ....   Date: ☐☐ / ☐☐ / ☐☐

Your Surname: ☐☐☐☐☐☐☐☐☐☐☐☐☐☐☐☐☐☐☐☐☐☐☐☐☐

Your GMC Number: (Doctors only) ☐☐☐☐☐☐☐

Acknowledgements: mini-PAT is derived from SPRAT (Sheffield Peer Review Assessment Tool)   9787288212

Reprinted with permission of the United Kingdom Department of Health, Policy Research Programme (10/05).

Self mini-PAT (Peer Assessment Tool)

Please complete the questions using a cross: ☒   Please use black ink and CAPITAL LETTERS

Your Surname:

GMC Number: **YOUR GMC NUMBER MUST BE COMPLETED**

How do you rate yourself in your:	Below expectations for F1 completion	Borderline for F1 completion	Meets expectations for F1 completion	Above expectations for F1 completion		U/C*
	1	2	3	4	5	6	
Good Clinical Care							
1 Ability to diagnose patient problems	☐	☐	☐	☐	☐	☐	☐
2 Ability to formulate appropriate management plans	☐	☐	☐	☐	☐	☐	☐
3 Awareness of their own limitations	☐	☐	☐	☐	☐	☐	☐
4 Ability to respond to psychosocial aspects of illness	☐	☐	☐	☐	☐	☐	☐
5 Appropriate utilisation of resources e.g. ordering investigations	☐	☐	☐	☐	☐	☐	☐
Maintaining good medical practice							
6 Ability to manage time effectively / prioritise	☐	☐	☐	☐	☐	☐	☐
7 Technical skills (appropriate to current practice)	☐	☐	☐	☐	☐	☐	☐
Teaching and Training, Appraising and Assessing							
8 Willingness and effectiveness when teaching/training colleagues	☐	☐	☐	☐	☐	☐	☐
Relationship with Patients							
9 Communication with patients	☐	☐	☐	☐	☐	☐	☐
10 Communication with carers and/or family	☐	☐	☐	☐	☐	☐	☐
11 Respect for patients and their right to confidentiality	☐	☐	☐	☐	☐	☐	☐
Working with colleagues							
12 Verbal communication with colleagues	☐	☐	☐	☐	☐	☐	☐
13 Written communication with colleagues	☐	☐	☐	☐	☐	☐	☐
14 Ability to recognise and value the contribution of others	☐	☐	☐	☐	☐	☐	☐
15 Accessibility/Reliability	☐	☐	☐	☐	☐	☐	☐
16 Overall, how do compare yourself to a doctor ready to complete F2 training?	☐	☐	☐	☐	☐	☐	☐

*U/C Please mark this if you feel unable to comment.

PTO:

Acknowledgements: mini-PAT is derived from SPRAT (Sheffield Peer Review Assessment Tool)   6830612691

Anything going especially well?

Please describe any areas that you think you should particularly focus on for development:

Your Signature: ....   Date: ☐☐ / ☐☐ / ☐☐

8727612698

Reprinted with permission of the United Kingdom Department of Health, Policy Research Programme (10/05).

0287165885

NHS
SCOTLAND

PHAST
Diagnostic Questionnaire

NHS
SCOTLAND

PRHO Name

☐☐☐☐☐☐☐☐☐☐☐☐☐☐☐☐☐☐☐☐☐☐☐☐☐☐☐☐☐☐

Current Post (Ward/Department)

☐☐☐☐☐☐☐☐☐☐☐☐☐☐☐☐☐☐☐☐☐☐☐☐☐☐☐☐

Hospital

☐☐☐☐☐☐☐☐☐☐☐☐☐☐☐☐☐☐☐☐☐☐☐☐☐☐☐☐

Date Started Current Post

☐☐ - ☐☐ - ☐☐☐☐

Educational Supervisor

☐☐☐☐☐☐☐☐☐☐☐☐☐☐☐☐☐☐☐☐☐☐

Evaluator Name

☐☐☐☐☐☐☐☐☐☐☐☐☐☐☐☐☐☐☐☐☐☐

Evaluator Grade

☐ Educational Supervisor/Consultant/GP

☐ Registrar

☐ SHO

☐ Nurse

Date Form Completed

☐☐ - ☐☐ - ☐☐☐☐

0436165881

PRHO Diagnostic Questionnaire
Guidelines for completing this form

Do not complete this form if you have no direct knowledge of the PRHO's performance.
In this instance, please return the form immediately to the PRHO for re-distribution.

Background to contents

The items listed in this form identify key critical behaviours that doctors themselves have identified as separating the competent PRHO from those who are struggling. The questionnaire is being used as a diagnostic tool to help identify those who need additional support and to give feedback to all PRHOs. The items are grouped into four of the domains from Good Medical Practice:

1   Good Clinical Care   3 Effective Relationships with Patients
2   Maintaining Good Medical Practice   4 Effective Working with Colleagues

Completing the form

You have been asked to comment on the named PRHO's performance. Please ensure *your* name, status/grade and date are completed on the front page in addition to the PRHO's details.

For each item on pages 3 to 5 please rate the PRHO's performance based on <u>your observations</u> to date using the grade descriptors below:

Excellent: Competence exceeds reasonable expectations
          i.e. several outstanding features.

Good: Competence is above average for this stage of training
     i.e. occasionally exceeds reasonable expectations.

Satisfactory: Competence acceptable for this stage of training
             ie. room for improvement but no significant weaknesses.

Requires help/attention: Competence falls short of what expected at this stage of training.

If you are unable to give a rating on any particular item *due to having not observed the PRHO in relation to this item or because you are not in a clinical position to make such a judgement,* you should not hesitate to cross the **Cannot Evaluate** box.

Please make a cross for *all* the items. | X |

Page 6 gives the opportunity to raise any additional problems (if any). You are also asked to provide an overall *<u>impression</u>* of the PRHO's performance in the light of your own views plus that of others.

7257165889

Please give your professional opinion on the PRHO's performance by **crossing** the appropriate box for each of the items below (*see Page 2 for grade descriptors*):

GMC Domain: Good Clinical Care	*Mark with a Cross (X)*

	Requires help/attention	Satisfactory	Good	Excellent	Cannot Evaluate
1. History taking	☐	☐	☐	☐	☐
2. Recognition of significant signs/ symptoms in physical examination	☐	☐	☐	☐	☐
3. Ability to provide appropriate differential diagnosis	☐	☐	☐	☐	☐
4. Ability to present accurate and complete patient findings to colleagues	☐	☐	☐	☐	☐
5. Practical skills	☐	☐	☐	☐	☐
6. Prioritisation of tasks	☐	☐	☐	☐	☐
7. Selection of investigations	☐	☐	☐	☐	☐
8. Knowledge of requirements of the various investigation services (eg. blood tubes, patient preparation)	☐	☐	☐	☐	☐
9. Completion of request forms (eg. with all required information)	☐	☐	☐	☐	☐
10. Interpretation of test results	☐	☐	☐	☐	☐
11. Initiation of correct management for common conditions	☐	☐	☐	☐	☐
12. Use of working guidelines and protocols of different units	☐	☐	☐	☐	☐
13. Response to common medical and surgical emergencies	☐	☐	☐	☐	☐
14. Medical judgement	☐	☐	☐	☐	☐

8689165889

	Requires help/attention	Satisfactory	Good	Excellent	Cannot Evaluate
15. Maintenance of safe practice	☐	☐	☐	☐	☐
16. Ability to make clinical judgements calmly (ie. not running around like a headless chicken!)	☐	☐	☐	☐	☐
17. Identification of an appropriate person when seeking help	☐	☐	☐	☐	☐
18. Use of the multi-disciplinary team (eg. physiotherapy, social services)	☐	☐	☐	☐	☐
19. Prescribing skills (eg. drug selection, dosage, prescription writing)	☐	☐	☐	☐	☐
20. Record/note keeping	☐	☐	☐	☐	☐
21. Basic knowledge of clinical medicine	☐	☐	☐	☐	☐

GMC Domain: Maintaining Good Medical Practice

Mark with a Cross (X)

	Requires help/attention	Satisfactory	Good	Excellent	Cannot Evaluate
1. Maximisation of learning opportunities in the clinical area	☐	☐	☐	☐	☐
2. Recognition of own limitations	☐	☐	☐	☐	☐
3. Reaction to constructive criticism	☐	☐	☐	☐	☐
4. Admission of significant errors	☐	☐	☐	☐	☐
5. Learning from personal errors	☐	☐	☐	☐	☐
6. Implementation of relevant statutory procedures (eg. death certification/notification)	☐	☐	☐	☐	☐
7. Commitment to the job	☐	☐	☐	☐	☐
8. Command of the English language	☐	☐	☐	☐	☐

8017165884

GMC Domain: Effective Relationships with Patients   *Mark with a Cross (X)*

	Requires help/attention	Satisfactory	Good	Excellent	Cannot Evaluate
1. Oral communication with patients	☐	☐	☐	☐	☐
2. Oral communication with relatives	☐	☐	☐	☐	☐
3. Empathy with patients	☐	☐	☐	☐	☐
4. Respect for patients' privacy and dignity	☐	☐	☐	☐	☐
5. Patient confidentiality	☐	☐	☐	☐	☐
6. Attitude to patients and relatives	☐	☐	☐	☐	☐

GMC Domain: Effective Working with Colleagues   *Mark with a Cross (X)*

	Requires help/attention	Satisfactory	Good	Excellent	Cannot Evaluate
1. Oral and written communication with:					
a) nurses	☐	☐	☐	☐	☐
b) peers	☐	☐	☐	☐	☐
c) team members	☐	☐	☐	☐	☐
2. Efforts to contribute positively to the team	☐	☐	☐	☐	☐
3. Accessibility to team members	☐	☐	☐	☐	☐
4. Punctuality	☐	☐	☐	☐	☐
5. Attitude to colleagues	☐	☐	☐	☐	☐

3768165882

Other Areas of Concern

If you have observed that the PRHO has a performance problem(s) other than any already identified in this questionnaire, please specify below:

In Summary

Please briefly summarise your impressions of the PRHO's performance in the box below:

Please also summarise areas (if any) in which you feel the PRHO could benefit from further experiences or interventions. Please indicate whether this is to improve poor performance or to stretch already competent behaviour:

Reprinted with permission of the National Health Service (NHS) for Scotland, United Kingdom (10/05)

APPENDIX C

SAMPLE REPORTING FORMATS

Johns Hopkins University School of Nursing

- Course Evaluation Scale RESULTS
- Clinical Faculty Evaluation Scale RESULTS

Johns Hopkins University School of Nursing
Course Evaluation Scale
RESULTS

1/11/2005

Course: NR100.105.0201
Semester: Fall 2004
Instructor:
Response Rate: 104 of 105 (99%)

SON Norm

Course Content and Organization

	SD	D	A	SA	N	Instructor Mean	Md	'Masters' Mean	Md
1. Syllabus provided clear statement(s) of how you will be graded.	0.0%	0.0%	15.4%	84.6%	104	2.85	3.00	2.52	3.00
2. Syllabus provided clear statement(s) of course requirements.	0.0	1.0	17.3	81.7	104	2.81	3.00	2.49	3.00
3. Syllabus provided objectives/outcomes that reflected course content.	0.0	1.9	17.3	80.8	104	2.79	3.00	2.43	3.00
4. Course materials were useful in attaining course objectives/outcomes.	0.0	1.0	15.4	83.7	104	2.83	3.00	2.29	2.00
5. Course materials were at the appropriate level of difficulty for the course level.	0.0	1.9	21.2	76.9	104	2.75	3.00	2.28	2.00
6. Assignments were useful in understanding course content.	0.0	0.0	17.3	82.7	104	2.83	3.00	2.26	2.00
7. The course was well organized.	0.0	3.8	18.3	77.9	104	2.74	3.00	2.16	2.00
8. The course requirements were appropriate for the number of credits.	0.0	0.0	19.2	80.8	104	2.81	3.00	2.24	2.00

Subscale Score Range = 0 - 24, Mdpt = 12
Instructor Mean / Md. = 22.39 / 24.00 where N = 104
SON Norm Mean / Md. = 18.66 / 19.00 where N = 493

Evaluation Methods (e.g., exams, projects, presentations)

	SD	D	A	SA	N	Instructor Mean	Md	'Masters' Mean	Md
9. Evaluation methods measured course objectives/outcomes.	0.0%	0.0%	18.3%	81.7%	104	2.82	3.00	2.31	2.00
10. Evaluation methods were fair.	0.0	0.0	12.5	87.5	104	2.88	3.00	2.30	2.00
11. Evaluation methods were appropriate for the course level.	0.0	1.0	13.5	85.6	104	2.85	3.00	2.34	2.00
12. Evaluation methods covered important content, not trivial information.	0.0	1.0	13.5	85.6	104	2.85	3.00	2.25	2.00
13. Evaluation methods required critical thinking/problem solving, not just memorization.	0.0	1.9	14.4	83.7	104	2.82	3.00	2.37	2.00

Subscale Score Range = 0 - 15, Mdpt = 7.5
Instructor Mean / Md. = 14.20 / 15.00 where N = 104
SON Norm Mean / Md. = 11.58 / 11.00 where N = 493

Learning Outcomes

	SD	D	A	SA	N	Instructor Mean	Md	'Masters' Mean	Md
14. Attending classes in this course was worthwhile.	1.0%	1.0%	12.5%	85.6%	104	2.83	3.00	2.19	2.00
15. This course positively changed my thinking about the subject area.	1.0	11.5	21.2	66.3	104	2.53	3.00	2.12	2.00
16. I learned new information in this course.	1.0	0.0	25.0	74.0	104	2.72	3.00	2.35	3.00
17. What I learned in this course will be useful in my career.	3.8	8.7	27.9	59.6	104	2.43	3.00	2.25	2.00

Subscale Score Range = 0 - 12, Mdpt = 6
Instructor Mean / Md. = 10.51 / 12.00 where N = 104
SON Norm Mean / Md. = 8.91 / 9.00 where N = 493

Course: NR100.105.0201
Semester: Fall 2004
Instructor:
Response Rate: 104 of 105 (99%)

Johns Hopkins University School of Nursing
Course Evaluation Scale
RESULTS

1/11/2005

Instructional Methods (*Instructor/Course Coordinator:*)	Instructor							'Masters'	
	SD	D	A	SA	N	Mean	Md	Mean	Md
18. Encouraged self-directed learning.	0.0%	1.0%	24.0%	75.0%	104	2.74	3.00	2.40	3.00
19. Utilized useful audiovisuals, where appropriate.	0.0	0.0	7.7	92.3	104	2.92	3.00	2.33	2.00
20. Facilitated critical thinking/problem solving.	0.0	1.9	17.3	80.8	104	2.79	3.00	2.32	2.00
21. Appeared knowledgeable about course content.	0.0	0.0	6.7	93.3	104	2.93	3.00	2.57	3.00
22. Demonstrated clear relationships between theory and practice.	0.0	3.8	18.3	77.9	104	2.74	3.00	2.33	2.00
23. Provided relevant examples to illustrate content.	0.0	1.9	16.3	81.7	104	2.80	3.00	2.37	2.00
24. Paced instruction to facilitate learning.	0.0	3.8	14.4	81.7	104	2.78	3.00	2.26	2.00
25. Encouraged questions, comments, and discussion.	0.0	0.0	9.6	90.4	104	2.90	3.00	2.49	3.00
26. Provided timely feedback on assignments and/or tests.	0.0	0.0	6.7	93.3	104	2.93	3.00	2.34	3.00
27. Provided helpful feedback on assignments and/or tests.	0.0	1.0	11.5	87.5	104	2.87	3.00	2.35	3.00
28. Encouraged students' participation in learning during class.	0.0	0.0	10.6	89.4	104	2.89	3.00	2.46	3.00
29. Made clear and understandable presentations.	0.0	0.0	16.3	83.7	104	2.84	3.00	2.23	2.00
30. Was thoroughly prepared for each class.	0.0	0.0	5.8	94.2	104	2.94	3.00	2.35	3.00

Subscale Score Range = 0 - 39, Mdpt = 19.5
Instructor Mean/Md. = 37.08 / 39.00 where N = 104
SON Norm Mean/Md. = 30.79 / 33.00 where N = 493

Learning Atmosphere (*Instructor/Course Coordinator:*)	Instructor							'Masters'	
	SD	D	A	SA	N	Mean	Md	Mean	Md
31. Was available for individual assistance.	0.0%	0.0%	17.3%	82.7%	104	2.83	3.00	2.48	3.00
32. Demonstrated respect for each student.	0.0	0.0	9.6	90.4	104	2.90	3.00	2.53	3.00
33. Was responsive to students' needs.	0.0	1.0	8.7	90.4	104	2.89	3.00	2.46	3.00
34. Was approachable out of class to answer questions.	0.0	1.0	11.5	87.5	104	2.87	3.00	2.51	3.00
35. Demonstrated sensitivity to gender and cultural differences.	0.0	0.0	11.5	88.5	104	2.88	3.00	2.56	3.00
36. Displayed enthusiasm for teaching.	0.0	0.0	2.9	97.1	104	2.97	3.00	2.57	3.00

Subscale Score Range = 0 - 18, Mdpt = 9
Instructor Mean / Md. = 17.35 / 18.00 where N = 104
SON Norm Mean / Md. = 15.11 / 17.00 where N = 493

Total Scale Score Range = 0 - 108, Mdpt. = 54
Instructor Mean / Md. = 101.53 / 107.00 where N = 104
SON Mean / Md. = 85.06 / 88.00 where N = 493

Johns Hopkins University School of Nursing
Clinical Faculty Evaluation Scale
RESULTS

1/12/2005

Course: NR100.105.0201
Semester: **Fall 2004**
Clinical Instructor: **J. Doe**
Course Coordinator: J. SMITH
Response Rate: 2 of 4 (50%)

St. Agnes Hospital
Course Level: Baccalaureate

Instructional Methods

	Clinical Instructor							Course Norm	
	SD	D	A	SA	N	Mean	Md	Mean	Md
1. Provided adequate orientation to my clinical requirements.	0.0%	0.0%	0.0%	100.0%	2	3.00	3.00	2.53	3.00
2. Clarified my learning needs.	0.0	0.0	50.0	50.0	2	2.50	2.50	2.52	3.00
3. Provided timely written and/or verbal feedback, as appropriate.	0.0	50.0	0.0	50.0	2	2.00	2.00	2.50	3.00
4. Mentored me in my nursing role.	0.0	0.0	50.0	50.0	2	2.50	2.50	2.50	3.00
5. Evaluated me fairly.	0.0	0.0	100.0	0.0	2	2.00	2.00	2.53	3.00
6. Communicated regularly with me.	0.0	0.0	50.0	50.0	2	2.50	2.50	2.59	3.00
7. Was available for individual advising and counseling.	0.0	0.0	0.0	100.0	2	3.00	3.00	2.53	3.00
8. Provided assistance when I had questions or was having difficulty.	0.0	0.0	0.0	100.0	2	3.00	3.00	2.59	3.00
9. Demonstrated respect for me.	0.0	0.0	0.0	100.0	2	3.00	3.00	2.69	3.00
10. Facilitated my critical thinking and problem solving.	0.0	0.0	0.0	100.0	2	3.00	3.00	2.57	3.00

Subscale Score Range = 0 - 30, Mdpt. = 15
Instructor Mean / Md. = 26.50 / 26.50 where N = 2
Course Mean / Md. = 25.55 / 29.00 where N = 136

Clinical Experiences

	Clinical Instructor							Course Norm	
	SD	D	A	SA	N	Mean	Md	Mean	Md
11. Provided experiences useful in attaining course objectives/outcomes.	0.0	0.0	50.0	50.0	2	2.50	2.50	2.60	3.00
12. Assisted me in applying theory and research to clinical practice.	0.0	0.0	50.0	50.0	2	2.50	2.50	2.57	3.00
13. Provided experiences to meet my learning needs.	0.0	0.0	50.0	50.0	2	2.50	2.50	2.60	3.00
14. Encouraged me to collaborate with my healthcare team.	0.0	0.0	50.0	50.0	2	2.50	2.50	2.63	3.00
15. Demonstrated current clinical knowledge.	0.0	0.0	50.0	50.0	2	2.50	2.50	2.61	3.00
16. Demonstrated skill proficiency.	0.0	0.0	50.0	50.0	2	2.50	2.50	2.65	3.00
17. Was a positive role model.	0.0	0.0	50.0	50.0	2	2.50	2.50	2.63	3.00
18. I would recommend continued use of this clinical site for this	0.0	0.0	50.0	50.0	2	2.50	2.50	2.68	3.00

Subscale Score Range = 0-24, Mdpt. = 12
Instructor Mean / Md. = 20.00 / 20.00 where N = 2
Course Mean / Md. = 20.96 / 23.00 where N = 136

Total Score Range = 0-54, Mdpt. = 27
Instructor Mean / Md. = 46.50 / 46.50   where N = 2
Course Mean / Md. = 46.51 / 52.00   where N = 136

APPENDIX D

COMMERCIALLY PUBLISHED STUDENT RATING SCALE SYSTEMS

1. *Course/Instructor Evaluation Questionnaire (CIEQ)*
   Developed by Laurence Aleamoni.
   Contact: Laurence M. Aleamoni, President
   Comprehensive Data Evaluation Services, Inc.
   6730 N. Camino Padre Isidoro
   Tucson, AZ 85718
   Phone: (520) 621-7832
   Fax: (520) 297-9427
   E-Mail: aaleamoni@aol.com
   Web: http://www.cieq.com

2. *IDEA—Student Reactions to Instruction and Courses*
   Developed by William Cashin
   Contact: William H. Pallett, Director
   IDEA Center
   211 South Seth Child Road
   Manhattan, KS 66502-3089
   Phone: (800) 255-2757; (785) 532-5970
   Fax: (785) 532-5725
   E-Mail: idea@ksu.edu; pallet@ksu.edu
   Web: http://www.idea.ksu.edu

3. *Student Instructional Report II (SIR II)*
   Developed by John Centra.
   Contact: Student Instructional Report II
   Educational Testing Service
   Mail Stop 55-L
   Rosedale Road
   Princeton, NJ 08541-0001
   Phone: (800) 745-0269
   Fax: (609) 771-7255
   E-Mail: highered@ets.org
   Web: http://www.ets.org/hea

4. *Purdue Instructor and Course Evaluation Service (PICES)*
   Developed by Purdue University faculty.
   Contact: Marne Helgesen, Director
   Center for Instructional Excellence
   Young Hall, Room 730
   302 Wood Street
   Purdue University
   West Lafayette, IN 47907-2108
   Phone: (765) 496-6422
   Fax: (765) 496-1749
   E-Mail: cie@purdue.edu; helgesen@purdue.edu
   Web: http://www.cie.purdue.edu/data/pices.cfm

5. *Instructional Assessment System (IAS Online)*
   Developed by the Office of Educational Assessment (OEA),
        University of Washington.
   Contact: Nana Lowell, Director
   Instructional Assessment System
   Office of Educational Assessment
   University of Washington
   4311 11th Avenue, NE
   430 Roosevelt Commons B
   Box 354987
   Seattle, WA 98195-4987
   Phone: (206) 543-9847 (543-1170)
   Fax: (206) 543-3961
   E-Mail: iasuw@u.washington.edu; nlowell@
   u.washington.edu
   Web: http://www.washington.edu/oea/ias1.htm

6. *Student Evaluation of Educational Quality (SEEQ)*
   Developed by Herbert Marsh.
   Contact: Beverley Oliver, SEEQ Coordinator
             Centre for Educational Advancement
             Building 105, Rm. 164
             GPO Box U1987
             Perth, Western Australia 6845
             Phone: +61 89266 2292
             Fax: +61 89266 3051
             E-Mail: b.oliver@curtin.edu.au
             Web: http://www.lsn.curtin.edu.au/seeq

INDEX

W

X

Y

Z